Debates in Citizenship Education

Edited by
James Arthur and Hilary Cremin

 Routledge
Taylor & Francis Group

LONDON AND NEW YORK

First published 2012
by Routledge
2 Park Square, Milton Park, Abingdon, Oxon OX14 4RN

Simultaneously published in the USA and Canada
by Routledge
711 Third Avenue, New York, NY 10017

Routledge is an imprint of the Taylor & Francis Group, an informa business

British Library Cataloguing in Publication Data
A catalogue record for this book is available from the British Library

Library of Congress Cataloging in Publication Data
Debates in citizenship education / [edited by] James Arthur and Hilary Cremin.
p. cm.
Includes bibliographical references and index.
1. Citizenship--Study and teaching. I. Arthur, James, 1957- II. Cremin, Hilary
LC1091.D36 2011
372.83'044--dc23
2011017195

ISBN: 978-0-415-59765-4 (hbk)
ISBN: 978-0-415-59766-1 (pbk)
ISBN: 978-0-203-59710-1 (ebk)

Typeset in Galliard
by Taylor & Francis Books

Printed and bound in Great Britain by the MPG Books Group

Contents

Author biographies

Professor James Arthur, Head of the School of Education, University of Birmingham. He has written widely on the relationship between theory and practice in education, particularly the links between communitarianism, social virtues, citizenship, religion and education. He is Director of citizEd, sits on the executive of the Society for Educational Studies and is editor of the *British Journal of Educational Studies*.

Dr John Beck, formerly Director of Studies in Education, Homerton College, University of Cambridge. He taught mainly in the areas of Sociology of Education and Professional Studies on undergraduate and Masters courses, as well as supervising and examining doctoral students. His main research interests include: citizenship and citizenship education; social theory and social policy within the sociology of education; and work on the continuing relevance of the work of Basil Bernstein.

Dr Kathy Bickmore, Associate Professor, OISE, University of Toronto. She teaches Social Foundations of Education, Geography/Social Studies Curriculum and the Politics/Practices of Democratic Citizenship and Conflict Resolution Education. Her research focuses on field development on the politics and practice of conflict resolution, and education for equity/democracy in public school contexts.

Dr Max Biddulph, Lecturer, University of Nottingham. He is a member of the Centre for Research in Schools and Communities. He has a particular interest in the field of sex and relationships education and a strong interest in activism and LGBT politics and in sexuality issues in the workplace.

Dr Hilary Cremin, Senior Lecturer, University of Cambridge. She researches and teaches in the areas of citizenship education and conflict resolution in schools and communities in the Faculty of Education. She chairs the Centre for Youth and Democracy, and is an editor of the *British Educational Research Journal*. She has worked in the public, private and voluntary sector as a school teacher, educational consultant, project coordinator and academic, and has research interests in the USA, New Zealand and Japan.

Professor Ian Davies, Professor in Education, University of York. He is the editor of the citizED and CiCea journal *Citizenship Teaching and Learning*. Publications include the *Sage Handbook of Education for Democracy and Citizenship*.

Moira V. Faul, Doctoral Student, University of Cambridge. She has previously held the role of Head of Education and Youth Policy at Oxfam GB, been Education Team Manager at Oxfam and Director of Education at Sylvan Learning.

Tom Harrison, Research Student, University of Birmingham. He is a director of the Learning for Life project and also works as a consultant for several other educational organisations. He has been a tutor for the University of Leicester on their Citizenship Masters course, Director of the cross-curricula and community strands for the citizED programme and run various citizenship and community development projects for CSV, the UFA and the ASC. He is currently studying an MPhil at the University of Birmingham.

Professor Terry Haydn, Professor of Education, University of East Anglia. He is tutor for History, and has special responsibility for equal opportunities and diversity issues on the course. He has previously worked in the Department of History, Humanities and Philosophy at the Institute of Education, University of London, and was previously a head of Humanities in an inner-city comprehensive school in Manchester.

Dr Moira Hulme, Lecturer in Education Research, University of Glasgow. Her research interests are in policy studies in teacher education and development, practitioner inquiry and curriculum innovation.

Professor Rob Hulme, Professor of Education and Director of Research Unit for Trans-professionalism in the Public Services, University of Chester. He co-ordinates social policy research in the university and chairs the university's Research Forum. He teaches Research Methods on postgraduate and under-graduate programmes. He also teaches Education Policy (global, national and regional).

David Kerr, formerly Principal Research Officer at the National Foundation for Educational Research, he is currently at Birkbeck College, University of London. Having joined NFER in 1996, he has led work on citizenship and human rights education and pupil voice. He has acted as Director of the Citizenship Education Longitudinal Study (CELS) and Associate Director of the IEA International Civic and Citizenship Education Study (ICCS).

Alveena Malik, Chief Executive, The Young Foundation. She was formerly Principal Associate at the Institute of Community Cohesion (iCoCo) with lead responsibility on education and cohesion policy and intercultural dialogue. She was also Head of Communities and Integration Policy at the

Commission for Racial Equality (CRE) where she led the development of CRE policy on issues of migration, segregation, extremism, interfaith dialogue and conflict resolution and mediation.

Dr Carolynne Mason, Senior Research Associate, Loughborough University. With more than 15 years' experience as a researcher, she has managed and undertaken numerous large and small-scale research projects. Her particular research interests include engaging young children in the research process, engaging 'hard to reach groups' through active citizenship and sport and physical activity, and promoting social inclusion and wellbeing.

Dr Andrew Peterson, Senior Lecturer in Education, Canterbury Christ Church University. He works in the field of the education of citizenship teachers and has published in the field of civic and moral education. He sits on the executive of the Society for Educational Studies and on the editorial board of the *British Journal of Educational Studies*.

Dr Mark A. Pike, Reader in Education, University of Leeds. He is a reader in Educational Values and Pedagogy, having previously been a senior lecturer and lecturer in the School of Education, University of Leeds. He recently acted as Principal Investigator on an AHRC/ESRC project looking at reading and values formation in new academies.

Don Rowe, formerly Director of Curriculum Resources at the Citizenship Foundation, of which he was a founder member. He is an honorary research fellow at Birkbeck College, University of London. His research and development interests have included moral and philosophical approaches to the teaching and learning of citizenship as well as the development of evidence-based assessment.

Dr Paul Warwick, Teaching Fellow, School of Education, University of Leicester. He has worked in the field of curriculum development in education for citizenship and sustainable development (ESD) since 1995. He has a particular research interest in participatory pedagogy, and methods for engaging young people in dialogue and civic action. Presently he is Chair of the University of Leicester's Education for Sustainable Development Forum and a member of the United Nations Regional Centre of Expertise for ESD in the East Midlands.

Introduction to the series

This book, *Debates in Citizenship Education*, is one of a series of books entitled *Debates in Subject Teaching*. The series has been designed to engage with a wide range of debates related to subject teaching. Unquestionably, debates vary among the subjects, but may include, for example, issues that:

- impact on initial teacher education in the subject;
- are addressed in the classroom through the teaching of the subject;
- are related to the content of the subject and its definition;
- are related to subject pedagogy;
- are connected with the relationship between the subject and broader educational aims and objectives in society, and the philosophy and sociology of education;
- are related to the development of the subject and its future in the twenty-first century.

Consequently, each book presents key debates that subject teachers should understand, reflect on and engage in as part of their professional development. Chapters have been designed to highlight major questions, and to consider the evidence from research and practice in order to find possible answers. Some subject books or chapters offer at least one solution or a view of the ways forward, whereas others provide alternative views and leave readers to identify their own solution or view of the ways forward. The editors expect readers will want to pursue the issues raised, and so chapters include questions for further debate and suggestions for further reading. Debates covered in the series will provide the basis for discussion in university subject seminars or as topics for assignments or classroom research. The books have been written for all those with a professional interest in their subject, and, in particular: student teachers learning to teach the subject in secondary or primary school; newly qualified teachers; teachers undertaking study at Masters level; teachers with a subject coordination or leadership role, and those preparing for such responsibility; as well as mentors, university tutors, CPD organisers and advisers of the aforementioned groups.

Books in the series have a cross-phase dimension, because the editors believe that it is important for teachers in the primary, secondary and post-16 phases to look at subject teaching holistically, particularly in order to provide for continuity and progression, but also to increase their understanding of how children and young people learn. The balance of chapters that have a cross-phase relevance varies according to the issues relevant to different subjects. However, no matter where the emphasis is, the authors have drawn out the relevance of their topic to the whole of each book's intended audience.

Because of the range of the series, both in terms of the issues covered and its cross-phase concern, each book is an edited collection. Editors have commissioned new writing from experts on particular issues, who, collectively, represent many different perspectives on subject teaching. Readers should not expect a book in this series to cover the entire range of debates relevant to the subject, or to offer a completely unified view of subject teaching, or that every debate will be dealt with discretely, or that all aspects of a debate will be covered. Part of what each book in this series offers to readers is the opportunity to explore the inter-relationships between positions in debates and, indeed, among the debates themselves, by identifying the overlapping concerns and competing arguments that are woven through the text.

The editors are aware that many initiatives in subject teaching continue to originate from the centre, and that teachers have decreasing control of subject content, pedagogy and assessment strategies. The editors strongly believe that for teaching to remain properly a vocation and a profession, teachers must be invited to be part of a creative and critical dialogue about subject teaching, and should be encouraged to reflect, criticise, problem-solve and innovate. This series is intended to provide teachers with a stimulus for democratic involvement in the development of the discourse of subject teaching.

Susan Capel, Jon Davison, James Arthur and John Moss
December 2010

Editors' introduction

As the chapters presented in this book demonstrate, citizenship education is a diverse and dynamic area for debate. In both theory and practice, numerous different themes and interests produce varied and interesting responses from academics, researchers, practitioners and students alike. We have attempted to cover a range of such debates in this text, attempting to recognise those which are prevalent in the UK currently, as well as those that are generating discussion internationally and cut across local and national boundaries. The overall aim of this book is to provide an insight and exploration of these key debates that citizenship education sparks, and we have sought to do this in an informed and accessible way. We have looked to bring together a mix of experienced and new researchers and academics from both universities and non-academic institutions, and have asked them to contribute their ideas on particular topics within citizenship education.

We hope that the book will prove useful for teachers of citizenship, and those who advise and support citizenship in schools, as well as student teachers learning to teach citizenship, mainly on secondary initial teacher education courses in England. However, the book also addresses citizenship in the primary curriculum and will be of interest to tutors and trainees who wish to prioritise the learning area of history, PSHE, citizenship and social understanding. Citizenship teachers will encounter the debates raised in this book throughout their teaching careers, and we hope, therefore, that the book will be revisited at various times as citizenship teachers consider and reflect on issues relevant to citizenship education in order to reach their own informed judgements. We would like to thank each author for their considerable efforts in contributing to this project. They have made the process of editing this book far easier by delivering thoughtful and articulate work.

We hope that readers will find the chapters here of interest, and that their content, along with the questions posed, will provoke further critical thought and dialogue on topics around such a vital part of a young person's education.

Professor James Arthur, University of Birmingham
Dr Hilary Cremin, University of Cambridge

Part 1

History of citizenship education

Chapter 1

A brief history of citizenship education in England and Wales[1]

John Beck

FORMERLY UNIVERSITY OF CAMBRIDGE

Introduction: the strange absence of citizenship education in Britain

Britain is exceptional among modern Western democracies in having had, until recently, very little direct provision of citizenship education in state schools. One reason for this absence may be that between 1925 and 1988 there was, in England and Wales, almost no direct central government control of curriculum content. Another reason for this neglect is the character of citizenship itself in Britain. Many writers have argued that the British are 'subjects' rather than citizens. Historian David Cannadine contrasts the USA 'where the inhabitants are citizens' with the UK 'where the inhabitants are still subjects' (1998: 53–4). Sociologist Bryan Turner (1990) in his well-known typology put the UK in the category of 'citizen-as-subject'. And Tom Nairn has written scathingly of Britons having 'a surrogate national identity' in which the Crown and the Royal Family provided the key symbolic focus – 'a national-popular identity composed decisively "from above"' (1988: 136–7). In such a situation it is scarcely surprising that Britain has no developed *language of citizenship*, no discourse through which British people naturally think or speak of themselves as citizens, and no public rituals in which citizenship is explicitly the focus (Ahier, Beck and Moore, 2003).

Despite this, Britain presents a paradox in that, especially since the Second World War, UK citizenship has been *substantively* strong – in certain respects much stronger than, say, in the USA. In his celebrated lectures on 'Citizenship and social class' (1950) T.H. Marshall distinguished three 'elements' of citizenship each associated with distinct kinds of entitlements. These were, first, the *civic* element consisting of civic and legal rights and protections, secondly the *political* element comprising a range of rights associated with democratic participation and representation, and finally (and most innovative) the *social* element, which includes, *precisely as rights of citizenship*, a range of welfare entitlements protecting individuals against risks arising from ill health, unemployment, and poverty in old age, and also including free primary and secondary education. Marshall went on to argue the contentious thesis that the realisation of *full* citizenship in a modern democracy needed to include this social element – not least because a relatively high standard of education, health care, etc. was a precondition of citizens being able to exercise their civil and political rights effectively. In Britain, these social entitlements became strongly entrenched, especially through the welfare legislation of Clement Attlee's post-war Labour government (1945–51) and they have, despite some erosion, broadly remained so. It is illuminating in this respect to contrast attitudes to 'socialised' medicine in Britain and the USA. In the UK support for the publicly funded, free-at-the-point-of-delivery National Health Service has remained strong ever since it was introduced in the post-war years. This is so even among many who vote Conservative. On the other hand, there is in the USA a long history of resistance to extending free health care to all as an entitlement of citizenship.

Despite this absence of a developed discourse of citizenship, the education system in England and Wales has played a very significant role in political socialisation in a broader sense – especially in shaping a sense of a shared *British* identity. Historian Linda Colley (1986; 1996) has highlighted the longevity of efforts, going back well *before* the introduction of compulsory elementary schooling in 1870, to shape such a sense of Britishness – based on identifications with the monarchy, the Empire, 'glorious' military and naval victories and the like. Colley notes that this sense of national belonging was always defined *against* an array of 'others' – who epitomised all that was *not* 'British'. Inevitably, the nation's schools were in due course recruited to this task. In an illuminating study, John Ahier, discussing history and geography textbooks used in British elementary and primary schools in the period 1880–1960, has shown how various kinds of 'othering' worked to shape a sense of *national superiority* among British children. He notes that school texts in regional geography

> both established a national confidence and at the same time, a set of assumptions about other races. It located 'them' (native people of 'the colonies') firmly in their climates and in lands which inhibited their growth towards civilisation. ... In these books there is a clear implication of a natural hierarchy by which the British were given their place in the world. It is a place that demands hard work and delayed gratification but offers superiority.
>
> (Ahier, 1988: 163–4)

Ahier also draws attention to the peculiarly direct way in which these texts addressed the imaginary child reader whilst simultaneously positioning the text's author 'as teacher', and doing so in ways that silenced differences of social class or locality or gender – instead positioning these readers as 'unified children of the nation' (ibid.: 51). Ahier goes on to draw attention to a range of *contradictions* in the discourse of the two subjects – 'history books attempted to establish for the reader the primitive bonds of the Anglo-Saxon race yet the geography books belittled other, similar lives, as foreign and primitive' – yet he emphasises that despite such contradictions, 'the texts ... were always trying to stabilize and pull together the position of the reader as *child of the nation*' (ibid.: 59). In such ways and over many decades, key aspects of what was taught in schools, as well as a wide range of 'hidden curriculum' and extra-curricular influences (including youth movements such as Scouts and Guides, Boys' and Girls' Brigades, etc.), helped to shape a strong sense of British identity that created powerful solidarities, uniting what was then a largely ethnically homogeneous people into the 'imaginary community' of the nation (Anderson, 1983).

Yet this 'forming' of Britons happened very largely in the absence of a language of citizenship or of direct provision for citizenship education. Of course, explicit education for citizenship was not *wholly* absent in state schools. For example, a number of 'civics' texts were produced in the inter-war years, such as Kathleen Gibberd's *Young Citizens: Simple Civics for Boys and Girls* (1935). Also, both before and after the Second World War, wider political developments such as the formation of the League of Nations and concerns about the growth of communism and fascism had some educational impact, one example being the formation of the Association for Education in Citizenship in 1935. In the post-war period, concerns about threats to democracy from 'totalitarianism', the 'authoritarian personality' and the like, spurred the Ministry of Education in 1949 to publish a pamphlet entitled *Citizens Growing Up*. But as Derek Heater ruefully noted more than 20 years later, this document was far from radical: it claimed that 'citizenship is a matter of character' (ibid.: 3) and urged teachers to help lay the 'foundations of a healthy democratic society' by encouraging in their pupils 'the old and simple virtues of humility, service and respect' (ibid.: 4) – an emphasis Heater saw as preparing 'pupils to be citizens with duties rather than rights' (Heater, 1972, reprinted in Crick and Heater, 1977). In any event, Heater saw this weak post-war impetus towards citizenship education as quickly fading, adding that 'the Association for Education in Citizenship finally spluttered out of existence … in 1957' (ibid.).

'Political education'

The first concerted efforts to promote direct political education in schools in England and Wales resulted from the forming in 1970 of the Politics Association and the founding of the journal *Teaching Politics* in 1971 – all under the joint chairmanship of Bernard Crick and Derek Heater. In retrospect, two main things stand out about this period, during which Heater initially claimed to have detected a 'burgeoning of interest' in political education (Heater, 1977: 58–78). First, as Crick later acknowledged, it turned out to be 'a false dawn of the citizenship movement in the curriculum' (2000: 13), real progress having to wait another 30 years. Secondly, it is striking that in all the writing and advocacy of these years (from the late 1960s to the early 1980s) the vocabulary of 'citizenship' is conspicuous by its *absence*. The word does not appear at all in the index of Crick and Heater's 1977 book, nor in Crick and Porter's influential 'Political Education and Political Literacy' (1978), nor was it included among Crick's 'basic concepts for political education' (Crick, 1974) which were foundational to his key educational idea: the development of *political literacy* among young people. In most of the key essays of this time, the educational goal is described as the formation of 'a politically literate person' rather than a 'citizen'. This focus on 'political education' and 'political literacy' can partly be understood as a reaction against the aridity and descriptiveness of the then current examination syllabuses in 'British Constitution' and 'Civics'. Charmion Cannon of the London Institute of Education memorably described such approaches as 'cataloguing institutions' and Crick himself, in an early polemical essay, attacked them for their blandness and lack of political realism (1969). Various developments in the 1970s, however, helped foster a stronger interest in more open and critical forms of political education. These included the lowering of the voting age to 18 in 1970 and the raising of the school leaving age to 16 in 1972, changes coinciding with intensified concerns both about political *apathy* among young voters but also about the 'wrong kinds' of political *activism* (evident in student revolts, the growth of the National Union of School Students, etc.). All this increased the perceived need for the young to be educated to be *responsibly* engaged with mainstream political processes. The concept of 'political literacy', combining as it did an understanding of core political concepts and the developing a disposition to become actively but responsibly involved in political processes, directly addressed such concerns.

Yet despite this apparently propitious context, the efforts of the Politics Association met with little success. Explicit political education for the majority of pupils remained absent or at best marginal in most state schools throughout the 1970s and 80s. This period did see, at least in some of the more adventurous comprehensive schools, considerable curriculum innovation in which political *issues* were prominent – for example in schools that introduced courses in Integrated Humanities. This included certain schools that drew inspiration from, or directly implemented, national programmes like the Schools Council/Nuffield-sponsored Humanities Project, with its explicit focus on controversial thematic issues such as war, the environment, sex and relationships, etc. (Stenhouse, 1967; Schools Council/Nuffield Humanities Project, 1970) and its equally controversial pedagogy involving the teacher as the 'neutral chair' of the pupils' own discussion (see Bailey, 1971; Elliott, 1971; Stenhouse, 1972). Also, these years saw a dramatic growth in examined courses at CSE, and GCE O and A levels in Sociology and Social Studies, with some History syllabuses also moving away from conventional narrative approaches towards a stronger focus on historical interpretation, identification of bias, etc. This proliferation of developments in the broad area of the humanities, as well as significant rivalry between various teachers' subject organisations (notably between the Politics Association and the Association for the Teaching of the Social Sciences) probably further weakened the thrust for a more focused approach to political education. Revealingly, Bernard Crick himself was later critical of his failure at this time to engage with social studies teachers: 'less pardonable was my ignoring of social studies at that time' – contrasting this situation with 'the new citizenship' of the new millennium, which he saw as 'a creative synthesis of politics and social studies' (2000: 13). Growing political radicalism among teachers influenced by Marxist and feminist ideas (for example members of the Socialist Teachers' Alliance) was a further source of professional division in the 1970s and 80s. Importantly, this also gave force and legitimacy to a growing New Right critique of 'the politicization of the curriculum', which was promoted initially in the *Black Papers* on education, published between 1969 and 1977 (e.g. Cox and Dyson, 1969; Cox and Boyson, 1977), and later in the polemics of such lobbyists as the Hillgate Group. This led to calls for a curriculum of 'tried and trusted' traditional subjects grounded in a sense of Britain's distinctive cultural and Christian heritage – calls to which the National Curriculum of 1988 was, in certain ways, a clear response (see Hillgate Group, 1986).

The National Curriculum and citizenship education

The introduction of a National Curriculum in England and Wales as a central element of the 1988 Education Reform Act was a key turning point in the fortunes of citizenship education. It coincided with the setting up in 1987 of a Commission on Citizenship by the then Speaker of the House of Commons – an initiative resulting (once again) from growing concerns among parliamentarians about perceived political apathy among young people. Together, these developments led to Citizenship being introduced as a non-statutory 'Cross-curricular Theme' of the National Curriculum – supported by a useful 'curriculum guidance' document for schools (National Curriculum Council, 1990). Although this was a significant milestone, putting national citizenship education on the map for the first time, there were two main reasons why its impact was actually limited: first, many in the Conservative governments of the time were suspicious of what they saw as the social democratic and pro-European bias of the Speaker's Commission (see Graham with Tytler, 1993: 4); secondly and more importantly, the new 'theme' of citizenship was not merely non-statutory but competed for scarce curriculum time with four more such 'themes' in addition to the Core and Foundation subjects of the *statutory* curriculum.

There is good reason to believe that it was the appointment of David Blunkett as Secretary of State for Education in Tony Blair's first New Labour administration in 1997, and Blunkett's personal association with Bernard Crick who had been his tutor in Politics at Sheffield University, that led to Crick being appointed to chair a new Advisory Group on Citizenship. The group published its Final Report in September 1988, containing a strong recommendation that citizenship education should become a *statutory* element of the National Curriculum (QCA, 1988: 22), advice that Blunkett's support ensured became a reality. The new subject of Citizenship was introduced in 2002 as a statutory Foundation Subject in secondary schools and as part of the non-statutory PSHE framework in the primary sector. In Crick's words, Citizenship was 'a subject at last' – with Britain, in this respect, belatedly 'joining almost every other parliamentary democracy in the world' (2000: 1).

The 'Citizenship Order' that prescribed the 'programmes of study' for the new subject (see QCA, 1999) was deliberately less prescriptive than for other statutory subjects. Following the advice of the Advisory Group, the proposals for content were indicative not mandatory, with a high degree of autonomy for schools to determine their own approach in terms of content, pedagogy and whether the subject would be 'delivered' through dedicated Citizenship lessons, through other subjects, as part of PSHE (personal, social and health education), etc. The main justifications for this were a desire to avoid risks of direct government control in such a sensitive area but also to enable schools to reflect distinctive characteristics of their local situations and to teach to their strengths. In other respects, however, citizenship education was defined to reflect and promote a 'maximal' conception of citizenship (McLaughlin, 1992) which went beyond the narrowly cognitive to embrace the fostering of skills and dispositions to equip pupils to become active citizens:

> we aim ... for people to think of themselves as active citizens, willing, able and equipped to have an influence in public life and with the critical capacities to weigh evidence before speaking and acting ... [and] to extend radically to young people the best in existing traditions of community involvement and public service.
>
> (QCA, 1998: 7)

Also, the Advisory Group's recommendation that the programmes of study should be 'tightly enough defined so that standards and objectivity can be inspected by Ofsted' (ibid.: 2) was adhered to. The QCA subsequently provided a range of impressive advisory and support materials, beginning with *Citizenship at Key Stages 3 and 4: Initial Guidance for Schools* (2000).

In 2007, the QCA undertook a major review of the secondary curriculum that included not only Citizenship but also non-statutory PSHEE (physical, social health and economic education) (extended to embrace 'economic well-being and enterprise'). In the same year, the Ajegbo Report (*Curriculum Review: Diversity and Citizenship*) made an important recommendation, accepted by government, that a 'fourth strand' focusing on 'identities and diversity: living together in the UK' should be added to the statutory specification of citizenship education from September 2008 (DfES, 2007). In that same year, schools were also given a new statutory duty to 'promote social cohesion'. The intended content and balance of citizenship education was, in consequence, extended in the direction of a stronger focus on citizens' multiple and overlapping identities within a multicultural and multiethnic society (QCA, 2008) but also to include what the authors of the Seventh Report of the NFER Citizenship Education Longitudinal Study (CELS) referred to as 'educating not just for political literacy but increasingly for community cohesion', emphasizing that this involved 'a broadening of the role of citizenship education, both in schools and local communities' (Keating *et al.*, 2009: para 1.4.1.3).

To date, we have limited *evidence* about the content and character of citizenship education in English state schools – and unsurprisingly, very little yet about the impact of these most recent policy changes. The CELS Report of 2009 (Keating *et al.*, op. cit.) identified a mixed picture from its longitudinal sample of secondary schools. On the one hand, it cited evidence that in some schools the 'impetus of the revised and updated Citizenship curriculum' was reflected in plans 'for the introduction of a specialist team for CE (citizenship education) and/or an increase in the time allocated for delivery in 2009–10'. In less committed schools, however, and especially in those the report revealingly refers to as 'exam-rich', 'citizenship education is affected by lack of status and momentum, and by pressures on the timetable from core subjects', highlighting one instance where 'CE is being pushed out of the curriculum' so that 'the new curriculum is not expected to have much impact due to the low status of the subject' (ibid.: para 7.2.2). Overall however, the Report's conclusion was positive: 'CE has become increasingly embedded and established in secondary schools in England over the course of CELS and ... its status has improved, at least to date' (ibid.: para 7.2.3). The Report of the House of Commons Education and Skills Select Committee's enquiry into citizenship education in 2006–7 revealed a similarly uneven pattern of provision, noting that 'the evidence we have received on the ... quality of CE ... describes a field that is patchy at best: while there is evidence of good – and sometimes excellent – practice, viewed nationally the situation is profoundly uneven and in a minority of cases ... students are missing out on their entitlement entirely' (House of Commons Education and Skills Committee, 2007: 40). The Committee drew particular attention to inadequacies in dealing with issues of diversity:

> Scott Harrison of Ofsted told us: 'what we are finding is more teaching of what you might perceive as the central political literacy/government/voting/law area than, for example, the diversity of the UK, the EU, the Commonwealth, which are somewhat neglected ... I am talking about, for example, the diversity of the UK, which in the [Statutory] Order [describes as] 'the regional, national, religious, ethnic diversity of Britain'. Some people find that difficult to teach.
>
> (ibid.: 36)

The Committee's Report noted that the Ajegbo review had reached similar conclusions: 'issues of identity and diversity are more often than not neglected ... and when these issues are referred to, coverage is often unsatisfactory and lacks contextual depth' (ibid.: 36).

At the time of writing, the most representative data available about CE in English state schools was that contained in the Ofsted report *Citizenship Established? Citizenship in Schools 2006/9* (Ofsted, 2010a), based on a survey of formal inspections of 91 secondary schools. It too revealed a mixed pattern with just over half of the schools categorized as 'good' or 'outstanding' – which, however, means that almost half were graded 'unsatisfactory' or only 'satisfactory'. (Ofsted has frequently intimated that 'satisfactory' can be read as 'not really satisfactory' – and provision in 10 of the schools inspected was judged clearly unsatisfactory.) Discussing these weak schools, Ofsted's own summary stated:

> Students' knowledge was often uneven ... While students ... knew a good deal about some aspects (such as human rights) there were important gaps in their knowledge, for example in political understanding. This reflected an uneven quality of teaching, only partial coverage of the curriculum, and a lack of focused leadership. In schools found satisfactory or worse, the report found contributions from other subjects to citizenship were negligible and citizenship was often forced to share an inadequate curriculum slot with PSHE to the detriment of both ... The survey also identified a need for more in-service training ... with schools slow to take up places on continuing professional development courses ...
>
> (Ofsted, 2010b)

More positively, the summary report indicated that 'the best examples of citizenship education are often found in schools where citizenship has dedicated and regular space on the timetable' adding that schools that deal with the subject mainly by suspending the timetable periodically 'are most unlikely to meet National Curriculum requirements' (ibid.).

Some unresolved tensions in citizenship and citizenship education in England and Wales

Inevitably, some of the tensions around citizenship *education* are inseparable from problems surrounding citizenship itself – especially when, in a globalising world, Western European societies continue to experience radical changes on a variety of fronts whilst also becoming increasingly diverse internally, both culturally and ethnically. Some politicians have seen the promotion of *common national citizenship* as a means of engendering social cohesion in this changing context. New Labour Prime Ministers Tony Blair and Gordon Brown, for example, in the first decade of the 21st century, sought to focus such hoped-for unity around the idea of 'Britishness', with Brown seeking to rally support for what he claimed were 'the enduring ideas that Britain gave the world – a commitment to liberty ... a belief in fairness' (2006). However, as the authors of the Ajegbo Report, who discussed this approach with a wide sample of respondents, noted: 'throughout our consultations, concerns were expressed about defining 'Britishness', about the term's divisiveness, and how it can be used to exclude others' (DfES, 2007: 8). Other commentators have argued that despite well-meant intentions to shape a more *inclusive* form of Britishness, such proposals still risk being seen as assimilationist, and that in any case, the idea of shared British *citizenship* lacks both symbolic resonance and popular appeal, not least because of the long-standing problem that most Britons still do not think of themselves *as* 'citizens'.

A related preoccupation with British identity is associated with a tendency on the part of successive UK governments to promote a vision of Britain that is more focused on *local* identities and that seeks to reinvigorate a stronger sense of *community* and *civil society*. In such visions, power is said to be devolved from the central state to 'ordinary people on the ground', accompanied by efforts to encourage local citizen participation, a culture of volunteering, a stronger sense of community, with individuals taking greater personal and moral responsibility for their own actions. The most recent expression of this type of intervention is the idea of 'The Big Society' launched by Britain's new Conservative–Liberal Democrat coalition government in May 2010 and spear-headed by a newly created Minister for Civil Society. In rhetoric typical of this kind of agenda, Prime Minister David Cameron declared:

> we know instinctively that the state is often too inhuman, monolithic and clumsy to tackle our deepest social problems; we know the best ideas come from the ground up, not the top down ... when you give people and communities more power over their own lives ... great things happen.
>
> (Sparrow, 2010: 8)

The Big Society agenda included the creation of a National Citizens' Service Programme which, Cameron declared,

> will bring together sixteen year olds from across the country in a three-week programme where they can learn what it means to be socially responsible, to serve their community, to get on and get along with people from different backgrounds.
>
> (Cameron, 2009)

Other elements of the vision involve enhanced roles for 'social entrepreneurs' and 'community activists', greater opportunities for groups of parents and/or professionals to control local schools, increased local accountability and a culture that would develop 'a new can-do and should-do attitude where Britons once again feel in control of their lives' (ibid.).

A brief retrospective glance, however, proves very illuminating here. Only four years previously, Gordon Brown was claiming just this kind of local empowerment and community involvement as one of *New Labour's* key achievements in promoting active citizenship:

> Having talked to young people shaping youth services, parents who run schools and under-five services, and social entrepreneurs transforming their communities, I am convinced that Britain is seeing the rise of a new kind of citizen, involved in their neighbourhoods, and now demanding the right to set the agenda ... Britain is advancing liberty ... as empowerment.
>
> (Brown, 2006)

Going back even further, we find Conservative Foreign Secretary Douglas Hurd employing uncannily similar rhetoric, but in his case contrasting the supposedly core *Conservative* commitment to localism and voluntary participation with what he claimed was the Left's centralised 'bureaucratic definition of citizenship':

> Underpinning our social policy are the traditions – the diffusion of power, civic obligation, and voluntary service – which are central to Conservative philosophy and rooted in British (particularly English) history ... So (our) government policy is to shift power outwards, away from the corporatist battalions to the small platoons ... Thus parents will get a bigger say in education, council tenants will get more control over the management of their estates.
>
> (Hurd, 1988: 30)

As I have noted elsewhere, 'such discursive convergence speaks volumes' (Beck, 2008: 36) and as social theorist Gerard Delanty observes, such 'governmental communitarianism is often a superficial politics of legitimacy' (2003: 90). These recurring rhetorical appeals to what are represented as authentically British traditions of localism, individual empowerment and personal responsibility are, arguably, a feature of a changing world where, in reality, not only individuals but also national governments are increasingly *disempowered* – by the consolidation of trans-national corporations into ever larger global entities, by the growing power of 'too-big-to-fail' banks and financial markets, and by an environmentally reckless consumer culture. Yet politicians of all mainstream parties seem irresistibly drawn to these selective and nostalgic visions of 'a better British past' that can, somehow, apparently be recaptured through rhetorical interventions and efforts of political will. A further problem with such agendas, of course, is that they can legitimise government interventions to shape citizenship *education* in accordance with party-political agendas.

Another important area of tension surrounding citizenship in the modern world is that as citizenship discourse has been increasingly extended in association with various kinds of 'rights' agendas, a widening range of sub-groups have sought to use citizenship to promote their own particularistic claims – and not only for enhanced rights but also for 'recognition'. This typically includes demands that other citizens should not only acknowledge a group's right to pursue and promote its distinctive identity but that they should also acknowledge the *positive worth* of these identities. This sort of 'politics of recognition', however, has a potential, at least in some cases, to heighten *division* between citizens – for example between those who wish to strengthen legal restrictions against 'blasphemy' and those championing rights of free speech, including the right to offend other people's deeply held religious beliefs and commitments.[2] Derek Heater, who, as we have seen, spent several decades promoting citizenship education in Britain, recognised this emerging problem two decades ago, presciently commenting:

Citizenship as a useful political concept is in danger of being torn asunder and any hope of a coherent civic education left in tatters as a consequence. By a bitter twist of historical fate, the concept which evolved to provide a sense of identity and community is on the verge of becoming a source of communal dissension. As more and more diverse interests identify particular elements for their doctrinal and practical needs, so the component parts of the citizenship idea are being made to do service for the whole. And under the strain of these centripetal forces, citizenship as a total idea may be threatened with disintegration.

(Heater, 1990: 282)

These are just two examples of areas in which debates around citizenship continue to be vigorous but also contested. Indeed, it has often been argued that citizenship, at least in the modern world, is an *essentially contested concept* (Gallie, 1955) – i.e. one about which there will always be disagreement between equally well-informed and equally serious people. An important implication of this may be that it is difficult in modern pluralistic societies to justify educating *for* a specific 'thick' form of citizenship, and that efforts might better be focused on equipping pupils to understand what political questions are, and why they are often contested, and to prepare them to become, as far as possible, active participants in such debates – at every level from school and local community to the national and even the global.

Questions for further investigation

1 In what ways is citizenship a contested concept and what implications might this have for citizenship education?
2 What is meant by 'political literacy' and why did Sir Bernard Crick think this was so central to serious education for citizenship?
3 Should schools educate mainly *about* citizenship or should they also educate *for* citizenship?
4 What similarities and differences are there between New Labour's idea of 'active citizenship' and David Cameron's concept of 'The Big Society'?
5 What are the strengths and weaknesses of putting volunteering at the centre of schools' programmes of citizenship education?

Notes

1 In a brief chapter of this sort it is not really possible to consider developments in citizenship education across the UK as a whole. Scotland and Northern Ireland have for many decades enjoyed considerable autonomy in shaping their own curricula and pedagogy, and, more recently, devolution of responsibility for education to the Welsh Assembly has increased differences between provision in England and Wales.
2 I have discussed these issues in more detail in the final chapter of *Meritocracy, Citizenship and Education* (Beck, 2008, Ch. 8).

Suggested further reading

Beck, J. (2003) 'Citizenship and citizenship education in England', in Beck, J. and Earl, M. (Eds.) *Key Issues in Secondary Education*. (2nd Ed.) London: Continuum. pp. 158–71. This is a brief, relatively simple overview of some key conceptual issues relating to citizenship, and some contemporary challenges to both citizenship and citizenship education – arising from cultural and ethnic diversity, the revival of interest in communitarian theories and the influence of postmodernism.

Crick, B. (2000) *Essays on Citizenship*. London: Continuum. A key text that reprints most of Crick's seminal essays on political education as well as providing an 'insider's' account of the emergence of Citizenship in England as a statutory subject of the National Curriculum.

Heater, D. (1990) *Citizenship: The Civic Ideal in World History, Politics and Education*. Harlow: Longman. A classic text that traces the evolution of citizenship from the rise of Athenian democracy, through the development of the modern state to the expansion of democratic citizenship in the 20th century. It concludes with an examination of a range of challenges to citizenship as a useful political concept and an analysis of key issues for citizenship education.

Isin, E.F. and Wood, P.K. (1999) *Citizenship and Identity*. London: Sage. An excellent wide-ranging discussion of the extension of citizenship to include a growing range of identity issues – such as consumer citizenship, sexual citizenship, cultural citizenship and cosmopolitan citizenship.

References

Ahier, J. (1988) *Industry, Children and the Nation: An Analysis of National Identity in School Textbooks*. London: The Falmer Press.

Ahier, J., Beck, J. and Moore, R. (2003) *Graduate Citizens: Issues of Citizenship in Higher Education*. London: RoutledgeFalmer.

Anderson, B. (1983) *Imagined Communities: Reflections on the Origins and Spread of Nationalism*. London: Verso.

Bailey, C.H. (1971) 'Rationality, democracy and the neutral teacher', *Cambridge Journal of Education*, 1, 2, pp. 68–76, reprinted in Norris, N. (Ed.) (2008) *Curriculum and the Teacher: 35 Years of the Cambridge Journal of Education*. London: Routledge. pp. 118–24.

Beck, J. (2008) *Meritocracy, Citizenship and Education: New Labour's Legacy*. London: Continuum.

Brown, G. (2006) 'We have renewed Britain: now we must champion it', *The Guardian*, 15th February 2006, p. 27.

Cameron, D. (2009) *Our 'Big Society' Plan*. London: The Conservative Party.

Cannadine, D. (1998) *Class in Britain*. New Haven, CT: Yale University Press.

Colley, L. (1986) 'Whose nation? Class and national consciousness in Britain 1750–1830', *Past and Present*, 11, 3, pp. 115–27.

——(1996) *Britons: Forging the Nation 1707–1937*. London: Vintage.

Cox, C.B. and Boyson, R. (Eds.) (1977) *Black Paper 1977*. London: Temple Smith.

Cox, C.B. and Dyson, A.E. (Eds.) (1969) *Fight for Education: A Black Paper*. London: The Critical Quarterly Society.

Crick, B. (1969) 'The introducing of politics in schools', in Heater, D. (Ed.) *The Teaching of Politics*. London: Methuen, reprinted in Crick, B. (2000) *Essays on Citizenship*. London: Continuum. pp. 13–34.

——(1974) 'Basic political concepts and curriculum development', *Teaching Politics*, January 1974, reprinted in Crick, B. and Heater, D. (1977) *Essays on Political Education*. Ringmer: Falmer Press. pp. 81–112, and in Crick, B. (2000) *Essays on Citizenship*. London: Continuum. pp. 75–111.

——(2000) *Essays on Citizenship*. London: Continuum.

Crick, B. and Heater, D. (1977) *Essays on Political Education*. Ringmer: Falmer Press.

Crick, B. and Porter, A. (Eds.) (1978) *Political Education and Political Literacy*. London: Longman.

Delanty, G. (2003) *Community*. London: Routledge.

DfES (Department for Education and Skills) (2007) *Curriculum Review: Diversity and Citizenship*. London: Department for Education and Skills.

Elliott, J. (1971) 'The concept of the neutral teacher', *Cambridge Journal of Education*, 1, 2, pp. 60–67, reprinted in Norris, N. (Ed.) (2008) *Curriculum and the Teacher: 35 Years of the Cambridge Journal of Education*. London: Routledge. pp. 112–17.

Gallie, W.B. (1955) 'Essentially contested concepts', *Proceedings of the Aristotelian Society*, 56, pp. 167–98.

Gibberd, K. (1935) *Young Citizens: Simple Civics for Boys and Girls*. London: J.M. Dent.

Graham, D. with Tytler, D. (1993) *A Lesson for Us All: The Making of the National Curriculum*. London: Routledge.

Heater, D. (1972) 'Political education in schools: the official attitude', *Teaching Politics*, May 1972, reprinted in Crick, B. and Heater, D. (1977) *Essays on Political Education*. Ringmer: Falmer Press. pp. 27–33.

——(1977) 'A burgeoning of interest: political education in Britain', *International Journal of Political Education*, Autumn, 1977, reprinted in Crick, B. and Heater, D. (1977) *Essays on Political Education*. Ringmer: Falmer Press. pp. 58–78.

——(1990) *Citizenship: The Civic Ideal in World History, Politics and Education*. Harlow: Longman.

Hillgate Group (1986) *Whose Schools? A Radical Manifesto*. London: The Hillgate Group.

House of Commons Education and Skills Committee (2007) *Citizenship Education: Second Report of Session 2006–07*. London: The Stationery Office.

Hurd, D. (1988) 'Citizenship in the Tory democracy', *The Spectator*, 15 April 1988, pp. 29–30.

Keating, A., Kerr, D., Lopes, J., Featherstone, G. and Benton, T. (2009) *Embedding Citizenship Education in Secondary Schools in England: Citizenship Education Longitudinal Study Seventh Annual Report* (DSCF Research Report 172). London: Department of Children, Schools and Families.

McLaughlin, T.H. (1992) 'Citizenship, diversity and education: a philosophical perspective', *Journal of Moral Education*, 21, pp. 235–50.

Marshall, T.H. (1950) *Citizenship and Social Class*. Cambridge: Cambridge University Press.

Ministry of Education (1949) *Citizens Growing Up* (Pamphlet No. 16). London: HMSO.

Nairn, T. (1988) *The Enchanted Glass: Britain and Its Monarchy*. London: Radius.

National Curriculum Council (NCC) (1990) *Curriculum Guidance 8: Education for Citizenship*. London: National Curriculum Council.

Ofsted (Office for Standards in Education) (2010a) *Citizenship Established? Citizenship in Schools 2006/09*. London: Ofsted. Available at: http://www.ofsted.gov.uk/resources/citizenship-established-citizenship-schools-200609 (accessed 9th April 2010).

——(2010b) *Steady Progress for Citizenship Education*. Available at: http://www.ofsted.gov.uk/news/Steady-progress-for-citizenship-education (accessed 9th April 2010).

Qualifications and Curriculum Authority (QCA) (1998) *Education for Citizenship and the Teaching of Democracy in Schools: Final Report of the Advisory Group on Citizenship*. London: QCA.

——(1999) *Citizenship Key Stages 3–4*. London: QCA.

——(2000) *Citizenship at Key Stages 3 and 4: Initial Guidance for Schools*. London: QCA.

——(2008) *The Secondary Curriculum Review: Programme of Study (non-statutory): Citizenship: Key Stage 3 and Key Stage 4*. London: QCA.

Schools Council/Nuffield Humanities Project (1970) *The Humanities Project: An Introduction*. London: Schools Council Publications with Heinemann.

Sparrow, A. (2010) 'David Cameron's "big society" plan will give power to the people', *The Guardian*, 18th May 2010, p. 8.

Stenhouse, L. (1967) *Culture and Education*. London: Nelson.

——(1972) 'Teaching through small group discussion', *Cambridge Journal of Education*, 2, 1, pp. 18–24, reprinted in Norris, N. (Ed.) (2008) *Curriculum and the Teacher: 35 Years of the Cambridge Journal of Education*. London: Routledge. pp. 107–11.

Turner, B.S. (1990) 'Outline of a theory of citizenship', *Sociology*, 24, 2, pp. 189–217.

Chapter 2

Comparative and international perspectives on citizenship education

David Kerr

BIRKBECK COLLEGE, UNIVERSITY OF LONDON

Introduction

This chapter focuses on comparative and international perspectives on citizenship education, or civic education as it is sometimes described internationally. It begins by defining what is meant by 'comparative' and 'international' perspectives in education and considering the scope of such perspectives on citizenship education. It then sets out some of the key influences on how and why such perspectives are increasingly being sought on citizenship education. This is followed by a short overview of the main ways in which such perspectives are being obtained. The chapter concludes with a review of some of the current debates concerning comparative and international perspectives on citizenship education. The chapter aims to provide a concise introduction to a vibrant and fast-growing dimension of citizenship education. It is hoped that this will enable the reader to explore such perspectives further.

What are comparative and international perspectives on citizenship education?

Comparative and international perspectives are, in fact, two interrelated, multi-disciplinary fields of educational theory and research. They attract researchers, policy-makers, stakeholders and practitioners from a range of disciplines including education, political science, sociology, economics, social sciences, history and psychology, among others. There is 'comparative' and alongside it 'international' education. The leading scholars who work in both fields state that the main distinction, though it remains fluid, is that comparative includes 'the more academic, analytic, and scientific aspects of the field, while international is related to cooperation, understanding and exchange elements' (Rust, 2002). Or put another way 'while comparative education advances our understanding of education through comparative research, international education as an endeavour is normative; it helps develop attitudes of tolerance and understanding of different cultures' (Epstein, 1994).

Put simply, 'comparative' entails the study of more than one unit of comparison. Given that the field developed when the nation-state was prominent, the nation-state/national education system has been the primary unit of study and comparison. However, in recent times the interpretation has broadened with some researchers insisting that the unit can also mean samples from different cultures and/or samples from at least two different points in time.

Meanwhile, 'international' involves the advancement of international understanding more generally, as well as specifically in relation to education. It has been characterised by a tradition of promoting humanitarian principles and seeking to bring improvement. Those involved in international education have long had a concern about promoting human rights and the principles of equality, equity and justice.

In reality, the fields of comparative and international education have become increasingly interlinked. This process has accelerated in the last two decades with the desire of policy-makers and researchers to explore and better understand the implications of globalisation for education. It has served to fuse and blur the traditions and practices of both fields as those in comparative education adopt an increasingly internationalist approach in response to the question: 'what is the comparative advantage of comparative education in understanding the changing social context of education and some of the secular dilemmas of equity, equality, and quality of education throughout the world?' (Torres, 2001).

The upshot of these developments is that the impact of globalisation on society and education has succeeded in opening up new areas and topics for research and investigation and brought increasing comparative and international perspectives in those areas (Raby, 2005). One of these new areas is civic and citizenship education. Indeed, it is no surprise that the trajectory of developments in comparative and international education is mirrored by that in the field of citizenship education. It explains why research and investigation of citizenship education over the past two decades has been marked by the increasing appearance and use of comparative and international perspectives.

As a consequence of such perspectives, citizenship education has become an increasingly complex field of study attracting multidisciplinary and multiple methodological approaches on a wide range of topics. This is apparent if you look at the contributors to and contents of the recent landmark *Sage Handbook of Education for Citizenship and Democracy* (Arthur, Davies and Hahn, 2008). The *Handbook* contains contributions from political scientists, philosophers, historians and educationalists on a range of topics and themes, of which many have a comparative and international perspective. The sections of the *Handbook* comprise: key ideas underlying citizenship education – including social justice, philosophy, democracy, diversity, equity and globalisation; geographically based overviews from countries and regions – the specific comparative component; key perspectives – including religion, gender, antiracism, sustainable development and history; characterisations and forms – including community, multicultural, peace, human rights and global education; and, finally, a section on pedagogy – including curriculum, school and community settings and active citizenship. Producing such a handbook for citizenship education would have been unthinkable 20 years ago. The *Handbook* highlights how embedded comparative and international perspectives have become in citizenship education, a trend that will continue apace as the 21st century progresses.

Why are comparative and international perspectives on citizenship education becoming more prominent?

The last two decades have been marked by increased international dialogue about and interest in citizenship education. As Hahn notes in a recent review of citizenship education research, 'clearly, the field of comparative and international civic education has gone global' (Hahn, 2010). The period has witnessed increased consensus, within and across countries and regions, about the importance of citizenship education for the strengthening of democratic societies and for protection against the rise of xenophobia, racism and injustice. This increased importance has been accompanied by the growing prominence of comparative and international perspectives in dialogue about and developments in citizenship education. Policy-makers, practitioners, stakeholders and researchers have shown a keen appetite for learning more about what others are doing in citizenship education and using that learning to progress their own actions.

This development begs the question stated in the sub-title above. The main reasons are summed up in the opening statement from a recent international collection on comparative education:

> The 21st Century has brought to the field [of comparative education] new perspectives, tools and forums for scholarly exchange. The new perspectives include those arising from the forces of globalisation and the changing role of the state. The new tools include ever-advancing information and transportation technology; and the new forms for scholarly exchange include the internet and electronic journals.
>
> (Bray, Adamson and Mason, 2007)

These new perspectives, tools and forums are being driven by four key, interrelated thrusts at both macro and micro levels of society, namely:

- impact of globalisation;
- advances in scientific theory and methodology;
- pragmatic desire to know more;
- deepening international and global understanding.

Impact of globalisation

The increasing interconnectedness in the world, as the 'global village' gets smaller under the impact of globalisation, means that political, social and economic events across the globe are having an increasing and rapid impact on societies and on education policy and practice. Regions, countries and communities around the world now face similar issues, particularly those concerning forms of governance and international relations, equality in society and participation in civic and political life. These issues are bringing altered contexts and new challenges for countries, which, in turn, are testing traditional views of and practices concerning civic and citizenship education.

As the recent *International Report* from the comparative IEA (International Association for the Evaluation of Educational Achievement) International Civic and Citizenship Education Study (ICCS) points out in its introduction (Schulz *et al.*, 2010) these altered contexts and new challenges for countries include:

- Changes in the external threats to civil societies through increases in terrorist attacks and debates about the response civil societies should make have resulted in greater importance being attached to civic and citizenship education (Banks, 2008; Ben-Porath, 2006).
- The migration of peoples within and across continents and countries is challenging notions of identity and bringing increased focus on the role of civic and citizenship education in facilitating social and community cohesion in society (Osler and Starkey, 2008).
- In many countries people are according greater value to democracy as a system of government but, at the same time, social and economic inequalities are threatening the functioning of democratic governments (Gorard and Sundaram, 2008; Reimers, 2007).
- There has been an increase in the importance of non-governmental groups (NGOs) serving as vehicles through which active citizenship can be exercised. New forms of social participation serve a variety of different purposes, ranging from religious to issues such as protection of human rights or protection of the environment (Zadja, 2009; Wade, 2007).
- Modernisation and globalisation of societies, more universal access to new media, increasing consumer consumption and transformation of societal structures (individualism) has continued (Roth and Burbules, 2007; Zadja, 2009).

As countries and communities face up to these challenges and look for solutions, so interest in civic and citizenship education, and in comparative and international perspectives has grown.

Advances in scientific theory and methodology

The challenges brought by globalisation have triggered a revisiting of theories, concepts and practices associated with citizenship and citizenship education. This has seen the construction of more complex theories and concepts for citizenship in attempts to find answers to these challenges. This is because these challenges go from the local to the global. They demand help to explain citizenship issues within and across societies at local, national, regional and international level.

They also require exploration of increasingly complex relationships that lie at the heart of civic and political society and the preparation of people (particularly young people) to undertake their roles and responsibilities as citizens in a rapidly changing world.

This advancement in theory has been particularly in relation to citizenship concepts and practices concerning: rights and responsibilities, engagement, access, identity and belonging. On-going theoretical debates address, among other things, concepts of national identity and belonging, how national identity can be identified and what might be done to confirm national identity (see for example White and Openshaw, 2005; Banks, 2008). This has resulted in a challenge to the nation-state as the unit of collective identity and brought increased investigation of other types of identity formation, such as personal, regional (e.g. European), global and cosmopolitan/multiple and units of comparison (Osler and Starkey, 2008). It has also served to challenge the nation-state/national education system as the main unit of comparison in perspectives on citizenship education.

Scientific advancement in citizenship education has also seen growing research interest in the competencies required of active and informed citizens – i.e. civic knowledge, skills, attitudes, values and behaviours – and in the influences on the development of those competencies, particularly among young people (Hoskins et al., 2006). Researchers and policy-makers are increasingly seeking answers to research questions such as: that has the greater impact on young peoples' civic knowledge, attitudes and behaviour that they experience through education/ school or factors beyond, in their family and local community? What is the extent of interest and disposition to engage in public and political life among young people? And what is the nature of the relationship between civic knowledge and civic attitudes, and action – what is commonly referred to as 'active citizenship'? They are interested in investigating contexts across the world that can help to provide answers to these key questions.

The developments in scientific theory have been matched by advances in methodological approaches. In particular, improvements in research methods and statistics have increased the range of methods that can be used to research and report on citizenship education within and across countries. Whereas previously the individual, qualitative case study, often at national level, was the main unit of comparison for citizenship education, recent statistical advances have increased the ability of researchers and policy-makers to collect and analyse larger quantitative datasets concerning citizenship education in more complex ways.

A notable example of the combined effect of advances in scientific theory and methodology on comparative and international perspectives on citizenship education is the conduct over the past four years of the groundbreaking IEA International Civic and Citizenship Education Study (ICCS). ICCS is the largest comparative study ever undertaken on civic and citizenship education. It has addressed six key research questions, underpinned by a complex assessment framework organised around three dimensions – content, affective-behavioural and cognitive (Schulz et al., 2008). It has collected and begun reporting on a mass of quantitative data from young people, teachers and school leaders in the 38 participating countries, as well as contextual data on policies and practices from policy-makers (Schulz *et al.*, 2010; Kerr *et al.*, 2010).

Pragmatic desire to know more

As the scientific theories underpinning citizenship education have evolved and the range of methodological approaches widened, so the size and appetite of audiences who want to know more about citizenship education has grown. The spread of comparative and international perspectives on citizenship education, accompanied by developments in information and communication technologies (ICTs), has succeeded in increasing the number and range of audiences who are interested in citizenship education. These audiences include:

Policy-makers – at international, regional, national and local level who want to know more about the most effective practices of citizenship, both in and beyond their context, in order to improve their own policy-making in the area.

International and regional agencies – including UNESCO, World Bank and OECD, as well as European Commission (EC) and Council of Europe (CoE) who are interested in international and regional comparisons of citizenship education to ascertain which countries or aspects are more advanced than others and to bring about improved standards.

Academics/researchers – at universities and other research institutions who have an interest in conducting research on citizenship education to strengthen the evidence base and sharing the outcomes through their teaching programmes and networking with other academics across the globe.

Practitioners – teachers and school leaders who are interested in learning more about effective practices in citizenship education so that they can improve their own approaches in the classroom, school and communities beyond the school.

Parents/young people – who, in an increasingly global market environment, want to know about the quality of education overall as well as that provided by individual institutions (schools, colleges and universities) including the nature of their citizenship education policies, practices and outcomes.

These audiences have a voracious appetite for information and data, which is helping to fuel the growth of comparative and international perspectives on citizenship education.

Deepening international and global understanding

The similar agendas and issues of policy-makers and international and regional agencies on citizenship education are leading to deepening international and global understanding of citizenship education. This has seen strengthened international consensus about the significance of citizenship education for modern societies and fuelled the desire to know more about the field. It has encouraged approaches that look to share local and national developments in citizenship education with others while, at the same time, learning from developments elsewhere at regional and international level. The 'two-way' learning that emerges from engagement with comparative and international perspectives on citizenship education is neatly summed up in the following observation: 'Many people who undertake comparative study of education find not only that they learn more about other cultures and societies but also that they learn more about their own' (Bray, Adamson and Mason, 2007).

Such two-way learning has taken time to emerge in citizenship education. Comparative and international perspectives in the field were originally initiated by western countries, particularly the UK and USA. It is only recently that countries in other regions of the world, notably in Asia and the Pacific, and Latin America, have become involved in contributing to and sharing such perspectives. The original western bias has led to the charge that it has encouraged 'educational borrowing' (Phillips and Ochs, 2004; Steiner-Khamsi, 2004). This is where countries in other regions of the world directly copy a policy or practice from a western country to their own context.

The engagement in recent times of policy-makers and researchers from all regions of the world on citizenship education means that there is now much more international and global interchange and understanding about citizenship education. Developments in regions beyond western countries are beginning to inform and transform global approaches to citizenship education. This happens, for example, where western civic republican and liberal traditions of citizenship interact with eastern Confucian-based traditions of duty and reciprocity in associations and relationships.

A good example of such interchange is the inclusion of innovative regional modules as part of the recent IEA ICCS study. All countries participated in the international core of the study. However, countries could also sign up to take part in regional modules for Europe, Latin America and Asia that focused on specific civic and citizenship issues at regional level. What is interesting is the influence of culture and context on the foci of these regional modules. The European module investigated levels of civic knowledge about the EU and attitudes towards movement of peoples, language learning and political co-operation across Europe. Meanwhile, the Asian module focused on issues of trust, duty and national versus personal identity, while the Latin American module concentrated on issues of corruption, violence in society, community action and attitudes towards minority groups. Taken together, the regional modules provide a fascinating snapshot of the diversity of regional comparative perspectives on citizenship education that are currently emerging.

What are the main approaches to comparative and international perspectives on citizenship education?

Given the growth and diversity of the field there is not the space here to review all the comparative and international perspectives on citizenship education, or to detail all the places where such perspectives can be found. Rather the intention here is to highlight, with a few examples, the main approaches to comparative and international perspectives on citizenship education. A useful starting place is a recent review article by Hahn (2010) which points out that there are two main approaches to comparative and international perspectives on citizenship education:

In or within country perspectives – descriptions of policies, practices and aspects of citizenship education in particular countries that are *within* national borders.

Across country comparative and international perspectives – studies where attempts are made to make direct and explicit comparisons *across* national borders and that take into account cultural, historical, social and educational contexts.

The former approach chiefly generates international perspectives and insights between nations, thereby adding to international and global understanding, while the latter provides comparative perspectives across national borders.

In or within country perspectives on citizenship education

These comprise descriptions or case studies of policies and practices on citizenship education from within the borders of countries. They provide opportunities to investigate and draw out similarities and differences in approach across national contexts. In or within country case studies remain the most common approach in providing international perspectives on citizenship education. They include both whole-country descriptions of policy and practice in citizenship education (Torney-Purta, Shwille and Amadeo, 1999; Arthur, Davies and Hahn, 2008), as well as case studies of particular aspects, such as active citizenship, student voice and assessment (Kerr, Keating and Ireland, 2009; Davies, 2002).

The history of comparative and international perspectives on citizenship education shows them beginning in western countries and spreading to other regions. It is, therefore, not surprising that the volume of in or within country perspectives is greater for North America (Canada and the USA) and Europe (including the UK) than for other regions of the world. However, in recent years there has been an increasing number of within country perspectives from Asia and the Pacific (including Australia), Latin America and Africa and the Middle East (Grossman, Lee and Kennedy, 2008; Reimers, 2007; Finkel and Ernst, 2005; Ichilov, 2005). The within country perspectives are often included in edited volumes or special editions of research journals and can have a region, cross-region or aspect-specific focus.

Across country comparative and international perspectives on citizenship education

These comprise direct comparisons of data and case studies on citizenship usually across countries and regions. They provide opportunities to investigate issues and aspects of citizenship from the same perspective across countries in order to provide comparative international perspectives and findings. Perspectives across national borders on citizenship education are less prevalent than those within country. However, across country perspectives have become more common in the past two decades, spurred by the twin thrusts of advances in theory and methodologies and the appetite of policy-makers and international and regional agencies to know more about citizenship education policies and practices around the world. The potential to build more sophisticated analytical models to investigate citizenship education, along with the ability to collect and analyse large, complex datasets and the willingness of countries across the globe to take part in such activities has increased the number and scale of across country perspectives on citizenship education.

The across country comparisons tend to be of three types. First, large-scale, comparative studies undertaken by the International Association for the Evaluation of Educational Achievement (IEA), with the active support of policy-makers at national, regional and international level. Though small in number they have had tremendous reach and impact. The IEA has conducted two landmark studies in the past 15 years that provide the largest and most comprehensive comparative and international perspectives on citizenship education ever undertaken. The first, the Civic Education Study (CIVED), was conducted in 1999 and included case studies of citizenship education in the first phase and questionnaires to nationally representative samples of 14-year-olds, their teachers and school leaders in the second phase (Torney-Purta, Schwille and Amadeo, 1999; Torney-Purta et al., 2001). CIVED provided groundbreaking evidence of the state of citizenship teaching and learning and of the civic competencies of young people at the end of the 20th century.

The second, the recent International Civic and Citizenship Education Study (ICCS), conducted from 2006 to 2010, has built upon CIVED and re-examined the influences on the civic development of young people and their readiness to participate in civic and political life both in and beyond school at the start of the 21st century (Schulz et al., 2008). Thirty-eight countries from across the globe have participated in the study and data has been collected from over 160,000 14-year-olds, their teachers and school leaders in those countries. The study has also included innovative regional modules for Europe, Latin America and Asia alongside the core international instruments. To date, the study has published an International and European report with further regional reports and a contextual encyclopaedia planned (Schulz et al., 2010; Kerr et al., 2010). These reports are currently being pored over by policy-makers and researchers worldwide.

The second type of across country perspectives are comparative studies involving comparison of particular citizenship aspects across a number of countries. These are often commissioned by regional agencies who want to know more about citizenship education across the region. For example, the European Commission sponsored a survey of citizenship education in schools and has plans for a similar survey of active citizenship across Europe (Eurydice, 2005). Meanwhile, the

Council of Europe has undertaken a study of citizenship policy-making in Europe, as well as produced a cross-European tool on citizenship and human rights education for policy-makers (Birzea *et al.*, 2004; Kerr and Losito, 2010). The third type of across country perspectives concern secondary analysis of groups of countries using existing datasets, such as those from the IEA studies (Kennedy, Hahn and Lee, 2008).

What are the current debates concerning comparative and international perspectives on citizenship education?

The current debates concerning comparative and international perspectives on citizenship education mirror broader debates about the nature of comparative and international education. Many of the debates have already been touched on in this chapter. Some of the main debates are around six interrelated areas: perspective, measurement, methodology, interpretation and reach, costs and benefits, and gaps in knowledge and understanding. I want to outline briefly the debates in each area, in turn.

Perspective – centred around two issues: units of comparison and scale of comparison. The units of comparison debate is concerned with whether the nation-state/ national education system remains the best unit of comparison and analysis, both within and across countries, or whether there are more appropriate units of comparison that take into account the impact of globalisation and increasing interconnectedness in the world. The scale of comparison debate concerns whether large-scale, broad comparative studies, such as the IEA studies, produce richer international and regional perspectives, compared with smaller scale, more focused, case-study approaches. It is an issue of breadth versus depth of perspective.

Measurement – two related issues: rigour of measurement and ability to measure civic competencies. The rigour of measurement debate relates to whether the theories and methodologies employed in comparative and international studies on citizenship education meet the same standards as studies in other areas, such as mathematics, science and literacy. The recent IEA ICCS study is proof that it is possible for citizenship education studies to meet such standards. The ability to measure civic competencies concerns whether it is possible to accurately measure and compare both the range of components that make up civic competencies and the factors that impact on them. There is an on-going debate about how far it is possible to measure 'active citizenship' components and also to isolate the impact of in-school and out-of-school factors on the acquisition of civic knowledge and development of civic attitudes and behaviours.

Methodology – the issue of what is the most appropriate methodology to provide rich comparative and international perspectives on citizenship education. There is a debate about whether large-scale, across nation studies are more suitable than smaller-scale, within country studies. There is a secondary debate as to whether it is more appropriate to undertake more bottom-up, in-depth case studies of actual citizenship practices compared with top-down overviews of citizenship policies. There is also an emerging debate about how best to tap into the potential of new media and technologies, particularly the internet, social networking and media, to provide comparative and international perspectives on citizenship education that are different from what already exists.

Interpretation and reach – two issues: the nature of bias in interpretation and the extent of reach of perspectives. The debate about bias in interpretation centres on the extent to which there is still an element of western bias in the collection and interpretation of comparative and international perspectives on citizenship education and how far such bias may influence policies and practices in countries in other regions of the world. The question arises as to how far developing countries still engage in 'educational borrowing' from western countries, in terms of looking for solutions to challenges from Europe and the USA. It begs a further question about whether there is sufficient voice for and attention given to perspectives from other countries and regions of the world, such as Latin America, Asia and Africa. There is a further subsidiary question as to how far the findings from comparative and international perspectives on citizenship remain the preserve of particular audiences, notably international and regional agencies and national policy-makers, at the expense of others. Or to put it another way, how can such findings be made available to practitioners, young people and the general public, in ways that are meaningful to them?

Costs and benefits – the question of what represents best value for money in terms of delivering useable comparative and international perspectives. These debates will become more prominent in the coming years as we enter a tougher economic climate globally. The debate concerns scale and outcomes and whether it is more productive for countries to take part in larger cross-national, comparative studies, such as ICCS, or to support a number of smaller within country studies.

Gaps in knowledge and understanding – where the biggest gaps are in knowledge and understanding on citizenship education and how they can be plugged. Hahn (2010) sets out a wish list of further research that is required. It includes more within country and cross-national research on the engagement of ethnic groups with citizenship concepts, the effects of school instruction in citizenship, the effects of gender and sexuality, the approach of transnational students to citizenship, the forms of teacher education that work best and the impact of globalisation on the meaning and concepts of citizenship. I would add the impact of new technologies on civic discourse to this list.

Conclusion

This is a fascinating era in which to be interested and engaged in citizenship education. The area has come to prominence as societies, policy-makers and researchers across the globe struggle to respond positively to the challenges posed by rapid, on-going changes. Chief among these challenges is the desire to foster safe, cohesive societies comprised of active, critical and informed citizens and how to educate people for such roles and responsibilities. The fact that societies across the world face similar challenges has fuelled the appetite to know more about citizenship education policies and practices within and across countries. It explains why comparative and international perspectives on citizenship education have grown exponentially over the past 20 years and become part of the fabric of the area. It is a trend that will continue as the 21st century progresses. Indeed, as Hahn notes in her recent review of the field: 'It is an exciting time to be working in the field [of citizenship education] as scholars spanning the globe share experiences and viewpoints, and increasingly form teams to examine questions using varied methods and both insider and outsider viewpoints' (Hahn, 2010).

I could not have put it better. Comparative and international perspectives on citizenship education are very much here to stay.

Questions for further investigation

1 What do you think is the distinction between comparative and international education? How far is it possible to pick out that distinction in the research reports, journals, books and other outputs that provide such perspectives on citizenship education?
2 In what ways is the 'impact of globalisation' affecting the nature and scope of comparative and international perspectives on citizenship education? On balance is this impact negative or positive for citizenship education?
3 Which audiences are the main drivers behind the growth of comparative and international perspectives on citizenship education; and which audiences benefit least and most from this growth? How much is growth still down to western influences and how much is it continuing to fuel 'educational borrowing' of policies and practices?
4 What do you think are the main gaps in knowledge and understanding about citizenship education and how far can comparative and international perspectives help to plug them? Do we need more large-scale, cross-national studies, such as ICCS, or more smaller, within country case studies, or both?

Suggested further reading

Arthur, J., Davies, I. and Hahn, C. (Eds.) (2008) *The Sage Handbook of Education for Citizenship and Democracy*. London: Sage. This *Handbook* is a labour of love and provides an invaluable introduction and overview to the main themes, issues, debates and developments in citizenship education across the world. Well-written and accessible, it has a truly international and comparative feel with short contributions from most of the leading scholars in the field. It is testimony to the reach and scope of citizenship education in modern societies.

Hahn, C. (2010) 'Comparative civic education research: what we know and what we need to know', *Citizenship Teaching and Learning*, 6, 1, pp. 5–23. An accessible review of the field which benefits from the breadth and depth of the author's own research and networks across the world. It provides an introduction to all the main studies in the field, both within country and cross-national, and a summary of the key findings. An excellent starting point for those wishing to get a feel for the range of comparative and international perspectives on citizenship education.

Kerr, D. (1999) *Citizenship Education: An International Comparison.* London: QCA/NFER. One of the first attempts to review citizenship education policies and practices cross-nationally. It grew from a desire in England to learn more about effective policies and practices in other countries to help inform the work of the Crick Group in drawing up proposals for the inclusion of citizenship in the National Curriculum. The report provides an overview of the different approaches taken by countries to citizenship education in terms of definition, curriculum approach, textbooks and resources and assessment and quality assurance among others. A good example of how within country requirements can be informed by cross-national perspectives.

Schulz, W., Ainley, J., Fraillon, J., Kerr, D. and Losito, B. (2010) *ICCS 2009 International Report: Civic Knowledge, Attitudes and Engagement among Lower Secondary School Students in Thirty-eight Countries.* Amsterdam: International Association for the Evaluation of Educational Achievement (IEA). Available at: http://iccs.acer.edu. au/uploads/File/Reports/ICCS_InternationalReport.pdf (accessed 21st January 2011). This report provides the most comprehensive comparative and international perspective on the current state of civic and citizenship education across the globe. It covers the context of citizenship education in the 38 participating countries as well as detailing the level of civic knowledge and civic attitudes of over 140,000 14-year-olds in those countries. Essential reading for all interested in citizenship education.

References

Arthur, J., Davies, I. and Hahn, C. (Eds.) (2008) *The Sage Handbook of Education for Citizenship and Democracy.* London: Sage.

Banks, J. (2008) 'Diversity and citizenship education in global times', in Arthur, J., Davies, I. and Hahn, C. (Eds.) *Education for Citizenship and Democracy.* London: Sage. pp. 57–70.

Ben-Porath, S.R. (2006) *Citizenship under Fire: Democratic Education in Times of Conflict.* Princeton, NJ: Princeton University Press.

Birzea, C., Kerr, D., Mikkelsen, R., Pol, M., Froumin, I., Losito, B. and Sardoc, M. (2004) *All-European Study on Education for Democratic Citizenship Policies.* Strasbourg: Council of Europe.

Bray, M., Adamson, B. and Mason, M. (2007) *Comparative Education Research: Approaches and Methods.* Hong Kong: Springer.

Davies, L. (2002) 'Pupil voice in Europe', in Schweisfurth, M., Davies, L. and Harber, C. (Eds.) *Learning Democracy and Citizenship: International Experiences.* Oxford: Symposium Books.

Epstein, E. (1994) 'International education', in Husen, T. and Postlethwaite, N. (Eds.) *International Encyclopaedia of Education* (2nd Ed.). Oxford: Pergamon Press. pp. 918–29.

Eurydice (2005) *Citizenship Education at School in Europe.* Brussels: Eurydice.

Finkel, S.E. and Ernst, H.R. (2005) 'Civic education in post-apartheid South Africa: alternative paths to the development of political knowledge and democratic values', *Political Psychology*, 26, 3, pp. 333–64.

Gorard, S. and Sundaram, V. (2008) 'Equity and its relationship to citizenship education', in Arthur, J., Davies, I. and Hahn, C. (Eds.) *Education for Citizenship and Democracy*. London: Sage. pp. 57–70.

Grossman, D., Lee, W. and Kennedy, K. (Eds.) (2008) *Citizenship Curriculum in Asia and the Pacific*. Hong Kong: Comparative Education Research Centre and the University of Hong Kong/Springer.

Hahn, C. (2010) 'Comparative civic education research: what we know and what we need to know', *Citizenship Teaching and Learning*, 6, 1, pp. 5–23.

Hoskins, B., Jesinghaus, J., Mascherini, M., Munda, G., Nardo, M., Saisana, M., Van Nijlen, D. and Villalba, E. (2006) *Measuring Active Citizenship in Europe*. CRELL Research Paper 4. Ispra, Italy: Joint Research Centre/CRELL.

Ichilov, O. (2005) 'Pride in one's country and citizenship orientations in a divided society', *Comparative Education Review*, 49, 1, pp. 44–61.

Kennedy, K., Hahn, C. and Lee, W. (2008) 'Constructing citizenship: comparing the views of students in Australia, Hong Kong and the United States', *Comparative Education Review*, 52, 1, pp. 53–91.

Kerr, D., Keating, A. and Ireland, E. (2009) *Pupil Assessment in Citizenship Education: Purposes, Practices and Possibilities. Report of a CIDREE Collaborative Project*. Slough: NFER/CIDREE.

Kerr, D. and Losito, B. (2010) *Policy Tool for Education for Democratic Citizenship and Human Rights Education*. Strasbourg: Council of Europe.

Kerr, D., Sturman, L., Schulz, W. and Burge, B. (2010) *ICCS 2009 European Report: Civic Knowledge, Attitudes, and Engagement among Lower-Secondary Students in 24 European Countries*. Amsterdam: International Association for the Evaluation of Educational Achievement (IEA).

Osler, A. and Starkey, H. (2008) 'Education for cosmopolitan citizenship', in Georgi, V. (Ed.) *The Makings of Citizens in Europe: New Perspectives on Citizenship Education*. Bonn: Bundeszentrale für politische Bildung.

Phillips, D. and Ochs, K. (2004) 'Researching policy borrowing: some methodological challenges in comparative education', *British Educational Research Journal*, 30, 6, pp. 773–84.

Raby, R.L. (2005) 'Reflections on the field: a review of the *2004 Comparative Education Review* bibliography', *Comparative Education Review*, 49, 3, pp. 410–18.

Reimers, F. (2007) 'Civic education when democracy is in flux: the impact of empirical research on policy and practice in Latin America', *Citizenship and Teacher Education*, 3, 2, pp. 5–21.

Roth, K. and Burbules, N.C. (2007) *Changing Notions of Citizenship Education in Contemporary Nation-states*. Rotterdam: Sense Publishers.

Rust, V. (2002) 'The place of international education in the Comparative Education Review', *Comparative Education Review*, 46, 3, pp. iii-iv.

Schulz, W., Ainley, J., Fraillon, J., Kerr, D., and Losito, B. (2010) *ICCS 2009 International Report: Civic Knowledge, Attitudes and Engagement among Lower Secondary School Students in Thirty-eight Countries*. Amsterdam: International Association for the Evaluation of Educational Achievement (IEA).

Schulz, W., Fraillon, J., Ainley, J., Losito, B. and Kerr, D. (2008) *International Civic and Citizenship Education Study: Assessment Framework*. Amsterdam: International Association for the Evaluation of Educational Achievement (IEA).

Steiner-Khamsi, G. (Ed.) (2004) *The Global Politics of Educational Borrowing and Lending*. New York, NY: Teachers College Press.

Torney-Purta, J., Schwille, J. and Amadeo, J.A. (1999) *Civic Education across Countries: Twenty-four Case Studies from the IEA Civic Education Project*. Amsterdam: International Association for the Evaluation of Educational Achievement (IEA).

Torney-Purta, J., Lehmann, R., Oswald, H. and Schulz, W. (2001) *Citizenship and Education in Twenty-eight Countries*. Amsterdam: International Association for the Evaluation of Educational Achievement (IEA).

Torres, C.A. (2001) 'Globalization and comparative education in the world system', *Comparative Education Review*, 45, 4, pp. iii–ix.

Wade, R.C. (2007) *Community Action Rooted in History: The CiviConnections Model of Service Learning*. Silver Spring, MD: National Council for the Social Studies.

White, C. and Openshaw, R. (2005) *Democracy at the Crossroads: International Perspectives on Critical Global Citizenship Education*. Lanham, MD: Lexington Books.

Zadja, J. (2009) 'Globalisation, nation-building and cultural identity: the role of intercultural dialogue', in Zajda, J., Daun, H. and Saha, L. (Eds.) *Nation-Building, Identity and Citizenship Education*. Frankfurt: Springer.

Chapter 3

Perspectives on citizenship education

Ian Davies

UNIVERSITY OF YORK

Introduction

In this chapter I discuss perspectives about citizenship education by drawing attention to two broad questions that are currently debated with some vigour: 'what is citizenship?' and 'how may citizenship be taught, learned and assessed?' In relation to the first question I discuss six overlapping areas that focus on rather fundamental matters about citizenship emerging from philosophy, politics, location, morals, identity and action. In relation to the second question (about teaching and learning) I refer to the three areas of status, form (or framing) and method. The complexities and controversies of citizenship education cannot all be covered within the space of one rather brief chapter but it might be possible to sketch in a rather cursory manner some aspects of the key debates.

What is citizenship?

In this part of the chapter I argue that we can begin to get a sense of the perspectives that are brought to bear on citizenship by examining six areas of debate. I will tackle each in turn but, of course, these matters become really meaningful when seen as overlapping sets of dynamic ideas and practices.

Fundamental philosophical perspectives: the liberal and/or the civic republican

Citizenship can be seen as an arena in which there are two competing perspectives that focus variously on rights and duties in private or public contexts. These have been characterized as the liberal, in which a private citizen has his or her rights and the expectation that government will, in many ways, leave them alone. The civic republican perspective, on the other hand, emphasizes the duties or responsibilities of citizens to those in the community. It is too simplistic to see these positions as the only possibilities in relation to a characterization of citizenship (there are some, for example, who from a communitarian position would see the need for something that is distinct from or a refinement of these rather general positions). It would be misleading to see the liberal and the civic republican as capable of being labelled simplistically as, for example, 'right-wing' or 'left-wing', or to see them as mutually exclusive options. I agree with Derek Heater that 'by being a virtuous, community-conscious participant in civic affairs (a republican requirement), a citizen benefits by enhancing his or her own individual development (a liberal objective). Citizenship does not involve an either/or choice' (Heater, 1999: 177). But, broadly, the liberal and civic republican perspectives allow us to develop a window into the heart of what citizenship is and could be.

The political: is citizenship inclusive or exclusive?

It would be too simplistic to see citizenship as being wholly inclusive or exclusive but this sort of binary divide allows for some insight into the nature of the debates about citizenship. Some who are involved with developing citizenship education and who are passionately committed to education as a force for improving the world have been at times rather sceptical about the wisdom of characterizing belonging or membership in formal terms. They feel that although there are many advantages to the legal and political status of citizenship in which rights may be guaranteed, it is also possible to identify through this process those who do not belong. At a time when there are fierce disagreements about immigration, refugees and asylum seekers those who do not have the required status can more easily be removed. Such action would obviously not be possible (or, at least the elision between belonging and status could not be made so easily) if we had chosen to emphasize human rights as opposed to citizenship. (This, of course, is not to suggest that emphasizing human rights is entirely free from its own philosophical and practical challenges.)

Location: local, national, international, global

Citizenship is often seen to suggest membership of a community and all communities have 'place'. This place may be seen in concrete terms and is most easily given expression in the form of the legal and political status that has been referred to above. The status of citizenship is often – but not exclusively – related to a nation state (Sears, Davies and Reid, 2010). Citizens, of course, do have many legal rights and responsibilities in local circumstances (e.g. the right to vote in local elections) and there are transnational frameworks which are highly significant. But these rights and responsibilities are often accorded in light of a national status. For example, as a result of my British citizenship I am also a European citizen. The meaning of such citizenship is at times debated. In relation to European citizenship it is important to see the literal nature of the use of the word *international* – or, *between* the nations – and to reflect on whether other forms of citizenship – with more overarching global perspectives – are possible (see Held, 1995). But even when these sub-national, national and supra-national forms of citizenship operate within a legal and political framework there are other matters beyond the expression of formal rights and responsibilities that are important. Anderson (1991) famously saw the nation as 'an imagined community' and this is obviously also true for one's membership of local and other communities such as the global. There is, in the global context, significant work that takes place by, for example, the United Nations, but often citizenship can be seen as an act of imaginative, perhaps emotional, identification and commitment. It should not, of course, be assumed that commitment to a particular community is in itself necessarily more democratic or just than a declaration of support for another group. That would be dependent on many other things including the goals and purposes that are explicitly declared and actually worked for and achieved.

Morality, religion and doing the 'right' thing

Many of the motivations for and formulations of citizenship are connected to the business of thinking and doing the right thing. The Crick Report (QCA, 1998), for example, included social and moral responsibility as one of the three key features of citizenship and it is clear from comments about almost all aspects of citizenship and why it was being introduced by politicians that the notion of goodness or justice was seen as being vitally important. In some ways this is very welcome. One would not wish to make an argument opposed to virtue. And yet there is a worrying lack of clarity about the debates over these matters. Some of these matters in relation to religion (e.g. Gearon, 2004; Arthur, Gearon and Sears, 2010) have been discussed. The nature of morality and its specific connection with citizenship has been explored (e.g. Beck, 1998). Very usefully, Sandel (2009) has drawn together and discussed conceptions of justice by contrasting utilitarianism in which the happiness of the largest number is targeted with the 'blind' process models of scholars such as Kant and Rawls and the virtue-based approaches in which particular versions of the good society are pursued. In educational contexts these matters seem to revolve around two key questions: where does morality come from (i.e. to what extent do we wish to rely on spirituality and an external power)?; and, do we know the 'right' answer (are we engaged in a process of moral clarification or, as some US character educators would claim, should we tell people the 'right' answer)?

Identity

Closely connected to issues of belonging and morality are debates about identity (Isin and Wood, 1999). When the Crick Report was published there were some who welcomed its avoidance of specific commitment to precise contexts. In other words, Crick seemed to support an approach to politics which saw matters broadly in a commitment to justice and did not go through what some would see as a long and, perhaps inevitably, incomplete list of citizenship and gender, disability, sexual orientation, ethnicity and so on. Crick also was always keen to make clear the distinction between personal and social education and citizenship education. With the latter public issues were always at the forefront. And yet, some felt deeply uncomfortable with what was perceived to be a failure to recognize the need to celebrate and develop multiculturalism which may have emerged from a rather traditional sense of politics. Osler went so far as to claim that the Crick Report 'contains albeit unwittingly an example of institutionalized racism in its characterization of minorities' (Osler, 2003: 49). These are highly charged matters. Perhaps all that can be said is that elaborations of Crick's arguments can be seen in his writing which followed the publication of the Crick Report (e.g. Crick, 2000), the National Curriculum was later revised to include a focus on identity and diversity, key work on the nature of citizenship has come to include 'personal' matters (e.g. Kiwan is undertaking work on 'Intersecting Identities: Women's spaces of sociality in post-colonial London') and Crick himself perhaps shifted his position towards the end of his life (e.g. see Crick, 2008).

Action, involvement and engagement

Citizens are often exhorted to do something. This seems to be the thrust of what was suggested by Oliver and Heater:

> Individuals are citizens when they practise civic virtue and good citizenship, enjoy but do not exploit their civil and political rights, contribute to and receive social and economic benefits, do not allow any sense of national identity to justify discrimination or stereotyping of others, experience senses of non-exclusive multiple citizenship and, by their example, teach citizenship to others.
>
> (Oliver and Heater, 1994: 6)

This is something to which I feel a strong attachment. If we want a vibrant democracy then people have to engage. And yet, we need to be cautious about what is meant by that engagement. It would not be helpful to propose that rights are only available when responsibilities are enacted. The seemingly obvious positions about justice in a democracy break down very readily if this sort of exchange is accepted too easily. It is no good, for example, trumpeting a slogan such as 'no taxation without representation' without also making clear our position on indirect and direct tax paid by young people today who are ineligible to vote. But, more widely, if citizenship and its attendant rights are given only to those who take part actively we effectively exclude many people including the very young, the very old, those with disabilities and so on. The privileging of physical engagement over cognitive reflection may not always be entirely wise (if we do not recognize this then we will find ourselves in the same difficulties as those who proposed active learning without seeming to include critical analysis). Further there are very many well-known examples of seeming non-engagement that are highly effective political weapons (e.g. Gandhi's non-violence). In this light, although I would like simply for there to be clearer evidence of engagement, the concern expressed about declining voter turnout is perhaps insufficiently alert to the possibility of informed voters who put forward a particular political position by not going through the ritual of representative politics but who may be simultaneously very active in forms of participatory democracy through pressure groups.

How may citizenship be taught, learned and assessed?

In this part of the chapter I suggest that we can establish a sense of the key debates in education for citizenship by considering three issues: status, form (or how citizenship education is framed) and method.

Status

A curious seeming contradiction, or at least inconsistency arises in relation to the status of citizenship education. The aims of citizenship about understanding, and helping to develop, contemporary society in ways that are consistent with democratic society are, broadly stated, the aims of schooling as a whole. And yet, citizenship education has experienced long periods of neglect, there are insufficient numbers of people trained to teach it and it tends to occupy low status positions on the timetable and in relation to examining. While there may be disadvantages in seeing citizenship as a subject it is possible to say that this situation is improving (see Ofsted, 2010). There are, however, a number of factors to consider in relation to this debate. It may, of course, be advantageous not to see citizenship as a subject if that were to mean that we would avoid unhelpful government bureaucracy. But the problems of the status of an explicit form of citizenship itself emerge from more significant concerns. Some may feel that it may not be appropriate for the government to identify what might be learned about democracy. There have also been attacks on the coherence and academic respectability of citizenship education which may weaken the case for it to appear as a separate subject on school timetables. Those who operate within longer established disciplines such as history are not always sympathetic to the claims of citizenship educators and may occasionally see them as rivals for timetable space. Struggles over space (hours on the timetable which mean jobs and career paths; rooms; purchasing teaching materials; continuous professional development opportunities, etc.) can be conducted fiercely and even if citizenship is 'just' a subject we know already how difficult it is for something new to be established (see Goodson, 1993).

The form of citizenship education

The comments above about school subjects are directly relevant to the issues that are important in considering how citizenship education should be 'packaged'. For some citizenship is something that is relevant to all teachers and attempts to make it into a school subject should be resisted. There are, broadly, four positions: it is a subject in its own right; it is something that can and should be infused through other subjects; it is a matter of atmosphere or ethos in which the interactions between members of the school community allow for citizenship to be 'caught not taught'; it is achieved through activity with the community (local, national and/or global). At times these positions, which are not mutually exclusive, are highlighted as discussions about three 'Cs': curriculum, culture and community. The issues that are at stake can be seen in longstanding debates about the cross-curricular nature of citizenship, with England and Scotland deciding to follow very different paths. In England Crick's failed attempts to introduce political education in the 1970s and more recent research outcomes (e.g. Whitty, Rowe and Aggleton, 1994) led to implementing citizenship as a specialist subject. Scotland, on the other hand, perhaps due to the absence of a National Curriculum in the same form as in England and the existence of Modern Studies decided to pursue in curricular matters the expectation that a specialist subject would not be necessary (see Global Citizenship section of Learning and Teaching Scotland, 2010; online). The risks of developing a specialist subject regarding the imposition of the possibly narrow political perspective of the current government, an over-bearing bureaucracy and the 'ghetto-ization' of citizenship in one small and neglected subject area need to be considered against the possible lack of specialist knowledge and in practice a return to the complete absence of any real work on citizenship if cross-curricular work is attempted.

Methods for teaching citizenship

The issues raised above about curriculum, culture and community are relevant here. Overviews of research findings (e.g. Osler and Starkey, 2005) consistently point to the importance of ethos which allows for a reasonable and respectful collaboration between teachers and learners in which significant and relevant questions may be considered. Such a collaborative atmosphere can be drawn from in the development of whole-school structures (e.g. school councils and mock elections) and links can be built between schools and communities (not just in face to face volunteering but virtually and, possibly, in alignment with action groups). The importance of a particular style of teaching and learning is often referred to in lists of desirable features. For example, Huddleston and Kerr (2006: 10) highlight the following:

Active – emphasizes learning by doing;
Interactive – discussion and debate;
Relevant – focuses on real life issues;
Critical – encourages young people to think for themselves;
Collaborative – employs group work and co-operative learning;
Participative – gives young people a say in their own learning.

These and other similar lists have at times led some to fail to make a distinction between the need for teachers to be authoritative and to avoid being authoritarian (Kakos, 2007). In the confident expression of their subject knowledge and appropriate development of assessment procedures teachers of citizenship education need to be able to able to deal with five things.

Contemporary content – citizenship is about today and history education and other subjects can only go so far in providing what is needed;

Public context – as mentioned above there are many advantages to be gained from a realization that fixed and simple barriers between the personal and the political will not help. But citizenship is about the public and when developing citizenship education we need to avoid those – valuable – lessons that focus on friendship and health in ways that relate only to individuals;

Relevant substantive concepts (e.g. power, authority, justice, representation, community) – citizenship must have a strong conceptual base. It needs to be about something and these substantive concepts provide the bedrock of our understandings and actions. This is not to say that we should stop discussing which substantive concepts we should focus on or that we should stop debating what is meant by the concepts we have selected;

Procedural concepts that are directly relevant to citizenship (e.g. significance, interpretation, chronology, toleration, evidence, participation) – in other words we need to be able to think about how citizenship is studied and enacted. If we can think clearly about how we operationalize citizenship then we will be much better able to guide students as they develop their knowledge, understandings, skills and dispositions;

Taking part and reflecting on taking part – citizenship is – with the caveats mentioned above – about taking part and we need to provide opportunities for students to think about what that means, to have opportunities to do things and, very important, to reflect on how they have worked.

All the above need to be informed by students, by teachers' professional reflections on the progress that is being made by students, and by teachers' and students' reflections on how well the learning process is being supported. In other words, there should be a clear and explicit approach to assessment and evaluation. Testing for bureaucratic purposes and meaningless tick sheets about matters which students in the real world of schools will never be able to influence should be treated with some considerable caution. But careful assessment for learning by students and teachers can be enormously beneficial.

Conclusion

It would not be realistic or desirable to expect a simple resolution to the debates about perspectives that have been highlighted in this chapter. The continuation of democratic discussion about what citizenship means is entirely necessary. Similarly, the simplicities of the 'what works' agenda should be resisted in education and especially in citizenship education where, although there will be continuing commitment to key principles and procedures, the nature of what those things are and judgments about whether success is being achieved must vary. It is doubtful that a teacher from the 1950s would be discussing controversial issues in the same way as a teacher would in the 21st century and this interchange between our vision of good education and the good society needs always to be adjusted. In order to achieve such adjustment we need to be able to ensure that citizenship is taken seriously and that we know more about its operation. At this particular moment I suggest we need more debates about subject knowledge, discussion techniques and assessment methods. More particularly, I suspect that we will need to focus more on debates about the content and processes of global societies that are characterized and developed by means of new technologies.

Questions for further investigation

1 To what extent do you think teachers are influenced by fundamental political and philosophical perspectives about citizenship? Is it necessary for teachers to develop forms of subject knowledge that are dependent on reflecting on these ideas?
2 To what extent are the reflections about democratic citizenship education a contradiction in which we fail to recognize the exclusive nature of what societies look for in their citizens?
3 How can you explain the apparent disjunction between the aim of schools to help young people grow into good citizens and the low status of forms of citizenship education?
4 Is it necessary to teach and assess citizenship education in so-called progressive ways in which, for example, learners may be involved as co-constructors of the curriculum?

Suggested further reading

Crick, B. (1962) *In Defence of Politics.* Harmondsworth: Penguin. A classic book by the person who was the key influence in England (and around the world) for the contemporary version of citizenship education. Crick's commitment to politics as the means by which engagement should occur is cogently presented.

Heater, D. (1999) *What is Citizenship?* Cambridge: Polity Press. This is a very well-written book that identifies the main features of many of the debates about citizenship education. The author certainly makes his own position clear but there is a very attractive and stimulating even-handedness about key ideas and issues within a historical context. It is not to be used for the detail of teaching and learning.

Huddleston, T. (2004) *Citizens and Society: Political Literacy Teacher Resource Pack.* London: Hodder and Stoughton. This is a collection of very good practical resources for teaching and learning. These resources emerged from a thoughtful and original project led by the Citizenship Foundation which focused on the development of public discourse. The resources are designed to help people learn how to engage with public issues. As such there is an implied argument that many other forms of social studies (academic political science, personal and social education, etc.) are not an entirely appropriate or sufficient form of citizenship education.

Sandel, M.J. (2009) *Justice: What's the Right Thing to Do?* London: Allen Lane. This is a very intelligently written book that explores the roots and practice of justice. It is terrifically engaging: great insights, stimulating and often very funny as the reader is invited to work out what to do in scenarios where the 'right' thing is by no means straightforward.

References

Anderson, B. (1991) *Imagined Communities.* London: Verso.

Arthur, J., Gearon, L. and Sears, A. (2010) *Education, Politics and Religion.* London and New York, NY: Routledge.

Beck, J. (1998) *Morality and Citizenship in Education.* London: Cassell.

Crick, B. (2000) *Essays on Citizenship.* London: Continuum.

——(2008) 'Foreword', in Kiwan, D. *Education for Inclusive Citizenship.* Abingdon: Routledge.

Gearon, L. (2004) *Citizenship through Religious Education.* London: Routledge.

Global Citizenship. Learning and Teaching Scotland (2010) Available at: http://www.ltscotland.org.uk/citizenship/index.asp (accessed 20th May 2010).

Goodson, I. (1993) *School Subjects and Curriculum Change.* Lewes: Falmer Press.

Heater, D. (1999) *What is Citizenship?* Cambridge: Polity Press.

Held, D. (1995) *Democracy and the Global Order: From the Modern State to Cosmopolitan Governance.* Cambridge: Polity Press.

Huddleston, T. and Kerr, D. (Eds) (2006) *Making Sense of Citizenship: A Continuing Professional Development Handbook.* London: Hodder Murray.

Isin, E.F. and Wood, P.K. (1999) *Citizenship and Identity.* London: Sage.

Kakos, M. (2007) 'The interaction between students and teachers in citizenship education'. Unpublished PhD thesis, University of York.

Ofsted (2010) 'Citizenship established', *Citizenship in Schools 2006/9.* Available at: http://www.ofsted.gov.uk/resources/citizenship-established-citizenship-schools-200609 (accessed 20th May 2010).

Oliver, D. and Heater, D. (1994) *The Foundations of Citizenship.* London: Harvester Wheatsheaf.

Osler, A. (2003) 'The Crick Report and the future of multiethnic Britain', in Gearon, L. (Ed.) *Learning to Teach Citizenship in the Secondary School.* London: RoutledgeFalmer. pp. 42–53.

Osler, A. and Starkey, H. (2005) *Education for Democratic Citizenship: A Review of Research, Policy and Practice 1995–2005.* London: BERA.

Qualifications and Curriculum Authority (QCA)(1998) *Education for Citizenship and the Teaching of Democracy in Schools: Final Report of the Advisory Group on Citizenship.* London: QCA.

Sandel, M.J. (2009) *Justice.* London: Allen Lane.

Sears, A., Davies, I. and Reid, A. (2010) 'From Britishness to nothingness and back again: looking for a way forward in citizenship education', in Mycock, A., McAuley, J.W. and McGlynn, C. (Eds) (in press) *Britishness, Identity and Citizenship: The View from Abroad.* Oxford: Peter Lang.

Whitty, G., Rowe, G. and Aggleton, P. (1994) 'Subjects and themes in the National Curriculum', *Research Papers in Education*, 9, 2, pp. 159–81.

The social and political context of citizenship education

Part II

The social and political context
of citizenship education

Chapter 4

The policy context of citizenship education

Rob Hulme[1] and Moira Hulme

UNIVERSITY OF CHESTER AND UNIVERSITY OF GLASGOW

Introduction

This chapter considers the range of influences on education policy for citizenship education. We advocate the adoption of a policy sociology approach to highlight the political nature of policy making. We draw on the notions of 'travelling' and 'embedded' policy (Ozga and Jones, 2006; Jones and Alexiadou, 2001) in outlining cross-national, national/regional and local influences on the enactment of policy. Consideration is given to the broader political context of citizenship education within contemporary debates about the 'new social democracy' and 'new localism'. At the local level, we identify some tensions in current policy frameworks that contain contradictory messages for practitioners and pupils, particularly the (mal-) alignment of the three message systems of schooling – curriculum, pedagogy and assessment (Bernstein, 1977).

Policy sociology

In order to understand the policy context of citizenship education, we start by adopting a theoretically-informed approach to education policy. Following Olssen *et al.* (2004: 3), policy is defined here as 'a politically, socially and historically contextualised practice or set of practices'. The case for theoretical engagement with policy has been strongly influenced by policy sociology; a term advanced by Ozga (1987: 144) to describe an approach to policy analysis that is 'rooted in the social science tradition, historically informed and drawing on qualitative and illuminative techniques'.

From this perspective the formation of curriculum policy is viewed as a process or a journey, subject to deliberation and contestation. Policy trajectory studies focus on the making and re-making of policy and challenge the traditional separation of policy, politics and practice. For example, through the case studies in *Politics and Policy Making*, Ball (1990) reveals how government departments are a 'changing amalgam'. The policy process involves 'refraction', 'filtering' and 'resistance'. Some policy making is 'haphazard'. Discrepancies and tensions become enmeshed in the debates and outcomes of policy. Self-interest, institutional

interests and political interests are played out. The study of citizenship education
as a policy process thus entails consideration of 'the who and how of policy production' (Gale, 2003) in an attempt to counter ahistorical and de-personalised
accounts of policy. 'When documentation is complete, human involvement seems
to be erased. Text seldom conveys the emotional, intellectual and ideological
endeavours, the arguments, debates, experiences and decisions of participants
involved in its creation' (Broadhead, 2002: 47).

Travelling and embedded policy

Education policy is increasingly subject to supra-national influences as policy
makers look to other education systems for new ideas to enhance the effectiveness
and efficacy of local education policy and practice. Dolowitz *et al.* (2000: 3) define
policy transfer as, '[a] process in which knowledge about policies, institutions and
ideas developed in one time or place is used in the development of policies,
institutions etc. in another time or place'.

Supra-national agencies shaping education policy include the World Bank, the
Organisation for Economic Cooperation and Development (OECD), the World
Trade Organisation and the European Union (EU) (Spring, 2009; Ball, 2008;
Hulme and Hulme, 2008). Citizenship curricula are influenced by the United
Nations Convention on the Rights of the Child (UN, 1989) and the activities of
a proliferation of non-governmental organisations, charities and aid organisations
including Greenpeace, Amnesty International and the United Nations Children's
Fund (UNICEF). The United Nations Educational, Scientific and Cultural
Organisation (UNESCO), the Council of Europe and the International Association
for the Evaluation of Educational Achievement (IEA) have targeted programmes
at the development of active citizenship at an international level. There is some
evidence of common elements within the developing frameworks for citizenship
education, including attention to 'the development of political literacy, critical
thinking and certain attitudes and values, and active participation' (Eurydice,
2005: 15). The promotion of active citizenship was a core objective of the
Lisbon Process.

Within these frameworks there is evidence of the interweaving of seemingly
contradictory influences. Citizenship education encompasses libratory discourses
of empowerment and critical pedagogy. It also reflects a view of the social role of
schooling as the management of risk and promotion of social cohesion through
responsible civic behaviour. Jones *et al.* (2008: 21) argue that citizenship education
is among an expanding number of priority tasks 'carried out in the name of
reconciling or controlling tensions that are thought to threaten European societies'.

Evidence from international studies suggests that the political culture of the
host country (or region) is significant in filtering and remodelling generic trans-
national policies. Global social policy is 'recontextualised' within local sites of
influence – national, regional and institutional (Ozga and Jones, 2006). Ozga and
Jones (2006: 2) explains that '[e]mbedded policy is to be found in "local" spaces,

where global policy agendas come up against existing priorities and practices'. Of particular significance is the role of the 'collective narrative' (Popkewitz *et al.*, 1999) or 'assumptive world' (McPherson and Raab, 1988) of the national policy community. For example, in Scotland a stable policy community has mediated external influences that have sought to 'Anglicise' education policy. The fact that policies travel does not mean that they are transferred without change. There is always a local politics in adapting a trans-national agenda.

Areas of divergence in citizenship education and the practice of citizenship in European schools include: pupil participation on school boards; the terms of reference for pupil councils; the level of pupil involvement in curriculum planning and school decision making; regional/national consultation and pupil unions; whether citizenship is constructed as a standalone school subject, integrated within a number of subjects or a school-wide educational theme; an elective or compulsory offering within the school curriculum; differing approaches to assessment; engagement at different levels of schooling – primary education, general lower secondary and upper secondary (Davies and Kirkpatrick, 2000; Eurydice, 2005).

Policy communities and local policy settlements

If travelling policy is 'fundamentally about learning' (Wolman and Page, 2002: 479), then that learning takes place within policy networks or policy communities. Policy networks are groups of actors aligned by mutual interest and resource dependence (Marsh and Rhodes, 1993). Jordan (1990: 327) defines a policy community as a 'special type of stable network which has advantages in encouraging bargaining in policy resolution'. Within stable policy communities participants have a commitment to work together to achieve settlement.

How travelling policy becomes embedded within specific 'local' contexts is influenced by a number of factors: the composition of the policy community; the history and tradition of the host education system; and local circumstances such as the balance of power between national or regional government and other agencies. It also reflects the relative influence of various actors within the policy and knowledge communities and their openness to learning. Policy entrepreneurs inside and outside formal schooling seek to influence the curriculum.

Political devolution has opened up new spaces for 'local' inflection of trans-national policy agendas in education in the UK. A separate Scottish Parliament and Scottish Executive were established following the Scotland Act of 1998. The Government of Wales Act 1998 set up a separate assembly with some devolved powers in Wales. The Belfast Agreement 1998 established the Northern Irish Assembly, suspended on 12th October 2002 and restored on 8th May 2007 following the Northern Ireland (St Andrews Agreement) Act 2007. For case studies of curriculum policy making in the post-devolution context see: Priestley and Humes (2010) for Scotland; Colwill and Gallagher (2007) for Northern Ireland; Daugherty and Elfed-Owens (2003) for Wales; and Wyse (2010) for

England. Home international studies of UK policy have noted that the differing political values and 'shaping myths' informing policy post-devolution support 'constrained divergence', especially with regard to values-based approaches to citizenship education, ethical literacy and the professional preparation of teachers (Raffe, 2005; Hulme and Menter, 2008).

The wider social policy context – the 'new localism' and citizenship

Neo-liberal political projects over the past thirty years, under both Conservative and Labour governments, have promoted the idea of active citizenship. There is continuity in the strong emphasis placed on social responsibility within New Labour's Third Way and the conservative 'civicism' or new 'localism' of the Coalition government's emphasis on voluntary and community organisations in the commissioning and delivery of public services. In a process of 'responsibilisation', the responsibility for risk minimisation is transferred to consumers, clients and service users. Whilst 'the Big Society' (Cabinet Office, 2010) receives much attention in the policy platform of the UK Coalition government formed in May 2010, governmentality studies over the last thirty years have provided detailed accounts of the use of 'self-governing' mechanisms of government to tackle a wide range of issues including community safety, welfare and health policies and local economic development (Flint, 2002; Allen, 2003; Marinetto, 2003). These studies bring to the foreground the obligations of citizenship. Allowing oneself to become sick, infirm, de-skilled or unemployed is a failure of self care. Responsible citizens have 'a duty to be well' (Greco, 1993: 361); to protect themselves from falling victim to risk.

Civic participation appears evidenced through a proliferation of citizens' panels, citizens' juries, crime prevention panels, focus groups, interactive websites, tele-democracy, community forums and roadshows to facilitate 'big conversations' on policy. In England, the re-organisation of local government under New Labour (1997–2010) drew extensively on the language of the 'politics of empowerment', 'community' and 'neighbourhood renewal' (Fairclough, 2000). David Miliband (2006), then Minister of Communities and Local Government, spoke of a 'new centre-local relationship' or 'double devolution', based on the twin principles of subsidiarity and neighbourhood empowerment as the solution to a perceived democratic deficit. However, despite the promotion of a 'new localism', Martin, among others, has observed that 'the educational space for "deliberative democracy", in which citizens learn, on their own terms, to be active in their own communities, workplaces and social movements as well as the wider body politic, has, in effect, been closed down' (Martin, 2003: 573–4). Policy interventions in the UK have constructed citizenship as a form of 'obligated freedom' within which 'incivility' is met with 'enforcement action' (Gillies, 2005). The *Respect and Responsibility* White Paper (Home Office, 2003) constructed the community as a legal 'place' governed by a new type of contract between citizen and society.

Good neighbour charters regulated behaviour in social housing by allowing the eviction or the withholding of housing benefits for transgressors, supported by the pastoral watch of neighbourhood wardens (Rodger, 2006). The Anti-social Behaviour Act 2003 introduced a range of education-related powers to reinforce parental responsibility. Local education authorities, youth offending teams, police and the courts were empowered to pursue parenting contracts, parenting orders and penalty notices for truancy and misbehaviour in schools. Whilst the *Respect Agenda* (January, 2006) addressed issues of 'fairness' and 'civility', it was silent on the issue of material inequality or the desirability of risk pooling strategies that involve mobilisation within collective organisations.

> While individuals are supposedly free to choose, they are not supposed to choose to construct strong collective institutions (such as trade unions) as opposed to weak voluntary organisations (like charitable organisations). They most certainly should not choose to associate to create political parties with the aim of forcing the state to intervene in or eliminate the market.
>
> (Harvey, 2005: 69)

The above review provides an overview of the wider social policy context within which education policy is located. The institution of the school is often characterised as a microcosm of society. Schools are cast as a 'hub' or another space where the tension between obligation and entitlement is played out. In the next section of this chapter we explore some of the ways in which teachers and pupils are enabled and constrained by policy and how policy shapes the context of school work.

Teacher agency

Braun *et al.* (2010: 547) use the term 'policy enactment' to refer to 'an understanding that policies are interpreted and translated by diverse policy actors in the school environment, rather than simply implemented'. What is played out in schools is the result of the messy interaction between situated activity within individual schools and the macro-environment within which they operate.

> The physical text that pops through the school letterbox does not arrive 'out of the blue' – it has an interpretational and representational history – and neither does it enter a social or institutional vacuum. The text and its readers and the context of response all have histories.
>
> (Ball, 1994: 17)

Approaches to policy that endeavour to 'engineer' change through top-down/centre-out policy prescription have tended to overstate the degree of control that is achievable over teachers and schools. Professionals in the public sphere, subject to strong central steering of policies, retain 'constrained' discretion. In other words, school leaders, teachers and other education workers shape curriculum policies as they are enacted at the local level. As Cuban (1998: 453) reminds us, 'schools change reforms as much as reforms change schools'. Practitioners are key change agents with the capacity to embrace, accommodate or resist policy direction. For example, during the introduction of the English National Curriculum, Bowe *et al.* (1992: 120) commented that programmes of study were 'not so much being "implemented" in schools as being re-created, not so much "reproduced" as "produced"'. Teacher unions have exercised industrial power through, for example, boycotting interventions on their work such as National Curriculum assessment measures in England (Jones, 1994) or working to contract and strike action ballots over 'readiness' for curriculum change in Scotland. Teachers, parents and local residents have offered occasional local resistance to school closures and to the Academies in England (Hatcher and Jones, 2006).

Pupil participation and school culture

Whether citizenship education is defined through its position in the official school curriculum and/or through its practice in school communities, it is influenced by the full range of educational policies that impact on teachers' work and pupil experiences of school. Policy influences on citizenship education require engagement with questions about the extent to which schools might be regarded as democratic learning organisations; the extent to which teachers are consulted as agents of change in school; and the extent to which democracy is practised at school. Policy on citizenship education, therefore, plays a part in ensuring that schools are constantly changing political environments.

Citizenship education is among a growing portfolio of initiatives that have sought to enhance pupil participation in UK schools in the last two decades. These include the promotion of curriculum flexibility to extend 'personalisation' and 'choice', debates about the removal of 'age and stage' barriers and an extension of opportunities for vocational learning. Enhanced pupil participation in planning and evaluating learning has been sought through national, local authority and school-level strategies including Assessment for Learning (AfL) (Black *et al.*, 2003), pupil self-evaluation and target-setting practices and the formation of schools' councils. Enhanced pupil participation underpins the promotion of particular forms of pedagogic practice. Critical skills, cooperative and collaborative learning feature strongly amongst continuing professional development for teachers. The involvement of young people has been promoted through a range of peer support and peer mediation schemes, including circle time, circles of friends, restorative practices and 'solution-focused approaches' (Kane *et al.*, 2007). Such trends reflect the influence in education of broader policies directed at social and personal well being. For example, Clarke (2005) has argued that the Scottish model of integrated community schools ('full service' schools) combined with health-promoting schools policies has promoted the development of participatory structures. Such policies position children and young people as service users and social actors.

Whilst this policy picture appears to be one of complementary and mutually reinforcing initiatives, research into the enactment of policies does not depict a uniform picture. A number of studies provide evidence that good practice in terms of pupil participation remains patchy (Hill *et al.*, 2004; Children in Scotland and University of Edinburgh, 2010). Ireland *et al.* (2006) suggest that citizenship education is most effective where it provides a living model of democracy. Many pupils are sensitive to contrived or 'tokenistic' opportunities that have little influence on school decisions (Mills, 2004; Wyse, 2001). Maitles and Deuchar (2006) suggest that pupil councils need to work alongside a wider range of other pupil committees and activities that together might constitute school-wide participative practice. Similarly, Allan *et al.* (2005) argue that effective participative practice involves opening up spaces for students to develop their *own* issue-specific initiatives.

Whilst research suggests a high level of involvement of pupils as participants in consultation and evaluation activities, influence as a consequence of participation is much lower (Cross *et al.*, 2009). There is a growing body of literature that highlights the need to avoid the co-option of pupil voice in forms of 'managed professionalism' (Whitty, 2006), or its 'confinement' in 'curriculum projects and elite forms of student leadership' (Thomson and Holdsworth, 2003: 372). Participation initiatives are frequently directed at activities external to pupils' day-to-day experience within classrooms, i.e. competitions and award bearing schemes, charitable work or national initiatives, e.g. healthy schools or Eco-schools. Such work rarely has a direct impact on the 'instructional core' of teachers' work (Elmore, 1996). There are difficulties with professional understandings of participation as an 'opt in' exercise or an option to be implemented in only a few areas of school life with a selection of pupils.

Significant 'culture work' would be necessary to embed participation as an enduring and meaningful aspect of day-to-day work in most schools (Fielding, 2001; 2007; Rudduck and McIntyre, 2007). There are tensions between the aspirations of 'democratic localism' (Bryk *et al.*, 2010) in education and established relations of 'linearity and control' (MacDonald, 2003), especially in secondary schooling. Maitles and Gilchrist (2006: 68), among others, have commented on 'the fundamentally undemocratic, indeed authoritarian, structure of the typical secondary school, where many teachers, never mind pupils, feel that they have very little real say in the running of the school'. Successive policy interventions have shaped school cultures characterised by performativity and compliance (Ball, 2003; Gewirtz, 2002; Gleeson and Husbands, 2001). At the same time teachers negotiate counter narratives of devolved leadership, collaboration, collegiality, creativity and professional autonomy. Developments in curriculum and pedagogy expound the virtues of personalisation, choice and active and enquiry-based learning for the knowledge society; whilst performance tables encourage a narrow definition of educational success. The tensions and apparent contradictions within this policy mix provide few clear guides for collective professional action.

Conclusion

In this chapter we have drawn attention to the politics of education policy making. We have identified some of the international, national/regional and local influences on citizenship education in schools. We have highlighted the interaction of ideas from different sources and considered how the school curriculum is influenced by wider social policy agendas. The practice of citizenship education is constrained, as well as enabled, by policies that are worked through in schools. This gives rise to tensions between participation and performance, collaboration and hierarchy, control and autonomy. In particular, 'high stakes' assessment regimes can work to undermine progressive aspects of the reform of the school curriculum and the democratisation of learning relations in the classroom. The alignment of these three message systems – curriculum, assessment and pedagogy – is one indicator of the purpose and value of a school system.

Questions for further investigation

1 Which social actors and organisations participate in curriculum policy making? (*Who* makes curriculum policy?) Identify the internal and external stakeholders within the citizenship education policy community.
2 Through what participative processes is policy for citizenship education made? (*How* is curriculum policy constructed?) What communication and consultation strategies are deployed (public consultation, expert authority, stakeholder engagement forums)? Is there a difference between consultation and engagement?
3 What are the main influences on decision making in relation to curriculum policy for citizenship education? What is the relative influence of *political* factors (public perception, media coverage, union stance and lobby groups), *economic* factors (public finance) and *pragmatic* factors (the range of feasible options available to decision makers at particular junctures)?
4 What role has *evidence* from curriculum agencies and commissioned research played in the construction and revision of the curriculum for citizenship education?
5 What has been the influence of trans-national 'travelling policy' on the domestic agenda for citizenship education? Is there evidence of policy learning (as well as policy borrowing)?
6 What mediating factors are involved in the translation of curriculum policy on citizenship and pupils' experience in education settings? What are some of the tensions between the formal or official curriculum and the curriculum in use?
7 To what extent are policies relating to curriculum, pedagogy and assessment in citizenship education congruent or divergent? How has assessment influenced other aspects of education policy making? How do sectoral differences (between primary and secondary education) influence policy and practice in citizenship education? To what extent is there an integrated and coherent citizenship curriculum across the stages (early, lower primary, middle, 14–19 years)?

Note

1 We are grateful to Emma Godding, University of Chester, for her efforts in assisting with the production of this chapter.

Suggested further reading

Ball, S.J. (2008) *The Education Debate*. Bristol: Policy Press. Important text which provides intellectual resources for understanding how education policy is produced, what it seeks to do and what its effects are.

Jones, K., Cunchillos, C., Hatcher, R., Hirtt, N. *et al.* (2008) *Schooling in Western Europe: The New Order and Its Adversaries*. Basingstoke: Palgrave Macmillan. Informative text which provides a comprehensive and coherent overview of recent policy developments in education and their impacts across Europe.

Ozga, J. (2000) *Policy Research in Educational Settings*. Buckingham: Open University Press. A text which argues for independent, critical research on education policy in the context of attacks on the quality and usefulness of educational research in general.

Spring, J. (2009) *Globalisation of Education. An Introduction*. Abingdon: Routledge. This text offers a comprehensive overview and synthesis of current research, theories and models related to the topic. Spring introduces readers to the processes, institutions and forces by which schooling has been globalised and examines the impact of these forces on schooling in local contexts.

References

Allan, J., I'Anson J., Fisher, S. and Priestley, A. (2005) *Promising Rights: Introducing Children's Rights in School*. Edinburgh: Save the Children Fund.

Allen, J. (2003) *Lost Geographies of Power*. Oxford: Blackwell.

Ball, S.J. (1990) *Politics & Policy Making in Education: Explorations in Policy Sociology*. London: Routledge.

——(1994) *Education Reform: A Critical & Post-Structural Approach*. Buckingham: Open University Press.

——(2003) 'The teacher's soul and the terrors of performativity', *Journal of Educational Policy, 18*, 2, pp. 215–28.

——(2008) *The Education Debate*. Bristol: Policy Press.

Bernstein, B. (1977) *Class, Codes and Control, Volume 3: Towards a Theory of Educational Transmissions*. (2nd Ed.) London: Routledge and Kegan Paul.

Black, P., Harrison, C., Lee, C., Marshall, B. and William, D. (2003) *Assessment for Learning. Putting It into Practice*. Maidenhead: Open University Press.

Bowe, R., Ball, S.J. and Gold, A. (1992) *Reforming Education and Changing Schools: Case Studies in Policy Sociology*. London: Routledge.

Braun, A., Maguire, M. and Ball, S.J. (2010) 'Policy enactments in the UK secondary school: examining policy, practice and school positioning', *Journal of Education Policy, 25*, 4, pp. 547–60.

Broadhead, P. (2002) 'The making of a curriculum: how history, politics and personal perspectives shape emerging policy and practice', *Scandinavian Journal of Educational Research, 46*, 1, pp. 47–64.

Bryk, A.S., Bender Sebring, P., Allensworth, E., Luppescu, S. and Easton, J.Q. (2010) *Organising Schools for Improvement*. Chicago, IL: University of Chicago Press.

Cabinet Office (2010) *Building the Big Society*. London: Cabinet Office. Available at: http://www.cabinetoffice.gov.uk/media/407789/building-big-society.pdf (accessed on 15th September 2010).

Children in Scotland and University of Edinburgh (2010) *Having a Say at School: Research Briefing Paper 2: Characteristics of Pupil Councils*. Available at: http://www.havingasayatschool.org.uk/documents/paper2_000.pdf (accessed on 18th August 2010).

Clarke, A. (2005) *The Voice of Children and Young People. Glasgow: HeadsUp Scotland. National Project for Children and Young People's Mental Health*. Available at: http://www.childreninscotland.co.uk/documents/ParticipationDiscussionDocument.pdf (accessed on 13th September 2011).

Colwill, I. and Gallagher, C. (2007) 'Developing a curriculum for the twenty-first century: the experiences of England and Northern Ireland', *Prospects*, *37*, pp. 411–25.

Cross, B., Hulme, M., Lewin, J., McKinney, S., Hall, J. and Hall, S. (2009) *Pupil Participation in Scottish Schools: Final Report*. Glasgow: Learning and Teaching Scotland/University of Glasgow. Available at: http://eprints.gla.ac.uk/49601/1/id49601.pdf (accessed on 13th September 2011).

Cuban, L. (1998) 'How schools change reforms: re-defining reform success and failure', *Teachers College Record*, *99*, 3, pp. 453–77.

Daugherty, R. and Elfed-Owens, P. (2003) 'A national curriculum for Wales: a case study in education policy-making in the era of administrative devolution', *British Journal of Educational Studies*, *51*, 3, pp. 233–53.

Davies, L. and Kirkpatrick, G. (2000) *The Euridem Project: A Review of Pupil Democracy in Europe*. London: Children's Rights Alliance for England.

Dolowitz, D. with Hulme, R., Nellis, M. and O'Neal, F. (2000) *Policy Transfer and British Social Policy*. Buckingham: Open University Press.

Elmore, R. (1996) 'School reform, teaching and learning', *Journal of Education Policy*, *11*, pp. 449–505.

Eurydice (2005) *Citizenship Education at School in Europe*. Brussels: Eurydice.

Fairclough, N. (2000) *New Labour, New Language?* London: Routledge.

Fielding, M. (2001) 'Beyond the rhetoric of student voice: new departures or new constraints in the transformation of 21st century schooling', *Forum*, *43*, 2, pp. 100–109.

——(2007) 'Beyond "voice": new roles, relations and contexts in researching with young people', *Discourse: Studies in the Cultural Politics of Education*, *28*, 3, pp. 301–10.

Flint, J. (2002) 'Return of the governors: citizenship and the new governance of neighbourhood disorder in the UK', *Citizenship Studies*, *6*, 3, pp. 245–64.

Gale, T. (2003) 'Realising policy: the who and how of policy production', *Discourse*, *24*, 1, pp. 51–65.

Gewirtz, S. (2002) *The Managerial School: Post-Welfarism and Social Justice in Education*. London: Routledge.

Gillies, V. (2005) 'Meeting parents' needs? Discourses of "support" and "inclusion" in family policy', *Critical Social Policy*, *25*, 1, pp. 70–90.

Gleeson, D. and Husbands, C. (Eds) (2001) *The Performing School: Managing, Teaching and Learning in a Performance Culture*. London: RoutledgeFalmer.

Greco, M. (1993) 'Psychosomatic subjects and the "duty to be well": personal agency within medical rationality', *Economy and Society, 22*, 3, pp. 357–72.

Harvey, D. (2005) *A Brief History of Neo-Liberalism*. Oxford: Oxford University Press.

Hatcher, R. and Jones, C. (2006) 'Researching resistance: campaigns against academies in England', *British Journal of Educational Studies, 54*, 3, pp. 329–51.

Hill, M., Davis, J., Prout, A. and Tisdall, K. (2004) 'Moving the participation agenda forward', *Children and Society, 18*, pp. 77–96.

Home Office (2003) *Respect and Responsibility: Taking a Stand against Anti-Social Behaviour*. London: The Stationery Office.

Hulme, M. and Menter, I. (2008) 'Learning to teach in post-devolution UK: a technical or an ethical process?', *Southern African Review of Education, 19*, 1–2, pp. 43–64.

Hulme, R. and Hulme, M. (2008) 'Transferring Global Education Policy', in Yeates, N. (Ed.) *Understanding Global Social Policy*. Bristol: Policy Press. pp. 49–72.

Ireland, E., Kerr, D., Lopes, J. and Nelson, J. with Cleaver, L. (2006) *Active Citizenship and Young People: Opportunities, Experiences and Challenges In and Beyond School Citizenship Education. Longitudinal Study: Fourth Annual Report* (DfES Research Report 732). London: DfES.

Jones, K. (1994) 'A new kind of cultural politics? The 1993 boycott of testing', *Changing English, 2*, 1, pp. 84–110.

Jones, K. and Alexiadou, N. (2001) 'Travelling policy: local spaces'. Paper to 'The global and the national: reflections on the experience of three European states' symposium at the European Conference on Educational research' (ECER), Lille, September 2001.

Jones, K., Cunchillos, C., Hatcher, R., Hirtt, N., Innes, R., Joshua, S. *et al.* (2008) *Schooling in Western Europe: The New Order and Its Adversaries*. Basingstoke: Palgrave Macmillan.

Jordan, G. (1990) 'Bringing policy communities back in? A comment on grant', *British Journal of Politics and International Relations, 7*, pp. 317–21.

Kane, J., Lloyd, G., McCluskey, G., Riddell, S., Stead, J. and Weedon, E. (2007) 'Full report of evaluation of restorative practices in three Scottish councils'. Available at: http://www.scotland.gov.uk/Publications/2007/08/24093135/0 (accessed on 20th June 2010).

Macdonald, D. (2003) 'Curriculum change and the post-modern world: Is the school curriculum-reform movement an anachronism?', *Journal of Curriculum Studies, 35*, 2, pp. 139–49.

McPherson, R. and Raab, C. (1988) *Governing Education: A Sociology of Policy*. Edinburgh: Edinburgh University Press.

Maitles, H. and Deuchar, R. (2006) 'We don't learn democracy, we live it! Consulting the pupil voice in Scottish schools', *Education Citizenship and Social Justice, 1*, 3, pp. 249–66.

Maitles, H. and Gilchrist, I. (2006) 'Never too young to learn democracy!: a case study of a democratic approach to learning in a religious and moral education secondary class in the west of Scotland', *Educational Review, 58*, 1, pp. 67–85.

Marinetto, M. (2003) 'Who wants to be an active citizen? The politics and practice of community involvement', *Sociology*, *37*, 1, pp.103–20.

Marsh, D. and Rhodes, R.A.W. (1993) *Policy Networks in British Government.* Oxford: Clarendon.

Martin, I. (2003) 'Adult education, lifelong learning and citizenship: some ifs and buts', *International Journal of Lifelong Education*, *22*, 6, pp. 566–79.

Miliband, D. (2006) 'Empowerment and the deal for devolution'. Speech to the annual conference of the New Local Government Network (NLGN), 18th January 2006.

Mills, I. (2004) 'Citizenship: pupil involvement in Scottish secondary schools', *Pedagogy, Culture and Society*, *12*, 2, pp. 259–80.

Olssen, M., Codd, J. and O'Neill, A.M. (2004) 'Education policy', *Globalisation, Citizenship & Democracy.* London: Sage.

Ozga, J. (1987) 'Studying educational policy through the lives of policy makers: an attempt to close the macro-micro gap', in Walker, S. and Barton, L. (Eds.) *Changing Policies, Changing Teachers.* Milton Keynes: Open University Press. pp. 138–50.

——(2005) 'Models of policy making and policy learning'. Discussion paper for the 'Seminar on Policy Learning in 14–19 Education' joint seminar of Education and Youth Transitions Project and Nuffield Review, 15th March 2005. Available at: http://www.nuffieldfoundation.org/14–19review (accessed 13th September 2011).

Ozga, J. and Jones, R. (2006) 'Travelling and embedded policy: the case of knowledge transfer', *Journal of Education Policy*, *21*, 1, pp. 1–17.

Popkewitz, T., Lindblad, S. and Strandberg, J. (1999) *Review of Research on Education Governance and Social Integration and Exclusion, Uppsala Reports on Education 35.* Uppsala, Sweden: Universitetstryckeriet.

Priestley, M. and Humes, W. (2010) 'The development of Scotland's Curriculum for Excellence: amnesia and déjà vu', *Oxford Review of Education*, *36*, 3, pp. 345–61.

Raffe, D. (2005) 'Devolution and divergence in education policy', in *Devolution in Practice: Public Policy Differences within the UK.* Newcastle upon Tyne: IPPR North. pp. 52–69.

Rodger, J.J. (2006) 'Anti-social families and withholding welfare support', *Critical Social Policy*, *26*, 1, pp. 121–43.

Rudduck, J. and McIntyre, D. (2007) *Improving Learning through Consulting Pupils.* London: Routledge.

Spring, J. (2009) *Globalization of Education: An Introduction.* Abingdon: Routledge.

Thomson, P. and Holdsworth, R. (2003) 'Theorising change in the educational "field": re-readings of "student participation" projects', *International Journal of Leadership in Education*, *6*, 4, pp. 371–91.

United Nations (1989) *Convention on the Rights of the Child.* New York, NY: United Nations.

Whitty, G. (2006) 'Teacher professionalism in a new era', General Teaching Council for Northern Ireland Annual Lecture, Queen's University, Belfast, 14th March.

Wolman, H. and Page, E. (2002) 'Policy transfer among local governments: an information-theory approach', *Governance*, *15*, 4, pp. 477–501.

Wyse, D. (2001) 'Felt tip pens and school councils: children's participation rights in four English schools', *Children and Society*, *15*, 4, pp. 209–18.

——(2010) 'The public, the personal, and national curricula: reform in England 1988 to 2010'. Paper presented at the ECER Conference, Helsinki, 25th–27th August 2010.

Chapter 5

Schools and their communities

Don Rowe

BIRKBECK COLLEGE, UNIVERSITY OF LONDON

Introduction

This chapter explores competing views of the nature and purpose of school communities as potential sites of social, moral and citizenship learning. Disagreements exist as to the extent to which such learning should take equal status with academic and vocational education and whether they are complementary or inimical to each other. The chapter then discusses various conceptualisations of the school as a paradigm of society and points out that, even where there are agreements on the importance of democratic and just schooling, there are widely differing views on how these should be operationalised. Schools also see themselves as communities within a range of local, national and international communities. However, they disagree on pedagogical approaches and priorities towards teaching about them and on whether, and if so how, to promote positive forms of cohesion and loyalty.

The contested nature of the school as a community

Schools are learning communities but disagreements exist as to what they should teach. Schools are also complex communities in their own right and as such they are rich sites of formal and informal, intended and unintended experiential social, moral and citizenship learning (Breslin, 2006; Arthur, 2003: 135). Schools have complex and sometimes conflicting sets of purposes, including the need, on the one hand, to prepare young people for economic competence and, on the other, to develop young people as rounded and socially competent beings able to participate in society as 'responsible citizens' (QCDA, 2008).

It is widely accepted that citizenship learning takes place experientially, cognitively and affectively (e.g. Osler and Starkey, 1996: 85). However, schools have differed in the extent to which they have recognised the contribution of these different modes of learning. Cleaver *et al.* (2006) noted the ways in which, when citizenship education was first introduced, some schools focused on the taught curriculum, ignoring the potential of the school community to offer practical experience of citizenship activities, whilst others argued that the ethos, values and structures of the school were the true site of citizenship learning, neglecting the crucial importance of the taught curriculum and viewing the introduction of a new subject as an unwelcome burden. A third group of schools recognised that citizenship education has both a cognitive and an experiential component (besides an affective component) and that these elements should all be seen as part of a coherent citizenship package or offer (Breslin, 2006: 342ff.). Even within this latter category, however, schools differ in the way they conceptualise the nature or thrust of this total learning package.

The recommendation of the so-called Crick Report (QCA, 1998) prior to the introduction of citizenship as a statutory subject in 2002, was that a major strand of citizenship education should be 'community involvement'. This focus was one of the features which distinguished the new citizenship education from what Crick called 'safe and dead, dead-safe, old rote-learning civics' (Crick, 2000: 119). However, there has not always been agreement amongst teachers as to how they might distinguish citizenship-rich activities from other forms of community involvement. Shortly after citizenship was introduced into schools, inspectors were offered a wide variety of citizenship-promoting activities in evidence of compliance with the National Curriculum. Many of these in Ofsted's (2006: 17) view were not citizenship activities, despite being forms of community involvement, including 'charity work, concerts and drama'. Having said that, Ofsted has noted (2003) that even school council activities can be so tokenistic as to contribute little or nothing to National Curriculum citizenship.

Breslin (2006: 342) has suggested that schools which embrace an holistic, whole-school approach to citizenship learning can be defined as 'citizenship-rich'. He suggests that these schools have five defining characteristics:

- citizenship education is clearly manifested in direct curriculum provision and can be identified in the timetable, in assessment frameworks, in the school's development plans;
- citizenship education is taught through a skills-based and learner-centred pedagogy;
- citizenship learning is explicitly acknowledged to take place through a range of opportunities both on and off the school site;
- the effective participation of all the school's stakeholders is encouraged, including students, teachers, parents and the wider community;
- it models in its day-to-day practices the principles it teaches through its citizenship curriculum.

An alternative way to conceptualise this is to suggest that citizenship schools should ensure consistency of message between the citizenship curriculum and the life of the school in respect of the key citizenship concepts which include rights, responsibilities, justice, democracy, power, equality, diversity and rules/laws (QCA, 2007 for a narrower set of key concepts).

Supporters of this whole-school view would no doubt count themselves amongst those who believe that a central purpose of education is the social, moral and spiritual development of young people (e.g. Ungoed-Thomas, 1997; Arthur, 2003). However, there are those who regard these aims as subsidiary to, or even a distraction from, the school's core business of promoting academic excellence in a social and political climate which appears not to value such wider ambitions (Arthur, 2003). Some regard schools who purport to teach social values of any kind as intruding on the private domain of parents (e.g. CRE, 2010) and, given that under the UN Convention of Human Rights parents have an explicit right to bring up children in their own beliefs, there is a genuine debate to be had about where, and in what way, the responsibilities of parents and schools overlap and where they may conflict (Arthur, 2003). That apart, those who claim a wider purpose for education often reconcile these competing views by arguing that academic learning is facilitated and enriched in schools which take seriously the task of creating humane, values-based learning communities (Harrison, 2010: 185).

In the following section, we look at how different conceptions of the school community have been used to shape its practices and ethos. These are all related to aspects of citizenship education but are perhaps open to the charge of privileging one strand of citizenship learning over others.

Schools as democratic communities

In recent years, as a result of legislation and other social factors, schools have increasingly embraced the need to involve students in the school's decision-making processes (Hannam, 2006: 248ff.), though as Hannam notes, there are frequently disparities between what school leaders claim they do and what students experience. However, even amongst schools which support student participation, the concept itself is contested and schools differ both in the way they conceptualise the meaning of democracy in the school setting and in the practical steps they take to put principle into practice (Rowe, 2003). For example, one head's previous experiences led him to believe that 'traditional' forms of school council were little more than shams because they implicitly claimed to offer students a degree of decision-making and influence over aspects of school life but in fact were little more than window dressing. To this extent they were more likely to create dis-illusionment with the 'real' democratic processes beyond the school gates. Because of this, the head refused to support the usual form of school council, opting instead for a kind of 'direct representation' in which all students were regularly interviewed by senior staff and given opportunities to raise issues of concern regarding school life. In addition, the head made himself very accessible to students during lunchtimes. In another school, concerns that the school council merely encouraged students to adopt a rights-based approach, focusing solely on student welfare and privileges, led the school's senior staff to promote a volunteer student council in the upper school, where all students who wished could volunteer to undertake work on behalf of the wider school community.

Whilst perhaps not widespread, these examples demonstrate that putting ideas of democracy into practice within the structures of hierarchical institutions like schools is problematic and controversial. Harber (1992: 10) has suggested that school democracy is meaningless without the real transference of *power* from staff to students and such practices regularly provoke anxiety and opposition amongst school staff, who feel this potentially threatens their authority and status. Even the question of *who* should have a say in running the school is contested and, beyond the head, school governors, students and teachers (who regularly complain of being left out), one could also include parents and community representatives amongst legitimate stakeholders. School leaders can face considerable problems in managing conflicting demands and expectations from these different groups. This debate points up the fact that students themselves, as members of the school community, can be seen to represent different roles (Rowe, 2010). Students are variously cast in the roles of:

subjects – more or less passive recipients of the education and schooling decided for them by the powers that be, on the basis that they are too young and lacking in experience to be able to contribute meaningfully to any discussion of what is best for them;

clients – the school has a duty to serve their educational interests and consulting students will help improve this provision;

experts – the school needs to ask students about the quality of life in school, e.g. about the quality of learning or about standards of behaviour which impinge on their rights;

partners – when teachers work with students as partners, e.g. in harnessing the majority voice to tackle issues such as bullying, their job in many respects becomes easier.

Schools as just and rights-based communities

An alternative conception of the school as a site of citizenship learning is that of a 'just community'. The term was famously used by Lawrence Kohlberg (Power *et al.*, 1989) when he established a school-within-a-school in a tough district of New York in order to examine whether an institution's complete commitment to the democratic participation of all its members could measurably raise the moral maturity of its participants and thus help them become more effective and committed citizens. Kohlberg's experiment had considerable success but critics of the model could argue that this was possible largely because of the small scale of the venture and the nature of the contract between the school and its tough, hard-to-reach students. Many would doubt that this is an approach that could work in large, mainstream schools for a number of reasons, though smaller communities, such as Pupil Referral Units, set aside for behaviourally challenging students, might aspire to it, based on the belief that its pupils need to improve levels of self-control and social functioning before their academic learning can improve.

Nonetheless, there are examples in the literature of the concept of justice being central to some conceptions of mainstream schools. Ungoed-Thomas (1997: 5) suggests that schools as institutions should uphold justice as their 'first virtue'. Cunningham (1992: 145), as a headteacher, was very concerned that the rules and behaviour policy in his school should be perceived by students to be fair and a paradigm of justice in wider society. Writing during the time citizenship was still a cross-curricular theme, he claimed:

> it is nonsense to aim to develop moral autonomy and democratic values [amongst students] within a rigidly authoritarian structure, and self-defeating to expect future citizens to deal fairly with the duties and rights of others unless they have experienced a model of a just society, or a determined attempt to portray one.
> (Cunningham, 1992: 145)

Cunningham also thought of his school as a 'human rights' school and based the behaviour and discipline policy for his school specifically on some of the most fundamental of human rights, including, for example, the right that no one shall be subjected to degrading treatment or punishment and everyone shall be pre-sumed innocent until proved guilty. Serious incidents in school were followed by a process of investigation (including the use of written statements), resolution (agreed by the parties, as far as possible), restitution (to provide opportunities for moral learning by the perpetrator), sanction (which must be fair and non-degrading) and communication (with parents and the victim). However, such procedures, Cunningham concedes, can be controversial, especially amongst staff in dispute with students, who feel that listening to the student in this way is tantamount to taking the student's side. As with the concept of democracy, disagreements exist as to exactly how schools relate to institutions and social practices beyond the school gates.

Proponents of just schools insist that school communities must be respectful of students because they are themselves rights bearers (Starkey, 2008; Osler, 2008). Recently the concept of the 'Rights Respecting School' has been gaining in currency through the work of the United Nations Children's Fund (UNICEF UK),[1] based on the UN Convention on the Rights of the Child (UNCRC) and the parallel work, called 'Rights, Respect and Responsibilities', in work by the Canadian educators Covell and Howe (2001). Starting with the primary school, children are explicitly taught about their rights under the UNCRC. Studies and anecdotal evidence report that even young children can utilise these concepts actively and teachers report improved classroom behaviours and school ethos.

Debates exist as to whether focusing on improving the quality of the life of the school community is a distraction from the school's core business of teaching and learning for economic functionality. Whilst many teachers may say this is a false dichotomy, there are nonetheless choices to be made by school senior leaders as to where to place the emphasis because this determines the allocation of finite time and resources. There are those who claim that improving the social and moral climate of the school brings instrumental benefits to learning and inclusion (Breslin, 2006; Hawkes, 2010; Trafford, 2008; Hannam, 2006). Others, such as Cunningham (1992) and Ungoed-Thomas (1997) favour more principled approaches to embodying civic virtues in the structures and practices of the school irrespective of any benefits.

The school in the wider community

Citizenship education, according to the Crick Report's tripartite model (QCA, 1998) should have a strong element of community involvement. However, the notion of community involvement is problematic and challenging for teachers and schools and there is a spectrum of involvement extending from intellectual engagement at one end to physical activities beyond the school gates at the other. Whilst teachers should ensure that all students engage to some extent with community affairs through structured lesson activities (QCA, 2007), it is by no means the case that all students will be able to participate in off-site citizenship activities. In the first place, schools vary considerably in the depth and type of community-based resources available to them. Schools serving students who mostly live locally will have much greater ability to engage with activities in the locality of the school than, say, rural schools where the students are widely dispersed. There are, in any case, practical limits to the number of community-based projects any one school could develop and sustain from one year to the next.

Such considerations require each school to develop its own definition of an entitlement offer and what activities may be offered to fewer pupils by way of enrichment activities. Ofsted (2006: 18) wrestled with this as a serious issue because if it transpired that, despite their best efforts, schools were unable to meet the requirement to teach through community involvement, this would undermine the whole basis of Crick's vision. Ofsted's response was to underline the fact that 'community involvement' may be offered to *all* students if the right activities are integrated into the teaching and learning programme. These might include:

- participation in class debates with pupils making responsible suggestions;
- written work taken to sensible conclusions and containing responsible suggestions;
- where appropriate, recommendations delivered in a responsible way to the management of the school or community-based bodies;
- drama and other presentations based on work undertaken in citizenship.

To some extent the way schools interpret this element of the citizenship curriculum is influenced by their own conception of the purpose of citizenship education and the contingent balance between imparting knowledge and developing skills. To a degree these are always in tension. Even when students' learning is real and relevant there is still a balance to be struck between developing action skills, e.g. campaigning skills (Pattisson, 2010), and developing students' knowledge and understanding of the social and political world without which campaigning will be ill-informed and ineffective. It is possible to conceive of a programme of citizenship education so heavily focused on skills that important areas of knowledge and understanding are neglected.

Experiential learning can have immediacy and impact but schools have a finite capacity to provide a range of practical community-based experiences which access the full range of social and political issues required by a broad and balanced curriculum. Additionally, well-taught teaching programmes focusing on key citizenship concepts have the capacity to broaden students' outlook on the world and to develop their sense of injustice which, along with human compassion, is a prime motivator of civic action.

Local, national and global communities

Schools are communities within communities and each school sits at the centre of an outwardly radiating series of concentric circles representing what are often described as local, national and international communities (QCA, 2007). To some extent these different communities compete for the attention of schools and there is a certain amount of evidence to suggest that the personal ideologies that teachers bring to the teaching of citizenship can result in the prioritisation of one or more of these communities over others. For example, citizenship in primary schools often focuses more on the local and global communities (Rowe *et al.*, 2011) at the expense of the national community, 'global citizenship' being interpreted as raising awareness of the needs of children and families around the world experiencing poverty, disease or human disaster.

Teachers who favour the active citizenship/campaigning model of citizenship may well look first and foremost to the local community for sites of action whereas teachers who favour an emphasis on curriculum content may see the need to focus more on the national level and the development of political literacy (Huddleston, 2006) amongst their students. Some citizenship teachers prioritise the concept of 'citizenship as service', and this can significantly influence course construction and favoured pedagogies. This service model of citizenship has a long tradition in this country which, arguably (Batho, 1990; Arthur, 2008), is strongly influenced by Judaeo-Christian values and, for many teachers, takes precedence over the teaching of political literacy and the practices of democratic participation.

At the level of international community involvement, two broad approaches are favoured. To a degree the term 'global citizenship' has been the term favoured by the aid agencies in their educational activities and thus it has come to be largely identified with specific kinds of international issue and driven by ethical concerns for human rights, social justice and democratic participation (Pike, 2008) closely allied to concepts of universal obligations towards humanity, and campaigns for justice and human rights. Strong elements of education for peace and international reconciliation also infuse this model. The dominance of this particular notion of global citizenship in the UK may be due to the predilection of citizens in Britain to conceptualise citizenship as service rather than as a rights-based status (Conover *et al.*, 1991) but may also be attributed to the fact that considerable resources have been put into this form of citizenship education by the major British aid agencies and the Department for International Development (Pike, 2008).

In contrast, the term 'world citizenship' has been more likely to attract a broader, more political and ideologically neutral meaning encompassing knowledge of world or international politics, including the nature of Britain's role in Europe, its relations with the Commonwealth and the international political community, including NATO and the UN. Given that teachers of citizenship are legally obliged under the Education Act 1996 to maintain non-partisan approaches towards political issues, it can be argued that ethical approaches towards the teaching of global citizenship run the risk of incorporating ideological bias into courses unless they are carefully balanced by alternative perspectives.

Citizenship, identity and patriotism

Ethical approaches towards global citizenship are based on the concept of solidarity with all peoples and universal human rights. However, whilst human rights values are widely supported throughout the world at inter-governmental level, there remain tensions between this approach and the treatment of the national community in many state citizenship education programmes. In many countries of the world, citizenship education is chiefly utilised for the purpose of nation-building, to promote a strong sense of allegiance to the national community for economic, cultural and militaristic purposes (see, for example, the case of Singapore: Boon-Yee Sim and Print 2005). Education for patriotism is widely regarded with suspicion in Britain and Europe. Hand (2011), for example, identifies the danger of sanitising history and argues that promotion of patriotism through 'peddling national myths and fictions' is too high a price to pay and, further, that the case has not been made that patriotism is an unmitigated good. It therefore ought to be treated as a controversial issue.

Notwithstanding these arguments, there have been calls in recent years from national political figures in Britain, especially following the London bombings of 2005, to present to students a clear notion of British heritage around which all citizens can unite, based not on ethno-nationalism but on cultural and political values including 'liberty, responsibility, fairness' (Brown, quoted by Osler, 2009) and belief in 'democracy, the rule of law, tolerance, equal treatment for all, respect for this country and its shared heritage' (Blair, 2006).

Conclusion

Controversies surround the relationship between schools and the communities they relate to in respect of the teaching of citizenship in schools. Not only are there differing views on the purpose of citizenship education and how it should be understood but also on its sites of learning. On a traditional view, citizenship education (or civics) is understood as education for future participation in the democratic life of the nation, but more recent and progressive models of citizenship, including that promoted in England by the Crick Report, see it as equipping young people with an understanding of their current rights and responsibilities requiring a dynamic interaction with the wider community, or rather communities. Nonetheless, even within the progressive citizenship camp, tensions exist regarding the extent to which the skills of participation through practical community involvement should take precedence over the development in students of political understanding through classroom-based, albeit active, learning. Further, underlying these debates are still deeper controversies relating to the purpose of education itself and the extent to which social, moral and political learning should have equal status with the more instrumental, vocational purposes of education. Whilst such differences persist, citizenship education will remain highly controversial.

Questions for further investigation

1 What weight do you place on the relative importance of social and citizenship learning compared with academic and vocational education? What factors should schools take into consideration when deciding how much time and effort to put into becoming 'citizenship-rich' schools at the possible expense of other priorities?
2 To what extent might efforts to promote active citizenship learning through community involvement detract from the development of broadly based political literacy?
3 To what extent do you agree with Ofsted's definition of participation as an entitlement? What are the strengths and weaknesses of this approach? Discuss the relative merits of conceptualising schools as either democratic, just, human rights-based or citizenship-rich.
4 How important is it to promote loyalty and affiliation to the community and what pedagogic approaches are justified in achieving this aim?

Note

1 See http://www.unicef.org.uk/tz/teacher_support/rrs_award_schools.asp

Suggested further reading

There is a wealth of literature on the subject of citizenship and community involvement. For this reason, readers new to this area could do worse than consult the range of excellent essays quoted from here which are to be found in two recent collections – *Developing Citizens,* edited by Breslin and Dufour (2006) and *Education for Citizenship and Democracy* edited by Arthur, Davies and Hahn (2008). For two very thorough discussions of the nature of school communities which promote social, moral and citizenship learning see Ungoed-Thomas's (1997) theoretical analysis of the virtues such schools should exemplify and Hawkes' (2010) empirical study of the benefits which accrue from making values explicit and living them out across the whole school.

References

Arthur, J. (2003) *Education with Character: The Moral Economy of Schooling.* London: RoutledgeFalmer.

——(2008) 'Christianity, citizenship and democracy', in Arthur, J., Davies, I. and Hahn, H. (Eds.) *The Sage Handbook of Education for Citizenship and Democracy.* London: Sage.

Arthur, J., Davies, I. and Hahn, H. (Eds) (2008) *The Sage Handbook of Education for Citizenship and Democracy.* London: Sage.

Batho, G. (1990) 'The history of the teaching of civics and citizenship in English schools', *The Curriculum Journal, 1,* 1, 91–100.

Blair, T. (2006) 'Our nation's future: multiculturalism and integration'. Speech given at 10 Downing Street, 8th December 2006. Available at: http://www.number10.gov.uk/output/Page10563.asp (accessed 1st September 2010).

Boon-Yee Sim, J. and Print, M. (2005) 'Citizenship education and social studies in Singapore: a national agenda', *International Journal of Citizenship and Teacher Education, 1,* pp. 58–73.

Breslin, T. (2006) 'The way forward: building the citizenship-rich school', in Breslin, T. and Dufour, B. (Eds) *Developing Citizens: A Comprehensive Introduction to Effective Citizenship Education in the Secondary School.* London: Hodder Murray.

Breslin, T. and Dufour, B. (Eds) (2006) *Developing Citizens: A Comprehensive Introduction to Effective Citizenship Education in the Secondary School.* London: Hodder Murray.

Campaign for Real Education (CRE) (2010) Available at: http://www.cre.org.uk/docs/pshe_and_citizenship.html (accessed 1st September 2010).

Cleaver, E., Kerr, D. and Ireland, E. (2006) 'Foundations and baselines for citizenship: the NFER Citizenship Education Longitudinal Study' in Breslin, T. and Dufour, B. (Eds.) *Developing Citizens: A Comprehensive Introduction to Effective Citizenship Education in the Secondary School.* London: Hodder Murray.

Conover, P.J., Crewe, I. and. Searing, D. (1991) 'The nature of citizenship in the United States and Great Britain: empirical comments on theoretical themes', *The Journal of Politics, 53,* pp. 800–32.

Covell, K. and Howe, R.B. (2001) 'Moral education through the 3R's: rights, respect and responsibility', *Journal of Moral Education, 30,* 1, pp. 29–42.

Crick, B. (2000) *Essays on Citizenship.* London: Continuum.

Cunningham, J. (1992) 'Rights, responsibilities and school ethos', in Baglin Jones, E. and Jones, N. (Eds) *Education for Citizenship: Ideas and Perspectives for Cross-curricular Study.* London: Kogan Page.

Hannam, D. (2006) 'Education for democracy and as a democratic process', in Breslin, T. and Dufour, B. (Eds) *Developing Citizens: A Comprehensive Introduction to Effective Citizenship Education in the Secondary School.* London: Hodder Murray.

Hand, M. (2011) 'Should we promote patriotism in schools?', *Political Studies, 59,* 2, pp. 328–47.

Harber, C. (1992) *Democratic Learning and Learning Democracy: Education for Active Citizenship?* Ticknall, Derbyshire: Education Now Publishing Cooperative.

Harrison, T. (2010) 'A curriculum full of character: developing character education in the classroom, culture and community of a school', in Arthur, J. (Ed.) *Citizens of Character: New Directions in Character and Values Education*. Exeter: Imprint Academic.

Hawkes, N. (2010) *Does Teaching Values Improve the Quality of Education in Primary Schools?* Saarbrücken: VDM Verlag Dr Müller Aktiengesellschaft & Co. KG.

Huddleston, T. (2006) 'From political education to political literacy: equipping young people for life in a more genuine democracy', in Breslin, T. and Dufour, B. (Eds) *Developing Citizens: A Comprehensive Introduction to Effective Citizenship Education in the Secondary School*. London: Hodder Murray.

Ofsted (2003) *National Curriculum Citizenship: Planning and Implementation*. London: Office for Standards in Education.

——(2006) *Towards Consensus? Citizenship in Secondary Schools*. London: Office for Standards in Education.

Osler, A. (2008) 'Human rights education', in Arthur, J., Davies, I. and Hahn, C. (Eds) *The Sage Handbook of Education for Citizenship and Democracy*. London: Sage.

——(2009) 'Citizenship education, democracy and racial justice 10 years on', *Race Equality Teaching*, 27, 3, pp. 21–27.

Osler, A. and Starkey, H. (1996) *Teacher Education and Human Rights*. London: David Fulton Publishers.

Pattisson, P. (2010) *Campaign Toolkit*. Association for Citizenship Teaching [online]. Available at: http://www.teachingcitizenship.org.uk/dnloads/campaign_toolkit_conference.pdf (accessed 1st September 2010).

Pike, G. (2008) 'Global education', in Arthur, J., Davies, I. and Hahn, C. (Eds) *The Sage Handbook of Education for Citizenship and Democracy*. London: Sage.

Power, F.C., Higgins, A. and Kohlberg, L. (1989) *Lawrence Kohlberg's Approach to Moral Education*. New York, NY: Columbia University Press.

Qualifications and Curriculum Authority (QCA) (1998) *Education for Citizenship and the Teaching of Democracy in Schools: Final Report of the Advisory Group on Citizenship*. London: QCA.

——(2007) *Citizenship: A Programme of Study for Key Stage 3 and 4*. London: QCA.

Qualifications and Curriculum Development Authority (QCDA) (2008) *A Big Picture of the Secondary Curriculum*. London: QCDA. Available at: http://www.teachingcitizenship.org.uk/dnloads/bigpicture_sec_05_tcm8_157430.pdf (accessed 13th September 2011).

Rowe, D. (2003) *The Business of School Councils*. London: The Citizenship Foundation.

——(2010) *Citizenship Education: A National CPD Course*. London: The Citizenship Foundation and Birkbeck College, University of London.

Rowe, D., Horsley, N., Thorpe T. and Breslin, T. (2011) *School Leaders, Community Cohesion and the Big Society*. Reading: CfBT Education Trust.

Starkey, H. (2008) 'Antiracism', in Arthur, J., Davies, I. and Hahn, C. (Eds) *The Sage Handbook of Education for Citizenship and Democracy*. London: Sage.

Trafford, B. (2008) 'Democratic schools, towards a definition', in Arthur, J., Davies, I. and Hahn, C. (Eds) *The Sage Handbook of Education for Citizenship and Democracy*. London: Sage.

Ungoed-Thomas, J. (1997) *Vision of a School: The Good School in the Good Society*. London: Cassell.

Chapter 6

Citizenship education, race and community cohesion

Alveena Malik

CHIEF EXECUTIVE, THE YOUNG FOUNDATION

Introduction

This chapter aims to explore the important role that the duty to promote community cohesion plays within our current British education system. It will discuss the key cohesion issues in Britain and the role of schools in tackling some of the most pressing social issues facing us now and in the future. This chapter will also explore the challenges for schools in promoting community cohesion and highlight good practice. In its conclusion, the chapter will raise some important issues for senior management, teachers and governors to consider in taking forward this agenda.

Current context

In Britain today, changes in lifestyle, advancements in technology, transport, different work patterns and globalisation have all re-defined the way we work, learn, live and play. The definition of 'community' has also undergone a radical redefinition with communities, or the social networks that make up these communities, not bound by any physical, geographical boundaries; more dispersed, diverse, short-lived and numerous than in the past. Furthermore, as a consequence of globalisation, people's relationship to their birth state has also changed. Most people now have multiple identities and are increasingly subject to diasporic influences, which have broken up traditional patterns of identification with the nation state.

Britain is defined by hyper-diversity and changing demographics, more so today than ever before. With an ageing population, the Office of National Statistics (ONS, 2011) has predicted that by 2034, 23 per cent of the population will be aged 65 and over, and just 18 per cent aged under 16. Ethnic minority groups have younger populations than average, with fewer than 20 per cent of people in such groups aged over 50, and less than 10 per cent aged 65 and over. With ethnic minority groups growing in size, religious affiliations to faiths other than Christianity can be expected over the coming years.

Whilst high levels of inward migration and a continued population churn have aided the increase in the national population, they have also placed greater demands on public services, increased disengagement with local and national politics and created frictions between communities of different cultures. Despite this, and an ever-decreasing voter turnout, the Citizenship Survey for 2009–10, commissioned by the Home Office, indicated that 85 per cent of people thought their community was cohesive, agreeing that their local area was a place where people from different backgrounds got on well together (HOCS, 2010). This was an improvement of 3 per cent from the 2007–8 survey (HOCS, 2008).

Perceptions of cohesion were generally higher among older age groups; in the 2010 survey, for example, 91 per cent of those aged 75 years and over thought their local area was cohesive, which was the same as the 2008 statistic, compared with 80 per cent of those aged 16 to 24 years, up from 76 per cent in 2008 (HOCS, 2008; 2010). However, younger people were more likely than older people to mix with people from different ethnic and religious backgrounds, with 93 per cent of people aged 16 to 24 years indicating that they had mixed in this way, compared with 53 per cent of people aged 75 years and over (HOCS, 2010).

What is community cohesion?

With the changes mentioned above has come the emergence of a new, interrelated cohesion and equalities paradigm. This new approach does two main things: firstly it recognises the need for protection on the grounds of age, sexual orientation, gender, gender reassignment, pregnancy and maternity, race, religion and belief, and disability. Secondly it recognises the urgency to promote interaction in addressing what Ted Cantle, in his Community Cohesion Report (2001), referred to as 'parallel lives'. Trevor Phillips, former Chair of the Commission for Racial Equality (CRE) shared Cantle's concerns regarding 'parallel lives' and in 2005 he warned 'We are sleepwalking our way to segregation. We are becoming strangers to each other, and we are leaving communities to be marooned outside the mainstream' (Phillips, 2005).

Schools and workplaces are places where people come together and interact on a daily basis, making them key arenas for promoting community cohesion. Schools are at the coal face of dealing with issues such as rapid population churn, segregated communities, extremism and manifestations of identity crises, including the rise of gang culture. Importantly too, due to increasingly globalised markets, future jobs will rely on employees being able to deal and work with difference. Whilst this presents a challenge for those who lack the opportunity to interact and learn about differences in race, culture and faith during formative years, it provides a great opportunity for young people to learn key skills which will enhance all aspects of their lives.

According to the most recent study into *Young People and Community Cohesion* (September 2010) commissioned by the Department for Education (DfE), the emphasis placed on schools as an agent of change reflects their recognised potential to serve as:

- sites of integration, bringing together young people from different backgrounds (race, ethnic, faith, gender, and social class);
- sites of citizenship training, promoting shared understandings and sense of belonging;
- and sites of knowledge and skills acquisition, promoting similar life opportunities.

(Demack *et al.*, 2010)

The duty to promote community cohesion

The Education and Inspections Act 2006 had already introduced a duty on maintained schools in England to promote community cohesion, and on the Office for Standards in Education, Children's Services and Skills (Ofsted) to inspect schools' work in this area. Such Ofsted guidance has since been revised, for the benefit of inspectors (Ofsted, 2009).

The Government's Department for Children, Schools and Families (DCSF) 'Community Cohesion – Guidance on Inspecting' document defines community cohesion as:

> working towards a society in which there is a common vision and sense of belonging by all communities; a society in which the diversity of people's backgrounds and circumstances is appreciated and valued; a society in which similar life opportunities are available to all; and a society in which strong and positive relationships exist and continue to be developed in the workplace, in schools and in the wider community.

(DCSF, 2009)

The community cohesion duty focuses on three strands:

> Teaching, learning and curriculum
> Helping pupils to learn to understand others, to value diversity whilst also promoting shared values, to promote awareness of human rights and to apply and defend them, and to develop the skills of participation and responsible action.
> Equity and excellence
> To ensure equal opportunities for all to succeed at the highest level possible, striving to remove barriers to access and participation in learning and wider activities and working to eliminate variations in outcomes for different groups.
> Engagement and extended services
> To provide reasonable means for children, young people, their friends and families to interact with people from different backgrounds and build positive relations: including links with different schools and communities and the provision of extended services with opportunities for pupils, families and the wider community to take part in activities and receive services which build positive interaction and achievement for all groups.

(DCSF, 2007)

The guidance outlines the term 'community' as having a number of dimensions, such as the school community, i.e. the pupils it serves, their families and the school's staff; but also the community within which the school is located, the school in its geographical community and the people who live or work in that area. In addition, the guidance indicates that the community of Britain, which all schools are a part of, and the global community, formed by the EU and international links, are two further dimensions.

The guidance also emphasises that because each school is different, each school's contribution to community cohesion will be different and will need to develop by reflecting the nature of the school's population, whether it serves pupils drawn predominantly from one or a small number of faiths, ethnic or socio-economic groups or from a broader cross-section of the population, or whether it selects by ability from across a wider area. Also, the location of the school, e.g. whether it serves a rural or urban area and the level of ethnic, faith and socio-economic diversity of the area, contributes to the school's cohesion.

The guidance is clear that community cohesion should not be limited to race and faith, and encourages schools to recognise other notions of equality. However, schools were reminded that the main focus of the duty is cohesion across different cultures, ethnic, religious or non-religious and socio-economic groups (DCSF, 2007: 5).

The guidance is unique to Britain and has generated much interest both across the Atlantic and within Europe. Importantly too, unlike previous agendas on race and diversity, the guidance places emphasis on the community as a whole to learn and interact with one another, regardless of race, faith or culture, as opposed to other approaches where a particular section of the community have been told to change or adapt. This provides a real opportunity to address local and societal cohesion challenges in a meaningful way through learning about difference within the curriculum, tackling inequalities and importantly providing a vital link between the school and its local community. In each community, the school can become (and indeed in many areas already is) the heart, providing a safe place for children, families and others to interact and break down prejudices, and teach everyone, not just the pupils, the confidence to become good neighbours and active citizens.

With the recent Comprehensive Spending Review, and related cuts in public sector budgets, it is more important than ever that this notion of the school as a 'safe place' remains, and is built upon in order to strengthen communities.

Inter-relationship between citizenship and cohesion

Citizenship education underpins and strengthens a school's ability to promote community cohesion. Through curriculum, ethos and good teaching, schools can facilitate exploration of one's identity and the 'other', illustrating different starting points but also common experiences and values.

The *Diversity and Citizenship Curriculum Review* foresaw the importance of citizenship education tackling cohesion issues, stating that: 'we passionately believe that it is the duty of all schools to address issues of "how we live toge-ther" and "dealing with difference" however controversial and difficult they might sometimes seem' (Ajegbo *et al.*, 2007). Citizenship education also strengthens community cohesion by its emphasis in advancing political and civic literacy amongst the younger generation. A sense of belonging, feeling valued and having opportunities to engage in civic life are important components of cohesive com-munities. The recent cohesion and young people study supports the correlation between cohesion and citizenship education, stating:

> judging from the relatively large proportion of young people reporting low levels of societal cohesion ... many young people do not perceive themselves to be accepted as worthy, valuable and responsible members of society. This finding reaffirms the importance of the citizenship agenda.
>
> (Demack *et al.*, 2010: 9)

The key combined outcomes of citizenship education and the cohesion duty should be to nurture responsible citizens in waiting who are confident in their own skins, who do not fear others who are different from them and who take actions which are beneficial to the whole community. These future citizens, from an early age, should acquire the necessary life skills to live and work with difference; they will be entering a world markedly different from the one that their parents entered and the patterns of education that they receive should reflect this. It is anticipated that the outcomes of citizenship and cohesion learning will be to improve life chances for many who will have to work and succeed in diverse workplaces. If such education is successful, we should also witness a trend towards less ethnically segregated areas around our communities as new citizens will be far less fearful of the 'other'.

Community cohesion in action

The duty to promote community cohesion places a central expectation on schools to know their local communities. In places of high population churn, knowing and understanding the demographic changes is very important to enable future planning and resourcing. Different schools will have different cohesion priorities based on the life experiences of their pupils. Therefore it is important that schools analyse their particular context and link it to the local, regional, national and international level. To do this effectively, schools need to understand the ethnic, faith and class dynamics of their local communities.

Importantly too there is a recognition that schools cannot meet the duty by themselves and need to connect with key local partners in order to understand the local context, the needs of the communities and any gaps in provision. Strong partnership is key to successful implementation of the duty; in some places local authorities are leading the agenda through sharing of local data, facilitation, support and promotion of best practice amongst schools in the local area.

The Institute of Community Cohesion (iCoCo) has pioneered an approach with a number of local authorities to set up clusters of primary, secondary and special schools in order to learn from each other's experiences and share knowledge of how to implement the different strands of the duty. The schools attend a number of group meetings to discuss different aspects of the duty, receive one to one support and celebrate their good practice through shared case studies, publications and showcase conferences. In the longer term, good practice databases and resources are developed and the learning networks continue, supported by the local authority.

The key issues that arise from the learning networks are:

- how to engage effectively with parents and/or governors;
- how young people can become active participants in making their schools and communities more cohesive;
- how to build the confidence and competencies of teachers to deal with controversial issues;
- what mechanism to develop in order to engage the wider community and encourage hard to reach families to use school facilities;
- what resources are available to support community cohesion;
- what cohesion activities fit within a very tight school timetable;
- how to engage with white British pupils on this agenda so that it is relevant to their circumstances;
- how to draw together the varied elements of cohesion work to evaluate overall effectiveness and identify potential improvements.

This list is not exhaustive and priorities are different for different areas. iCoCo works through each issue, identifying whether it is particular to one school or the local area, referencing relevant resources and approaches nationally, and then developing ways of working which tackle the issue and evidence the impact. iCoCo has developed several toolkits, audit tools, curriculum reviews and an extensive good practice database for parents, teachers, governors and local authorities to access. These provide ideas that will help schools to develop cohesion work relevant to their particular contexts whilst meeting the legal requirements of the duty.[1]

A recent community cohesion report by Ofsted (2010) supports iCoCo's approach at the local level. There are some clear recommendations regarding the role and responsibilities of local authorities in supporting schools. In addition, the report recommends that schools and colleges should:

- understand local community needs and opportunities for promoting social responsibility and community cohesion;
- explore ways to improve the transfer of information between schools and colleges about young people's attainment and previous achievements;

- monitor and evaluate participation rates in specific programmes and activities intended to promote social responsibility and community cohesion, and the impact they make;
- ensure that governing bodies have appropriate training so that they can discharge their duties to the whole community;
- provide regular opportunities for staff training, including for senior leaders, to develop their confidence in dealing with sensitive, topical and controversial issues with young people;
- develop learners' advocacy and participation skills to support them in making a positive contribution to their educational setting and the wider community;
- promote intergenerational activities that foster mutual understanding.

Community cohesion, at least at a policy level, is a relatively new idea which has been taken on board and encouraged at all levels of government over the last ten years. More recently, public sector services have become subject to national and local cohesion targets and indicators, and, within the education sector, to legislation.

There have been a number of government committees, research studies and policy reports produced on this subject. However because the agenda is an evolving one and sensitive to international as well as national events it is difficult to predict conclusively what determines or undermines cohesion at any given time. Laurence and Heath (2008) have provided an in-depth study into general factors that can undermine cohesion. They determined that, amongst others, feeling unable to influence decisions, ignorance of rights and responsibilities and a lack of places in which to mix socially were amongst the most popular reasons given by those questioned for a lack of community cohesion. In addition, a lack of volunteering opportunities, perceived inequality and disadvantage, a distrust in the fairness of authority and a dissatisfaction with the environment were also stated.

Through the three strands – teaching, learning and curriculum; equity and excellence; and engagement and extended services – the cohesion duty on schools aims to help tackle the factors identified by Laurence and Heath. Schools are ideally placed to provide young people with the necessary skills to recognise, address and overcome these threats to cohesion. Therefore they play a vital role in helping young people to successfully navigate the challenges of the modern world.

Good practice

Over the past three years there has been a significant body of good practice and tools built up around meeting the cohesion duty. The most successful schools are the ones that work closely with local authorities and other key local partners; adopt a whole school approach, ethos and vision; mainstream community cohesion across key agendas such as Every Child Matters; and actively engage parents; and whose stakeholders range from governors through to lunchtime supervisors. These are also the schools that understand and support the agenda.

Clearly, citizenship education plays a key role in tackling some factors undermining cohesion. There have been a number of initiatives across schools in England which have attempted to address the democratic deficit facing Britain today. Over many years schools have encouraged the development of 'pupil voice' on issues such as school environment, lunchtimes, uniform, charity work and links with local communities. More advanced practice has engaged young people at the centre of school improvement initiatives including reviews of teaching and learning, lesson observation, staff appointment procedures and discussion of fundamental school aims and long-term development. In these cases young people recognise that they can contribute to important aspects of their communities and in doing so they learn that important decisions are not 'only for important people'. Schools have set up peer training programmes for student councils, facilitated Model United Nations events and used critical inquiry methods such as Philosophy for Children/Communities or 'P4C' to promote the kinds of skills needed for democratic debate, with a focus on developing thinking skills, quality dialogue, and exploring pupils' values and emotions within a group or 'community of enquiry'.

Another successful approach which promotes both citizenship and cohesion is UNICEF's Rights Respecting School Award (RRSA) which is based on the rights and responsibilities enshrined in the articles of the United Nations Convention on the Rights of the Child (UNCRC). The RRSA is premised on the understanding that if children want to achieve they have to feel included, and have a sense of belonging and understanding that they matter. Children and young people can raise their achievement at school and improve the quality of their own and their families' lives, if they learn exactly what their rights and responsibilities are according to the UNCRC and use this understanding as a guide to living. Schools which promote the rights-respecting model as a basis for building learning communities in every classroom have found that self-esteem is improved, there is a reduction in prejudice and, overall, school improves due to less truancy and bullying and better learning and academic standards (UNICEF UK, 2007).

The 'Who Do We Think We Are?' project is a highly creative project to engage schools in the exploration of identity, diversity and citizenship with their pupils. A national, week-long activities programme entitled 'Who Do We Think We Are? week' has taken place each year since 2007, in which schools offered alternative timetable arrangements that encouraged cross-curricular explorations of identity and diversity through subject 'join up', extensive on-site enrichment activities and off-site visits to museums, archives, places of worship and other community-based venues.

Following the Diversity and Citizenship Curriculum Review the Schools Linking Network (SLN) was established to increase opportunities for pupils to mix with children who are different from them and, through well-planned linking work, to explore the concepts of community, identity and diversity. The process of linking (either within school, by geography, race, class or special needs) is followed by activities between the schools exploring four key questions:

- Who am I?
- Who are we?
- Where do we live?
- How do we live together?

Usually the projects begin with students being encouraged to reflect on how they see their own identities through names, cultures and communities. The parties involved in the link then exchange information about one another, which leads to the first meeting. This is followed by further work on identity, with an emphasis on reflecting on what has been learnt through working together. A second and third exchange of information and meetings follow, focusing on the key questions 'Where do we live?' and 'How do we all live together?' Children involved have demonstrated improved confidence, self-esteem, aspiration, communication and critical thinking skills.

Tackling inequality and disadvantage is what schools have been attempting to do for a long time. According to the most comprehensive study on equality and fairness in Britain produced by the Equality and Human Rights Commission (EHRC, 2010), students eligible for free school meals (FSM) are less than half as likely to achieve five GCSE passes (grade C or above), including English and Maths, than those not eligible for them. Yet ethnic differences at GCSE are narrowing, although the two top performing groups are still Chinese and Indian students. In England, Chinese girls perform best at GCSE level, and even Chinese girls eligible for FSM outperform all other ethnic groups whether on FSM or not. Gypsy and traveller children appear to struggle and results indicate that their performance is declining, with less than one in six students obtaining at least five GCSE passes.

A relatively new inequality has shown an increase in white working class boys failing to meet the accepted levels of achievement at GCSE. Currently there are only limited strategic focus and educational resources which tackle underachievement, or explore white British identity, culture and post-war history, and the challenge of providing a relevant curriculum to all sections of society whilst promoting active community cohesion is one which seriously needs to be addressed.

However, there are pockets of exemplar practice which attempt to address underachievement and explore white identity. Some secondary schools are adopting cutting-edge work to address white boys' underachievement through direct academic intervention. This has led to impressive results. These boys have been taken out of mainstream groups and put into a separate class to allow for individual attention and support. In addition they have been exposed to extra-curricular activities tailored to their needs in order to boost confidence and competence. Other schools have adopted the 'working solutions' model of assertive mentors[2] to raise attainment of this target group with very good results.

Many schools have used St George's day as a focus for celebrating England and English identities, carefully developing approaches that are inclusive and respectful of a diversity of perspectives. Importantly these approaches challenge the divisive use of St George as a symbol of 'ethnically white' England and challenge mythical notions of a historically homogenous culture. They help young people see how they belong and how other people belong around them.[3]

A new era

In 2010, with the change of government and the new direction of education policy, there are concerns that the Coalition government will repeal many duties, including the community cohesion duty, and slim down the Ofsted framework as part of its 'reducing bureaucracy' agenda. The stark difference between the previous government's and the new government's policies on education can be seen in the quotes below.

According to Barry Sheerman, former Chair of the Education Select Committee:

> Transforming the community is what a great school does.

However according to the new Secretary of State for Education, Michael Gove MP:

> I fear that duties on schools, and teachers, to fulfil a variety of noble purposes – everything from promoting community cohesion to developing relationships with other public bodies, trusts, committees and panels – gets in the way of their core purpose – education.
>
> (Gove, 2009)

It seems that the new Government's, or at least Rt. Hon. Gove's, aim for education is the promotion of educational excellence and academic attainment for all. It is likely, therefore, that Ofsted will no longer be required to inspect schools against the cohesion duty. However it is interesting to note that even though community cohesion was not included in the new Academies Act 2010 it remains a condition in the funding agreement, and conditions for the grant must be that: 'the school will be at the heart of its community, sharing facilities with other schools and the wider community'.

What will this mean for schools? Some schools will continue to see the school as the central hub of their local community, while others might see the new government's change in policy as an opportunity to move away from the agenda. Yet it is still relevant to note that with the Equality Act 2010 there is a re-emphasis on community cohesion priorities. The general duty which came into force on 1st October 2010 puts a statutory obligation on all public authorities including schools to:

- eliminate unlawful discrimination, harassment and victimisation;
- advance equality of opportunity between different groups;
- foster good relations between different groups.

All three strands of the general duty support the cohesion duty, however it is the third strand – fostering good relations – which is most closely aligned to the cohesion duty on schools. Indeed some would argue that the cohesion duty is a precursor to the new good relations duty and because of this that schools are ahead of the rest in meeting the new obligations. The Act outlines the necessity to foster good relations between persons who share a relevant protected characteristic and persons who do not share it; in particular, the need to (a) tackle prejudice; and (b) promote understanding.

Those schools which have been effectively promoting community cohesion for the past three years and equipping their pupils to live and thrive alongside people from many different backgrounds will be well placed to meet the new equality duty.

Conclusion

Even though the future of the cohesion duty is uncertain it is clear that community cohesion remains important both in terms of new legislation and evolving practice within the education sector. The new government should consider more deeply that if it wants to achieve its vision of the Big Society then this is wholly dependent on future generations being politically literate, active citizens. This requires schools to retain a focus on both the citizenship and cohesion agendas. Secondly if the new government recognises the growing international competition in job markets, ignoring the cohesion agenda in state schooling will deskill the future generation in the important life skills of dealing with difference and accelerating demographic changes. It will not matter that high academic excellence is achieved if young people lack the skills to communicate, interact and work in an increasingly diverse globalised workforce. Community cohesion actually matters more in this decade then it ever did in the previous decade. Politicians, policymakers and teachers would be wise to reflect on this before making any radical changes that undermine recent well-focused advances.

Acknowledgement

This chapter has been edited by Aidan Thompson, University of Birmingham.

Questions for further investigation

1 What do you think are the best ways to actively promote community cohesion in light of the Big Society agenda?
2 List the different types of potential frictions that can arise between different communities and suggest ways to address them.
3 What information can be routinely collected which provides up-to-date profiles of a changing population and workforce in local communities, and across the country? How can this information be used to enhance community cohesion?

Notes

1 See http://www.cohesioninstitute.org.uk/home
2 First pioneered by Hurworth School, Darlington. For further reading please see Farrar, E. (2008) *Using Assertive Mentoring to Counter Laddishness.* Darlington: NTRP.
3 See http://www.stgeorgesdayproject.org.uk

Suggested further reading

Cantle, T. *Parallel Lives.* Available at: http://www.eurozine.com/articles/2006-11-03-cantle-en.html Interesting online article about breaking down segregation in multicultural societies.

Institute of Community Cohesion (iCoCo) (2010). *DCSF Community Cohesion Toolkit.* Available at: http://www.cohesioninstitute.org.uk/Resources/Toolkits. iCoCo Toolkits offer practical advice and guidance to cohesion practitioners and feature top tips and checklists to help you plan your schemes and projects and to support you in your community cohesion initiatives.

Richardson, R. (2009) *Holding Together – Equalities, Difference and Cohesion – Guidance for School Improvement Planning.* Stoke-on-Trent: Trentham. This book shows ways that schools can harmonise their legal duties – to promote equality in relation to disability, ethnicity and gender and to promote community cohesion – with one another; and how they can be applied holistically to all curriculum subjects, and to a school's organisation and ethos.

References

Ajegbo, K., Kiwan, D. and Sharma, S. (2007) *Diversity and Citizenship Curriculum Review.* Nottingham: DfES.

Cantle, T. (2001) *Community Cohesion: A Report of the Independent Review Team.* London: Home Office.

Demack, S., Platts-Fowler, D., Robinson, D., Stevens, A. and Wilson, I. (2010) *Young People and Community Cohesion: Analysis from the Longitudinal Study of Young People in England* (LSYPE). Sheffield: Sheffield Hallam University, Centre for Regional Economic and Social Research and the Centre for Educational and Inclusion Research.

Department for Children, Schools and Families (DCSF) (2007) *Education and Inspections Act 2006.* London: HMSO.

——(2009) 'Community Cohesion – Guidance for Inspecting'. Available at: http://www.ofsted.gov.uk (accessed 22nd February 2011).

Equality and Human Rights Commission (EHRC) (2010) 'How Fair is Britain?', EHRC The First Triennial Review. London: EHRC.

Gove, M. (2009) 'What is Education For?' Speech to the Royal Society for the Arts 30th June 2009. Available at: http://www.thersa.org/_data/assets/pdf_file/0009/213021/Gove-speech-to-RSA.pdf (accessed 22nd February 2011).

Home Office Citizenship Survey (HOCS) (2008) 'Citizenship Survey 2007–8' [online]. Available at: http://www.communities.gov.uk/publications/communities/citizenshipsurveyaprmar08 (accessed 21st February 2011).

——(2010) 'Citizenship Survey 2009–10' [online]. Available at: http://www.communities.gov.uk/documents/statistics/pdf/164191.pdf (accessed 21st February 2011).

Laurence, J. and Heath, A. (2008) *Predictors of Community Cohesion: Multi-level Modelling of the 2005 Citizenship Survey.* London: Dept for Communities and Local Government.

Office of National Statistics (ONS) (2011) 'Key Population and Vital Statistics'. Available at: http://www.statistics.gov.uk/default.asp (accessed 22nd February 2011).

Ofsted (2009) *Non-Executive Board Meeting Minutes (29th September 2009).* Available at: http://www.ofsted.gov.uk (accessed 22nd February 2011).

——(2010) *Learning Together: How Education Providers Promote Social Responsibility and Community Cohesion.* London: Ofsted.

Phillips, T. (2005) Speech Given at Manchester Council for Community Relations Meeting, 22nd September 2005.

Richardson, R. (2009) *Holding Together – Equalities, Difference and Cohesion: Guidance for School Improvement Planning.* Stoke-on-Trent: Trentham.

Sheerman, B. *Barry Sheerman News [Online],* available at http://www.barrysheerman.co.uk (accessed 13th September 2011).

UNICEF UK (2007) *Rights Respecting School Award Summary.* London: UNICEF.

Chapter 7

The civic engagement of young people living in areas of socio-economic disadvantage

Carolynne Mason

LOUGHBOROUGH UNIVERSITY

Introduction

The introduction of citizenship education (CE) into the Secondary National Curriculum in England in 2002 was rooted in anxieties about levels of civic engagement amongst young people. This anxious starting point has very much influenced the ways in which attention has been paid to young people's civic engagement. Policy concerned with young people and civic engagement has been dominated by a view of young people as inadequate performers in civic society. By way of example both the current coalition government and the previous Labour UK government have each developed their own programmes aimed at encouraging a more civically engaged body of young people in Britain. Young people's lack of civic engagement is portrayed as manifesting itself in various guises, ranging from apathy to anti-social behaviour, each of which are generally held to be problematic for other members of society. By way of contrast, civic engagement is held to be beneficial for both individuals and society as a whole, and it is therefore generally perceived to be intrinsically rewarding behaviour that is to be encouraged amongst young people.

Those interested in pursuing social justice have turned their attention to examining the civic engagement of marginalised young people including those from socio-economically disadvantaged communities. This interest perhaps reflects a concern that whilst these young people potentially have the most to gain from being civically engaged, they are also often the young people facing the most challenges in their lives which may adversely affect their levels of civic engagement for a variety of reasons. This risk is heightened because some altruistic behaviours relevant to these young people are not traditionally regarded as indicative of civic engagement because they do not occur within the public, and therefore civic, domain. Instead, they occur in the private domain.

This chapter has a specific focus on young people living in areas of socio-economic disadvantage. It examines the evidence base that has focused on the civic engagement of young people. Then, having found the evidence base to be lacking, it argues that if we know little about the civic engagement of young people in general, then we know even less about the civic engagement of young people living in areas of socio-economic disadvantage. It finds that issues of epistemology and measurement are significant in explaining the diversity of views about whether or not young people are civically engaged. The chapter begins by addressing the question what is civic engagement?

What is civic engagement?

Civic engagement is a term that is variously defined (when it is defined at all). It is something that is often portrayed as synonymous with civic action and therefore with 'doing'. Interest in what young people 'do' in their leisure time is of great concern to policy-makers and this is reflected in the number of studies dedicated to exploring what young people 'do'. The Centre for Excellence and Outcomes in Children and Young People's Services (C4EO), for example, recently sought to explore and summarise the evidence base relating to young people's involvement in 'positive activities' which was, in this study, defined as 'participation in structured leisure-time activities outside of school and home'. Positive activities were varied but these were predominantly sports-based activities with arts and/or culturally based activities far less prevalent.

A report from the study (Adamson and Poultney, 2010) found that around three-quarters of young people participated in some form of positive activity but far fewer young people from lower-income families or from rural areas participated in these activities. The under-representation of young people from these two groups is concerning since a range of positive outcomes were reported to be delivered through young people's participation in positive activities including developing personal, social and emotional skills, improved relationships between young people and their peers and adults and improved educational outcomes. The more positive activities young people engaged in, the greater their resulting benefit. It was also recognised, however, that there was a lack of robust evidence in terms of social return on investment and on longitudinal outcomes and that much of the evidence was based on young people's self-reports.

The findings from the C4EO (Adamson and Poultney, 2010) study supports the belief that young people benefit from being engaged in positive activities; however, there was no suggestion that such engagement demonstrated 'civic engagement'. Civic engagement then is not confined to positive activities – it involves more than young people being positively occupied in socially acceptable activities.

Civic engagement is defined in this chapter as an umbrella term used to describe a collection of behaviours by either individuals or groups which contribute to the 'common good', often through promoting or delivering positive change. Specific behaviours that potentially fit under this umbrella include formal political participation, volunteering, campaigning, fundraising and participation in decision-making.

Focusing on 'civic' engagement is however potentially problematic because it can overlook activities which can be classified as 'contributing to the common good' but which may not occur within the public domain. Morrow (1994) found that 40 per cent of 11–16-year-olds had regular home responsibilities (minding siblings, cleaning, laundry, etc.) and almost as many helped in a family business or earned money outside the home. Some European children (unpaid usually) are the main carers of disabled parents or other family members (Becker *et al.*, 2001). In immigrant families children's language skills are frequently used by the family in dealing with officialdom (Orellana *et al.*, 2003). It is suggested here then that a definition of civic engagement that rests on actions for the 'common good' should include a broad range of activities that require young people to exert their energies to aid others since, it is argued, this enables a greater 'common good' to be achieved.

Civic engagement also has an implicit temporal dimension as not only does civic engagement benefit both young people and wider society in the immediate time-frame, it is also believed that having civically engaged young people will ensure positive outcomes for individuals and for wider society in the future. By ensuring our young people are civically engaged in the present there is a hope that the future will also be secured. A key issue here is of course young people's role in upholding democratic society through voting and other associated behaviours.

Young people living in areas of socio-economic disadvantage

This chapter is concerned with issues relating to the civic engagement of young people from socio-economically disadvantaged communities who are often marginalised and who face many challenges arising from poverty and other associated disadvantages. In Britain around 2.8 million children were living in relative poverty in 2008/09 (Department for Work and Pensions, 2010) leaving them vulnerable to a range of negative outcomes which frequently persist into adulthood, as noted by Darton *et al.* who stated that:

> [P]overty in Britain is inextricably intertwined with disadvantages in health, housing, education and other aspects of life. It is hard for people who lack resources to take advantage of the opportunities available to the rest of society.
>
> (Darton *et al.*, 2003: 9)

There is a greater risk of experiencing poverty for children living with lone parents, in workless households or for children from Pakistani, Bangladeshi or Black ethnic groups. Almost half of all children from minority ethnic families are in households experiencing income poverty (Kenway and Palmer, 2007). The lower a child's socio-economic group at birth, the greater the probability they will experience multiple deprivation in adulthood (Feinstein *et al.*, 2007). There is also an established link between educational under-achievement and low income. It is known that 11-year-olds eligible for free school meals are twice as unlikely to achieve basic standards in literacy and numeracy as other 11-year-olds and more than a quarter of White British boys eligible for free school meals do not obtain five or more GCSEs, a much higher proportion than any other group (Palmer *et al.*, 2008: 43).

If civic engagement is positively associated with being, and becoming, a 'citizen' then it is important to explore the civic engagement of young people living in socio-economically disadvantaged communities, recognising that they face more challenges than most young people. It is disappointing then to report that much research examining the civic engagement of young people is conducted with little or no reference to this issue. Some of the evidence that has examined young people's civic engagement is presented in the following sections. The evidence has been collated under three subheadings: civic engagement as formal political participation, civic engagement through volunteering, campaigning and fundraising and civic engagement as participation. The evidence base indicates that identifying civically engaged young citizens is a challenging task.

Civic engagement as formal political participation

Some authors have argued that young people's lack of engagement in formal politics is resulting in a 'democratic deficit' (Jowell and Park, 1998; Putnam, 2000). This viewpoint has however been contested by others arguing that it is not apathy that fuels young people's abstinence from formal political participation but instead disaffection with a political system that does not reflect contemporary youth culture (Loader, 2007). Other authors have argued that young people are no different to other adults in their variations in formal political participation processes (Edwards, 2007; Banaji, 2008). Kirshner *et al.* remind us of the complexity of young people's political positioning 'Young people are often cynical and hopeful, or both critical and engaged' (2003: 2).

The Young People's Social Attitudes Survey of 663 12–19-year-olds was conducted by the National Centre for Social Research. The study found that young people generally were disaffected about politics but were more likely to be interested in households where the adults in their house were interested in politics and where those adults were both educated and wealthy (Park *et al.*, 2004). They found that young people's attitudes were not static and varied across both time and age groups. Socio-economic status was more important than other factors in predicting the types of activities, such as voluntary and charity work, that young people were engaged in.

The Citizenship Education Longitudinal Study (CELS) was conducted by the National Foundation for Educational Research (NFER). The study aimed to examine the impact of citizenship education on students in England. The NFER produced annual reports on the findings from the study throughout its duration (2001–10). Using data from the 2004/05 survey of 13,646 English students aged 13/14, Lopes *et al.* (2009) explored the impact of citizenship education on four specific dimensions of young people's future intentions: voting in general elections, voting in local elections, volunteering time to help other people and collecting money for a good cause. Regardless of the reliability of these measures for predicting future action, the results reveal some interesting differences between groups of young people. Female students and those living in homes with more books (a proxy for socio-economic status) were more likely to indicate an intention to participate, as were Asian students. Importantly though, the strongest relationship identified was the relationship between perceived benefits of participation and intention to participate in the future. The authors suggest that future research could usefully explore the impact of both knowledge and self-efficacy on this relationship: 'Bringing out the personal advantages of participation through citizenship education and other initiatives may be desirable if young people's engagement in civic and political life is to be stimulated' (Lopes et al., 2009: 15). Some authors have suggested that a unique attribute of young people's political participation is their distinctive preference for single-issue political action (Haste 2005; Roker et al., 1999).

Civic engagement through volunteering, campaigning and fundraising

Volunteering, campaigning and fundraising are other behaviours that fit under the umbrella of civic engagement. Available evidence indicates that whilst young people may be disengaged from formal political participation there is evidence that they do get involved with actions that are concerned with a variety of activities which contribute to the 'common good' – activities including signing petitions, fundraising and donating money.

In the sixth Citizenship Education Longitudinal Study annual report the authors argue that young people's civic engagement is connected to 'near environment' experiences and issues (such as family, peers, school or neighbourhood) and away from national and European community issues (Benton et al., 2008). They argue that this creates the potential for new learning spaces or sites of civic engagement that are more personalised to the interests of young people and subsequently more accessible than traditional and more formal sites of civic engagement. Commuity Service Volunteers highlight the 'hidden volunteering' taking place, particularly among Black and Minority Ethnic communities, which is informal and not necessarily professionally organised, but is driven by communities or faith groups according to their needs (Hoodless, 2004: 11). Haste (2005) found that around a quarter of young people in England were very involved in their communities, and yet the study also found a similar number were disengaged and disaffected.

There is evidence that young people living in socio-economically disadvantaged communities are potentially excluded from formal volunteering opportunities by negative perceptions of volunteering and volunteers. Volunteers were seen by young people as hippies, affluent or old people and young people were dissuaded by these negative stereotypes (Pye et al., 2009) and many young people, particularly from socially excluded backgrounds, did not consider themselves as the sort of person who volunteers. Fiscal concerns also deterred young people from volunteering with costs such as membership fees and transportation costs being prohibitive (Roker *et al.*, 1999). Organisations that aim to facilitate formal volunteering recognise the challenges they face in engaging young people from diverse backgrounds.

Where young people from disadvantaged communities are recruited into volunteering opportunities there is however evidence that they can find these experiences beneficial. An example of this is the Young Volunteer Challenge project which targeted the recruitment of volunteers from more diverse backgrounds, as defined by factors including young people's socio-economic status, ethnicity and gender. The evaluation feedback from the young volunteers about the impact of the programme was overwhelmingly positive and young people who took part were also more likely to progress into education and employment (GHK Consulting Ltd, 2006).

Civic engagement as participation

There has in recent years been an increasing interest in hearing the voices of young people and notions of 'voice' are intrinsically linked with notions of civic engagement. Young people are encouraged to become civically engaged or to demonstrate their civic engagement through contributing to decision-making processes. There is a 'growing culture of participation' whereby young people's contributions are valued as having the potential to influence decisions that affect their lives and those of their communities (Halsey *et al.*, 2006). This culture of participation can have a positive impact on young people's sense of 'self-efficacy' which in turn has been found to be a key factor in influencing their levels of civic engagement (Benton *et al.*, 2008). Halsey *et al.* (2006) suggest, however, that the time has now come for organisations to move beyond concerns with 'participation as a process', in order to direct attention towards exploring the actual impact of young people's involvement. They report that there is a paucity of evidence about the actual impact of young people's involvement, prompting them to recommend that the outcomes of young people's involvement are properly evaluated through longitudinal research which prioritises young people's own perspectives.

Morrow examined the participation experiences of young people from socio-economically disadvantaged communities, exploring the nature of social networks, local identity, attitudes towards institutions and facilities in the community. She found that participation in community decision-making for young people in the study was limited:

> Overall, the study highlighted how a range of practical, environmental, and economic constraints were felt by this age-group; for example, not having safe spaces where they could play, not being able to cross the road because

of traffic, having no place to go except the shopping centre, being regarded with suspicion because of lack of money.

(Morrow, 2006: 145)

The report concluded that 'linking social capital', that is, connecting or bridging groups to influential others, enabling access to power structures, was clearly lacking for the young people in the study.

Another social change relevant to a discussion about young people's civic engagement is an increasing interest in the impact of technological advances on young people's civic engagement (Banaji, 2008; Coleman, 2007). Perhaps unsurprisingly some studies suggest that there are considerable variations between young people's opportunity to access the internet. The UK Children Go Online study of 9–19-year-olds' use of the internet concluded that socio-economic differences are sizeable (Livingstone *et al.*, 2005).

Discussion

The evidence presented within this chapter indicates that we have a long way to go in understanding the complexity of young people's civic engagement and this is even more so when we focus on young people living in areas of socio-economic disadvantage. This section explores some of the factors underpinning the gaps in our evidence base. These factors include methodological issues, 'adultism', questions about the beneficial nature of civic engagement and the nature of young people's 'citizenship'.

The evidence indicates that young people living in areas of socio-economic disadvantage are less likely to be engaged in many of the behaviours currently associated with civic engagement. However, it is important to offer some words of caution here. Qualitative methods usually suggest that young people have higher levels of social and civic participation than are recorded through quantitative methods (Whiting and Harper, 2003). In addition to young people's actions being under-recorded, survey data also typically underestimates the participation of socially marginalised groups because it fails to capture the fluid and unstructured forms of participation that are attractive to young people (Fahmy, 2006).

Another factor impacting on our understanding of young people's civic engagement is 'adultism' (Dalrymple and Burke, 1995: 141–42) which Roche (1999) argues is as pervasive a force as sexism and racism. Much of the attention that is paid to the civic engagement of young people is done from an adult viewpoint and it is therefore frequently structured according to the concerns of the adult rather than young people. Where authors have attempted to adopt research that is young-person led, a more complex picture emerges. For example, Haste found that young people have a different definition of what being a good citizen means, and also of what it means to be civically engaged. This report found that:

[Y]oung people's definition of the good citizen, as well as the pattern of their own motives, indicates a broader picture that includes both quasi-political activity related to specific issues they wish to make their voices heard on, and community involvement to help the disadvantaged and to support others. This latter kind of activity is not usually seen as explicitly 'political' – either by its practitioners or by political science – but it clearly plays a very important part in motivating civic involvement and perhaps in providing basic skills for action.

(Haste, 2005: 27)

Civic engagement is commonly perceived to be desirable and intrinsically beneficial for all. The indicated under-representation of young people from socio-economically disadvantaged communities in civic engagement opportunities is considered to be problematic *inter alia* because of the missed opportunities for development that are denied to the excluded young people and their communities. It is important to recognise that the assumption that all young people universally benefit from formalised civic engagement educational opportunities is one that again may not reflect the complexity of young people's lived experiences. In their paper 'Dead end kids in dead end jobs?' Quinn *et al.* (2008) challenge the notion that young people in 'jobs without training' would necessarily benefit from being encouraged into alternative educational pathways. Their assertions are based on a longitudinal, participative, qualitative project involving 182 interviews with 114 young people in jobs without training. The study attempted to challenge existing notions and respond to the lack of research that examined the complexity of these young people's needs, work experiences and priorities. They concluded that whilst young people in jobs without training face serious structural inequalities, this is not necessarily a deficit category and the term does not reflect their complex lives. Young people in 'dead end jobs' were learning, both in the workplace and in their social worlds outside of work, and these learning contexts were preferable to those previously offered by school or college. Quinn *et al.* therefore suggest trying to force these young people 'into formal, linear educational pathways is anachronistic and likely to be actively resisted' (2008: 185). This study highlights the importance of not assuming that 'civic engagement' opportunities are necessarily intrinsically or universally beneficial for all participants. It raises important questions about which young people learn what through being civically engaged.

Another issue relevant to this discussion about the civic engagement of young people living in areas of socio-economic disadvantage is the nature of citizenship and its link with aspirations of economic independence and financial contribution. The work of Lister *et al.* (2003) indicates that young people experiencing socio-economic disadvantage are less likely to see themselves as citizens. Lister *et al.* (2003) classified the 110 young people in their three-year, qualitative, longitudinal study of young people aged 16/17, 18/19 and 22/23 as 'insiders' and 'outsiders'. Insiders were studying A levels en route to university and graduate occupations whilst 'outsiders' had no qualifications and were mainly unemployed. Among the many conclusions they draw is that there are differences between the 'insiders' and 'outsiders' in terms of the way they perceive themselves to be citizens. 'At each wave, "outsiders" were less likely than "insiders" to identify themselves as citizens' (Lister *et al.*, 2003: 241).

The young people in their study recognised different models of citizenship which were more or less relevant to them and their experiences. Many felt that the link between being a 'good' citizen and earning money excluded them because of their age and lack of inclusion in the job market. This is an issue that is likely to become increasingly pertinent to young people's civic engagement as young people feel the impact of the current economic constraints disproportionally.

Conclusion

This chapter has raised many questions about current understandings of young people's civic engagement, particularly those living in areas of socio-economic disadvantage. Whilst it is possible to find evidence that supports the idea that young people are, or are not, civically engaged there is also much evidence to suggest that this is a much too simplistic approach. A broad definition of civic engagement was adopted in the chapter in order to explore the complexity of young people's civic engagement and in response to the problem that focusing on very narrow aspects of young people's behaviour simplifies their actions and ignores young people's viewpoints and realities. It is recognised that adopting this broad definition is of course problematic because such a broad definition is necessarily difficult to operationalise. It is also recognised that in some cases it is the absence of a behaviour that can be considered to signify young people's civic engagement and that some behaviour such as protesting can be perceived both as civic engagement or as civic disorder depending on the perspective taken.

Research evidence indicates that young people can be both civically engaged and civically disengaged simultaneously. It is also important to note, however, that there is considerable evidence which indicates that young people living in areas of socio-economic disadvantage are amongst the least likely to *appear* to be civically engaged. This is explained in part by the inadequacies in collating evidence of civic engagement resulting in part from utilising adult-led narrow definitions of civic engagement. It is likely also, however, to be a reflection of processes that discourage, or even prohibit, these young people from being civically engaged and it is these issues that are in need of further scrutiny.

Interest in young people's civic engagement is underpinned by a hope that young people 'care' enough to be, or to become, fully fledged citizens taking on both the rights and the responsibilities that this entails. This chapter has indicated that rather than searching for evidence that supports or refutes adult preconceptions of young people's civic engagement efforts are instead dedicated to recognising the complexity of issues surrounding young people's civic engagement. The studies presented here indicate that we learn more when we prioritise the voices of young people in research, challenge assumptions about what constitutes civic engagement and challenge the implicit universally beneficial nature of civic engagement opportunities for all young people.

Questions for further investigation

1 What are the implications of broadening our notions of civic engagement to include the private domain?
2 Does the nature of the motivation for civic engagement matter? If young people appear civically engaged is that enough?
3 What evidence is there that all young people benefit directly from their civic engagement activities and do some young people gain more than others?
4 What does civic engagement in the public domain offer that civic engagement in the private domain does not for young people and their communities?
5 How can we best learn more about young people's 'trajectories' of civic engagement?

Suggested further reading

Davis, J., Hill, M., Tisdall, E., Kay M. and Prout, A. (Eds.) (2006) *Children, Young People and Social Inclusion: Participation for What?* Bristol: Policy Press. This book explores social exclusion and participation research and theory and questions the progress that has been made in hearing marginalised young people and in tackling poverty issues.

France, A. (2007) *Understanding Youth in Late Modernity*. Maidenhead: Open University Press. This book places our understandings of youth within a historical context and examines contemporary debates in areas such as transitions, education, crime policy and criminology, consumption and youth culture.

Lister, R. (2004) *Poverty*. Oxford: Polity Press. Lister introduces readers to the meaning and experience of poverty in the contemporary world.

Percy-Smith, B. and Thomas, N. (Eds.) (2010) *A Handbook of Children and Young People's Participation, Perspectives from Theory and Practice*. London: Routledge. Drawing on examples from around the world this book explores the many ways in which young people's participation is understood in different contexts and the implications of this for theory and practice.

References

Adamson, J. and Poultney, J. (2010) *Increasing the Engagement of Young People in Positive Activities*. London: Centre for Excellence and Outcomes in Children and Young People's Services.

Banaji, S. (2008) 'The trouble with civic: a snapshot of young people's civic and political engagements in twenty-first-century democracies', *Journal of Youth Studies*, 11, 5, pp. 543–60.

Becker, S., Dearden, C. and Aldridge, J. (2001) 'Children's labour of love? Young carers and care work', in Mizen, P., Pole, C. and Bolton, A. (Eds.) *Hidden Hands: International Perspectives on Children's Work and Labour*. London: RoutledgeFalmer. pp. 70–87.

Benton, T., Cleaver, E., Featherstone, G., Kerr, D., Lopes, J. and Whitby, K. (2008) *Citizenship Education Longitudinal Study (CELS): Sixth Annual Report. Young People's Civic Participation In and Beyond School: Attitudes, Intentions and Influences.* London: DfES.

Coleman, S. (2007) 'How democracies have disengaged from young people', in Loader, B. (Ed.) *Young Citizens in the Digital Age: Political Engagement, Young People and the New Media.* Abingdon: Routledge. pp. 116–85.

Dalrymple, J. and Burke, B. (1995) *Anti-Oppressive Practice: Social Care and the Law.* Milton Keynes: Open University Press.

Darton. D., Hirsch. D. and Strelitz, J. (2003) *Tackling Poverty: A 20-year Enterprise.* York: Joseph Rowntree Foundation.

Department for Work and Pensions (2010) *Households Below Average Income (HBAI).* Available at: http://research.dwp.gov.uk/asd/index.php?page=hbai_arc (accessed 9th February 2011).

Edwards, K. (2007) 'From deficit to disenfranchisement: reframing youth electoral participation', *Journal of Youth Studies, 10*, 5, pp. 539–55.

Fahmy, E. (2006) 'Social capital and civic action – a study of youth in the United Kingdom', *Young, 14*, 2, pp. 101–18.

Feinstein, L., Hearn, B. and Renton, Z. (2007) *Reducing Inequalities: Realising the Talents of All.* London: National Children's Bureau.

GHK Consulting Ltd (2006) *Evaluation of the Young Volunteers Challenge Programme.* London: DfES.

Halsey, K., Murfield, J., Harland, J.L. and Lord, P. (2006) *The Voice of Young People: An Engine for Improvement? Scoping the Evidence.* Slough: National Foundation for Educational Research.

Haste, H. (2005) *My Voice, My Vote, My Community.* Swindon: Nestlé Social Research Programme, ESRC.

Hoodless, E. (2004) 'Russell Commission on youth action and engagement', Consultation Document Questionnaire Response from Community Service Volunteers. London: The Russell Commission.

Jowell, R. and Park, A. (1998) *Young People, Politics and Citizenship: A Disengaged Generation?* London: The Citizenship Foundation.

Kenway, P. and Palmer, G. (2007) *Poverty among Ethnic Groups: How and Why Does It Differ?* York: Joseph Rowntree Foundation. Ref 2042. Available at: http://www.jrf.org.uk/node/2594 (accessed 7th May 2010).

Kirshner, B., Strobel, K. and Fernandez, M. (2003) 'Civic involvement among urban youth: a qualitative study of "critical engagement"' [online]. Biennial Conference of the Society for Research on Adolescence, April 2002, New Orleans, LA. Available at: http://gardnercenter.stanford.edu/docs/SRA%20 conference%20paper%20-%20civic%20Involvement0402.pdf (accessed 13th September 2011).

Lister, R., Smith, N., Middleton, S. and Cox, L. (2003) 'Young people talk about citizenship: empirical perspectives on theoretical and political debates', *Citizenship Studies, 7*, 2, pp. 235–53.

Livingstone, S., Bober, M. and Helsper, E.J. (2005) *Inequalities and the Digital Divide in Children and Young People's Internet Use: Findings from the UK Children Go Online Project.* London: London School of Economics and Political Science.

Loader, B. (2007) 'Young people in the digital age: disaffected or displaced?', in Loader, B. (Ed.) *Young Citizens in the Digital Age: Political Engagement, Young People and the New Media.* Abingdon: Routledge. pp. 1–18.

Lopes, J., Benton, T. and Cleaver, E. (2009) 'Young people's intended civic and political participation: does education matter?', *Journal of Youth Studies*, *12*, 1, pp. 1–20.

Morrow, V. (1994) 'Responsible children? Aspects of children's work and employment outside school in contemporary UK', in Mayall, B. (Ed.) *Children's Childhoods: Observed and Experienced.* London: Falmer Press. pp. 128–43.

——(2006) 'Conceptualising social capital in relation to children and young people: is it different for girls?', in O'Neill, B.L. and Gidengil, E. (Eds.) *Gender and Social Capital.* London: Routledge. pp. 127–51.

Orellana, M.F., Dorner, L. and Pulido, L. (2003) 'Accessing assets: immigrant youth's work as family translators or "para-phrasers"', *Social Problems*, *50*, 4, pp. 505–24.

Palmer, G., MacInnes, T. and Kenway, P. (2008) *Monitoring Poverty and Social Exclusion 2008.* York: Joseph Rowntree Foundation and New Policy Institute. Available at: http://www.jrf.org.uk/publications/monitoring-poverty-and-social-exclusion-2008 (accessed 13th September 2011).

Park, A., Phillips, M. and Johnson, M. (2004) *Young People in Britain: The Attitudes and Experiences of 12–19 Year Olds*, Research Report No. 564. London: Department for Education and Skills.

Putnam, R. (2000) *Bowling Alone: The Collapse and Revival of American Community.* New York, NY: Simon & Schuster.

Pye, J., Lister, C., Latter, J. and Clements, C. (2009) *Young People Speak Out: Attitudes to, and Perceptions of, Full-time Volunteering.* London: vResearch.

Quinn, J., Lawy R. and Diment, K. (2008) '"Dead end kids in dead end jobs"? Reshaping debates on young people in jobs without training', *Research in Post-Compulsory Education*, *13*, 2, pp. 185–94.

Roche, J. (1999) 'Children: Rights, Participation and Citizenship', *Childhood*, *6*, 4, pp. 475–93.

Roker, D., Player, K. and Coleman, J. (1999) 'Young people's voluntary and campaigning activities as sources of political education', *Oxford Review of Education*, *25*, 1 & 2, pp. 185–98.

Whiting, E. and Harper, R. (2003) *Young People and Social Capital.* London: Office for National Statistics.

Chapter 8

Citizenship, inclusion, gender and young people

Hilary Cremin

UNIVERSITY OF CAMBRIDGE

Introduction

This chapter goes to the heart of the citizenship debate by asking what it is to be a good citizen, and who is included. The concept of citizenship changes over time, is influenced by culture and means different things to different people. It is therefore important to be clear about what is meant when we promote citizenship education. Whilst traditional notions of citizenship persist, there are newly emerging concepts of citizenship that challenge and add complexity to existing ideas about what it means to be a citizen. It is no longer tenable, for example, to universalise the citizen as white, male, heterosexual and middle-class. Various individuals and social groups continue to encounter barriers to claiming their citizenship rights as a result of disadvantage and/or discrimination based on ethnicity, religion, gender, sexuality, disability, poverty or a combination of these and other factors (Osler, 2003; Garrett and Piper, 2008). It is no longer credible either to claim that the acts of good citizens will bring about the emancipation of women, the working classes or minority ethnic groups. This chapter will explore the ways in which these struggles cast doubt on the traditional citizenship project.

Gender and citizenship

Perhaps the most sustained attack on traditional notions of citizenship has come from feminist theorists (e.g. Lister, 1997; Arnot, 2009) who highlight the fact that citizenship, like so many political concepts, has a gendered history. These theorists suggest that the public/private divide within traditional concepts of citizenship has resulted in the marginalisation of women from the public sphere, and the exclusion of the private sphere from discussion about rights, duties, justice and freedom. Whilst Lister argues that 'rejecting the false universalism of traditional citizenship theory does not mean abandoning citizenship as a universalist goal' (Lister, 1997: 41), both Arnot (2009) and Lister call for a radical rethink to ensure that citizenship continues to be of use as a contemporary cultural and social-scientific term. Arnot cautions that traditional notions of citizenship are premised on a patriarchal notion of civil society, statist and masculinist notions of what it means to be a citizen and a lack of regard for 'how different types of citizen are positioned within the polity, and what they receive from the government in terms of protection, support and provision' (Arnot, 2009: 45).

In the traditional masculinist view of citizenship, citizens are bound together by rational, often hierarchical, social or economic contracts rather than by a sense of interdependence and care (Cremin and Faulks, 2005). Noddings (2003) adds that these approaches to citizenship and politics often lead to conflict and violence in the name of some principle or another. Women (and some men), she argues, acting in accordance with feminised perspectives, 'can and do give reasons for their acts, but the reasons often point to feelings, needs, impressions, and a sense of personal ideal rather than to universal principles and their application' (Noddings, 2003: 3). As a result of this 'odd' approach, she suggests, women have often been judged inferior to men in the moral domain, and feminised perspectives have been ignored in the public sphere: 'One might say that ethics has been discussed largely in the language of the father: in principles and propositions, in terms such as justification, fairness, justice. The mother's voice has been silent' (ibid.: 1).

Plummer's (2003) concept of intimate citizenship helps bring together a number of theoretical approaches that have challenged masculinist assumptions. Intimate citizenship renders issues that have traditionally been seen as a matter of private choice and personal morality as directly relevant to the political world. Likewise, Barbalet (1998; 2002), in developing a systematic approach to the sociology of emotion, has made a useful contribution to our understanding of new concepts of citizenship. Any social action, voting or carrying out one's obligations for instance, cannot be understood purely in terms of a narrow definition of rationality. The exercise of effective citizenship presumes a series of underpinning emotions, such as trust, confidence and security. Similarly, negative emotions of fear, envy and shame will seriously undermine the capacity of citizens to exercise their rights and responsibilities. This 'is not an argument against reason, only against the inflation of reason at the expense of emotion' (Barbalet, 2002: 2). In a similar vein, writing from the perspective of psychoanalysis, Samuels (2001) criticises the neglect of the positive input psychological approaches can make to citizenship. An understanding of the emotional basis of one's political beliefs and prejudices can only help to improve communication across ideological, ethnic and class boundaries.

It would be misleading, however, to claim that there is consensus, even amongst feminists, about the ways forward in relation to more intimate, private and feminised perspectives on civic life. Many women now feel that gender equality exists, and there is little appetite in the UK and elsewhere to strive for the rights of women in the West. In a gender poll carried out by Ipsos Mori to mark the 100th anniversary of International Women's Day in 2011, a third of women and half of men believed that women are treated equally. This is not in accordance with the statistics, with gender inequalities persisting well into this century in the West as well as in the global East and South. Despite the fact that the majority of both women and men polled in the survey above believed that domestic tasks should be shared equally between men and women, women are still shouldering more responsibility than men for managing the home and looking after the family. Table 8.1 shows some statistics taken from the Equal Opportunities Commission's[1] (2006) *Facts about Women and Men in Great Britain*. The statistics compare key indictors for men and women in 1975, when the Sex Discrimination Act was first introduced, and in 2005, 30 years later, when many would feel that gender equality is greatly improved. Whilst some progress has been made in this time, it is nevertheless the case that women continue to earn less than men, and, for example, they make up less than 10 per cent of the judiciary and more than three-quarters of cleaners and domestics. This is despite girls consistently outperforming boys in their educational outputs. Domestic violence against women continues to be a key issue, with the British Crime Survey in 2008/9 showing that more than one in five women have experienced domestic abuse, and that almost half of all female murder victims are killed by a lover or ex-partner (Home Office, 2009).

It is interesting to reflect, therefore, on why so few women identify themselves as feminists in current times, and on why there is so little appetite amongst women and men to tackle these issues. Perhaps part of the reason behind this lack of interest lies in some of the failings of historical feminism. Critiques of feminism can be divided into two kinds: those based on the ideology of neoliberalism; and those based on the tendency of feminists (especially early feminists) to universalise female identities. In a critique of liberal feminism Arnot (2009) points out that liberal feminists fail to challenge the ideological premises of liberal

Table 8.1 Facts about women and men in Great Britain

In 1975
• Girls and boys achievements were almost identical. 25% of school leavers in England and Wales passed at least five O (GCSE) levels.
• 50% of mothers with dependent children worked.
• Men in full time work earned on average 29% more than women in full time work.
• 4.3% of MPs were women.
In 2005
• 49% of boys and 59% of girls in England and Wales passed at least five GCSEs (grade A–C).
• 66% of mothers with dependent children work.
• Men in full time work earn on average 17% more than women in full time work.
• 20% of MPs are women.
• 71% of students taking A level English literature are girls. 24% of students taking A level Physics are girls.
• 17% of directors and chief executives of major organisations are women.
• 33% of secondary head teachers and college principals are women.
• 9% of the senior judiciary are women.
• 76% of cleaners and domestics are female.

Source: Equal Opportunities Commission (2006).

democracy, and the ways in which schools, for example – even so-called demo-cratic schools – have become a regulating force linked to state agendas and the construction of gender identities. Writing with Harriet Marshall (Arnot, 2009) she argues that abstract notions of 'the citizen' can detract attention away from social inequalities, and citizenship education can become a political device to mask social hierarchies. The Crick Report (QCA, 1998) fails to address the dif-ferent relationship that men and women have to citizenship ideals. There is a silence about the historical legacy of marginalising family life. This failure, how-ever, goes deeper than a failure of politics at the time – it is a reflection of the underlying conceptual assumptions of both civic republicanism and liberalism within an Anglo-Saxon tradition. Whilst it may appear beneficial for women for the state to exclude the private domain from state control, it is disadvantageous for women to be marginalised and discursively subordinated as non-rational beings, and for a wider set of civic virtues to be ignored as part of citizenship education. This applies equally to the voices of lesbians and gay men.

Arnot (2009) also critiques 'maternal feminists', such as Noddings cited above, who argue that women's voices should inform greater recognition of the private sphere as a valid space for political activity. Whilst she recognises the validity of moving towards greater recognition of the centrality of the role of 'nurturer' in the construction of the public sphere, she criticises the unproblematic use of the universalising term 'woman' and the ways in which maternal feminists fail to take account of the differentiated identities of women. Socialist and black feminists have attempted to address gender politics in terms of the differences between and among women, rather than just in terms of the differences between women and men. Late modern and post-modern feminism has had to respond to these chal-lenges in radical ways, moving away from normalising ideas of what it means to be a woman towards greater recognition of the inadequacies of totalising dis-courses. In doing so, however, the feminist banner may have become rather faded and difficult to decipher. In short: feminists are caught between liberal ideology on the one hand (we simply need to ensure equal opportunities for all) and uni-versalising discourses on the other (women need greater recognition of the things that women value). To add complexity, there is the question of whether we should strive for equality of opportunity or equality of outcome. Does it matter if 90 per cent of the judiciary are male, provided that the barriers to women entering the judiciary have been removed? Does it matter if few men take extended paternity leave provided that there are no structural barriers to them doing so?

Citizenship and inclusion in times of high modernity and the digital age

These questions seem irresolvable, and yet shifts in patterns of engagement at family, local, national and international level amongst younger people may result in different questions being asked in the future. Giddens (1991) talks about these shifts in terms of 'high modernity' and 'life politics'. In these new times, he proposes, 'Life politics – concerned with human self-actualisation, both on the level of the individual and collectively – emerges from the shadow which emancipatory politics has cast' (Giddens, 1991: 9). He argues that the effects of modernity extend into all areas of personal, social and civic life, radically altering concepts of time and space in both the inner world of individuals, and the globalised world that they inhabit. In the current time of high modernity concepts of citizenship, community, connection, progress and causality are transformed and the 'reflexive project of the self' takes on a new importance. Authenticity is key. Being true to oneself as one goes through various life stages and transitions is part of a process of creating a personal belief system that forms an all-important narrative of the self. The public/private divide, once so central to concepts of citizenship, becomes less defined. As Giddens points out, 'Social circumstances are not separate from personal life, nor are they just an external environment to them. In struggling with intimate problems, individuals help actively to reconstruct the universe of social activity around them' (Giddens, 1991: 12). Thus, ideas of what it means to be a citizen may be evolving anyway, in ways that build on feminised perspectives of the fluidity of the public/private divide.

In a similar vein, Loader (2007) proposes that new forms of citizenship are de-institutionalised, less stable than traditional forms of social class, religious or national identities and more transitory in nature. Disconnection with social class and political institutions 'has led to a corresponding shift in social obligation and rights, such that individuals are being required to take more responsibility for managing their own lifestyle choices, risk assessment and life plans' (Loader, 2007: 7). Selwyn (2007) argues that we should move away from viewing young people as future citizen-workers or citizen-voters towards recognising them as citizen-consumers or citizen-lifestylers.

This fusing of the public with the private extends into politics and the ways in which politicians are judged, especially by young people. Coleman (2007) suggests that politicians have lost popular appeal through attempting (and often failing) to manifest ordinariness, as if they were offstage and being themselves. He reports on a study exploring the Big Brother television programme as a form of popular culture that engages young people in models of participation, including voting, very effectively. Two hundred Big Brother viewers and voters completed regular surveys during the 2005 general election campaign. The 200 Big Brother voters were neither inattentive nor inactive citizens during this time, but their experience of the campaign was that it was boring and did little to change their minds. Their feelings of political efficacy were low, and they did not believe that their involvement in the election could have much impact on political consequences. Asked with whom they would most like to have a discussion about the state of the world, 39 per cent of the Big Brother voters chose Tony Blair and 36 per cent selected Jamie Oliver. This favouring of television voting over voting in public elections is given by Coleman as evidence of the ways in which new forms of citizenship and engagement are emerging amongst many young people:

The relaxed and obligation-free relationships that the audience has with Big Brother, as entertained viewers, discriminating judges, interactive participants and empowered voters, signals a new kind of citizenship which combines autonomy and flexibility of the audience with the collective decision-making of the traditional political public.

(Coleman, 2007: 170)

In contrast, traditional political communication valorises the public over the private sphere, regarding the former as a space for shared rationality. The private world is seen as, 'atomised, feminised, emotive and inaccessible: a space of retreat from the civic and political world' (Coleman, 2007: 178). And yet, 'Politics is moving inside: spatially, to the observed private sphere in which duplicity cannot be sustained for long, and psychologically, towards an unprecedented public interest in the inner strengths, struggles and frailties of their leaders' (Coleman, 2007: 179).

Drawing on the work of Fairclough *et al.* (2006), Coleman (2007) asserts that citizenship in the digital age can best be described as a 'communicative achievement' which gets away from preconceptions about what citizenship is, and looks at how it is done – at the ways in which people position themselves as citizens in participatory events. This repositioning has three striking characteristics. It rejects high civic decoupling of participation and pleasure, it does not shy away from affective encounters with power and broad cultural judgements about the performances of power-holders and it represents informal as well as formal forms of discursive circulation.

Others have placed active and participatory communication as central to new forms of citizenship. For Lister (1997), communicative action is key to rescuing the notion of citizenship. Building on Habermas's 'communicative ethic', she argues for a politics of solidarity, grounded in dialogic, deliberative or communicative democracy. Public dialogue thus becomes a framework for the articulation of difference, which can promote the development of views from different perspectives. Giddens (1991) recognises that in a modern social world without final authorities, even the most cherished beliefs are open to revision. Communication between the individual and the group becomes increasingly important.

Conclusion

In thinking about ways forward, therefore, for both concepts of citizenship and related ideas of civic engagement amongst young people, it would appear that communicative action, personalised responses to civic issues and a fusing of the public and private are key.

Citizenship education in the UK might have flourished better since its introduction into the National Curriculum if these more feminised perspectives on citizenship had featured more strongly in the Crick Report (QCA, 1998). Much ground (perhaps?) has been covered since the days when John Major, the UK Prime Minister in the 1990s, stated at the 1992 Conservative Party Conference,

'Let us return to basic subject teaching and get rid of courses in the theory of education ... Our primary school teachers should learn how to teach children to read, not waste their time on the politics of gender, race and class' (cited in Chitty, 2004: 186). There is, however, much ground still to cover if citizenship education is to remain relevant to the needs of young people in the twenty-first century. Finally, to return to the concept of inclusion, citizenship educators can make a strong contribution by considering how they can create new civic and educative spaces that enable all young people to express their voices and partici-pate in civic life. Inclusion theorists have suggested that the twentieth century saw a move from segregation (you cannot be part of our mainstream provision) to integration (we will let you in if you can adapt) to inclusion (we need to rethink the nature of our mainstream provision to ensure that we do not exclude anyone). The challenge now is how to create inclusive schools, communities and cyber spaces that engage with young people in ways that take account of new identities in a digital age of high modernity.

Questions for further investigation

1 Do you believe that we should focus on equality of opportunity or equality of outcome when thinking about issues related to gender?
2 Is the feminist project over?
3 What can this chapter contribute to understandings of inclusion and citizen-ship from the point of view of ethnicity and/or social class?
4 Should the public/private divide in relation to citizenship be maintained?
5 Should we adapt concepts of citizenship to engage the Facebook generation? If so, how?

Note

1 The EOC became the CEHR (Commission for Equality and Human Rights) from October 2007.

Suggested further reading

Arnot, M. (2009) *Educating the Gendered Citizen: Sociological engagements with national and global agendas.* Abingdon: Routledge. Focusing on the relationship between gender, education and citizenship, this book explores, from a feminist perspective, how the concept of citizenship has been used in relation to gender, and how young people are being prepared for male and female forms of citizenship.

Loader, B. (Ed.) (2007) *Young Citizens in the Digital Age: Political engagement, young people and the new media.* Abingdon: Routledge. pp. 129–42. This book presents new research and the first comprehensive analysis of ICTs, citizenship and young people from an international group of leading scholars. It is an important book for students and researchers of citizenship and ICTs within the fields of sociology, politics, social policy and communication studies among others.

References

Arnot, M. (2009) *Educating the Gendered Citizen: Sociological engagements with national and global agendas.* Abingdon: Routledge.

Barbalet, J. (1998) *Emotion, Social Theory and Social Structure.* Cambridge: Cambridge University Press.

Barbalet, J. (Ed.) (2002) *Emotions and Sociology.* Oxford: Blackwell.

Chitty, C. (2004) *Education Policy in Britain.* Basingstoke: Palgrave.

Coleman, S. (2007) 'How democracies have disengaged from young people', in Loader, B. (Ed.) *Young Citizens in the Digital Age: Political engagement, young people and the new media.* Abingdon: Routledge. pp. 116–85.

Cremin, H. and Faulks, K. (2005) 'Citizenship education: past, present and future'. Paper presented at the British Education Research Association Conference: Glamorgan, 2005.

Equal Opportunities Commission (2006) *Facts about Women and Men in Great Britain.* Available at: http://www.equalbutdifferent.org.uk/pdfs/men%20and%20women.pdf (accessed 25th February 2011).

Fairclough, N., Pardoe, S. and Szerszynski, B. (2006) 'Critical discourse analysis and citizenship', in Hausendorf, H. and Bora, A. (Eds.) *Analysing Citizenship Talk.* Amsterdam: John Benjamins. pp. 98–123.

Garrett, D. and Piper, H. (2008) *Citizenship Education, Identity and Nationhood: Contradictions in practice?* London: Continuum.

Giddens, A. (1991) *Modernity and Self-identity: Self and society in the late modern age.* Cambridge: Polity Press.

Home Office (2009) *Crime in England and Wales 2008/2009.* Available at: http://data.gov.uk/crime-england-wales-2008–2009 (accessed 1st March 2011).

Ipsos Mori (2011) EQUALS International Women's Day Poll 2011. Available at: http://www.ipsos-mori.com/Assets/Docs/Polls/international-womens-day-topline-March-2011.pdf (accessed 13th September 2011).

Lister, R. (1997) *Citizenship: Feminist perspectives.* Basingstoke: Palgrave.

Loader, B. (2007) 'Young people in the digital age: disaffected or displaced?', in Loader, B. (Ed.) *Young Citizens in the Digital Age: Political engagement, young people and the new media.* Abingdon: Routledge. pp. 1–18.

Noddings, N. (2003) *Caring: A feminine approach to ethics and moral education.* Berkeley, CA: University of California Press.

Osler, A. (2003) 'The Crick Report and the future of multiethnic Britain', in Gearon, L. (Ed.) *Learning to Teach Citizenship in the Secondary School.* London: Routledge-Falmer.

Plummer, K. (2003) *Intimate Citizenship: Private decisions and public dialogues.* Washington: University of Washington Press.

Qualifications and Curriculum Authority (QCA) (1998) *Education for Citizenship and the Teaching of Democracy in Schools: Final report of the Advisory Group on Citizenship.* London: QCA.

Samuels, A. (2001) *Politics on the Couch: Citizenship and the internal life.* London: Profile Books.

Selwyn, N. (2007) 'Technology, schools and citizenship education', in Loader, B. (Ed.) *Young Citizens in the Digital Age: Political engagement, young people and the new media.* Abingdon: Routledge. pp. 129–42.

Chapter 9

Sexualities and citizenship education

Max Biddulph

UNIVERSITY OF NOTTINGHAM

> Sexuality – that absolute kernel of human experience that transcends all context, all cultural influence, any trace of fashion – to grip limbs and genitals into the same special feeling that all lovers have felt through time.
>
> (Bhattacharyya, 2002: 37)

Gargi Bhattacharyya's poetic observation about sexuality in the quotation above provides a thought provoking entrée into this chapter and her conceptualization suggests that sexuality is a core dimension of human experience. It is also a phenomenon that is dynamic, and in the twenty-first century the impact of developing communications technology has turned it into a global phenomenon that is experienced in an increasingly connected world. Sexuality is also an intriguingly difficult term to define. In the past, Foucault (1981) suggests that sexuality was just assumed to be some sort of 'given' aspect of human experience and that it was not until the late nineteenth century that a politics of sexuality emerged in the west, when classifications of sexuality emerged with the 'invention' of a binary construction of heterosexuality and homosexuality. In the twentieth century theorizing continued to evolve in debates between scholars who held essentialist perspectives (Dover, 1989; Norton, 1997) and those who assigned sexuality to social construction (Foucault, 1986; Weeks, 1981) and these in turn have led to a more fluid set of definitions in the twenty-first century, raising further questions about the constitution of sexuality. These new perspectives are also challenging assumptions that are bound up in issues of identity and power and the ways in which these relate to the evolving politics of sexuality. A potent focus for much of this debate is one constituent of sexuality, i.e. sexual orientation, defined by the American Psychological Association (APA) as follows:

> Sexual orientation refers to an enduring pattern of emotional, romantic, and/or sexual attractions to men, women, or both sexes. Sexual orientation also refers to a person's sense of identity based on those attractions, related behaviours, and membership in a community of others who share those attractions. Sexual orientation is commonly discussed as if it were solely a characteristic of an individual, like biological sex, gender identity, or age.

This perspective is incomplete because sexual orientation is defined in terms of relationships with others. People express their sexual orientation through behaviours with others, including such simple actions as holding hands or kissing. Thus, sexual orientation is closely tied to the intimate personal relationships that meet deeply felt needs for love, attachment, and intimacy.

(APA, 2009)

The mention of the word 'politics' necessarily makes sexuality the stuff of citizenship education and the discussion in this chapter focuses on how sexuality should be presented to children and young people. I will argue that in discussions relating to sexuality, an inclusive model should be used, acknowledging the plurality of sexual identities and orientations. In forming a case for this I begin by examining the evidence that in all societies in the world there *is* a plurality of sexuality. I then review the arguments made for not adopting an inclusive model, focusing specifically on the issue of morality. The costs of not adopting an inclusive approach are then considered in terms of the implications of withholding knowledge about sexualities from young people. Finally, I turn my attention to the ways in which an inclusive model might be operationalized in work in the classroom, reviewing approaches, teaching methods, strategies and resources.

A rationale for sexualities

In establishing a rationale for the concept of sexuali*ties*, research evidence can be traced back to the seminal work of Kinsey *et al.* (1948, 1953) who alerted the world (via what continues to be one of the largest empirical studies into human sexual behaviour) to the existence of same sex sexual behaviour. In their sample of approximately 18,000 participants, 37 per cent of males (Kinsey *et al.*, 1948: 650) and 13 per cent of females (Kinsey *et al.*, 1953: 475) reported instances of at least one same-sex experience to orgasm. The devising of the 'Kinsey scale', a seven point heterosexual-homosexual orientation rating scale suggested the potential for not only variations between individuals, but the possibility that this may vary within an individual over the life span. Kinsey *et al.* (ibid.) argued that even this distinction, separating the human population into heterosexuals and homosexuals may be too crude, and that in reality, human sexual behaviour is actually much more complex. They concluded that '[t]he world is not to be divided into sheep and goats. It is a fundamental of taxonomy that nature rarely deals with discrete categories ... The living world is a continuum in each and every one of its aspects' (Kinsey *et al.*, 1948: 639).

In the twenty first century the theorizing of sexuality has surfaced further complexity, Horowitz and Newcomb (2002) arguing that sexuality is constituted of three key domains, namely identity, desires and behaviours. At first glance it would be reasonable to assume that for any given individual these elements are synchronous in forming an overall sexual identity. In many societies in the world, a commonly held assumption is that the elements of sexuality are focused on persons of the opposite gender – in this way heterosexuality becomes the norm. But in the era post Kinsey, is this assumption borne out in reality? Since the 1980s the spread of the human immunodeficiency virus (HIV) has posed a new impetus to understand human sexual behaviour, and, given the prevalence of homosexual modes of HIV transmission, a new interest has focused on same sex activity, particularly between men. Research undertaken in sub-Saharan Africa (Smith *et al.*, 2009), Australasia (Saxton and Hughes, 2009), the UK (Hickson *et al.*, 2004) and India (Phillips *et al.*, 2010) once again reveals that for some individuals identity, behaviour and desire are far from synchronous. This has implications for the descriptors used to describe such individuals. The inadequacy of assigning the label 'gay' to a male who identifies as heterosexual, has sex with men and women and who desires both is clearly inaccurate and inadequate, hence the emergence of the descriptor MSM – men who have sex with men. The acknowledgement of this category is important because it not only widens our perception of the prevalence of same sex sexual activity within a population, but it also reveals a need for inclusive Sex and Relationships Education (SRE) and HIV Education.

Inherent in the teaching of sexuality are explorations of issues relating to morality and politics (Mead, 2010) – interestingly, this is also the core business of citizenship education. Mead (ibid.) implies that the aim of the liberal project of citizenship has been to produce the informed, tolerant citizen who has formulated their values system via a process of being exposed to, and engaged in, various debates relating to key issues within any society. This assumes though that there is a visible and audible debate to be accessed and that educators are willing to open up conversations with children and young people about the plurality of sexualities. On a global scale, recent history indicates that the prevalence of such debates is very mixed, and whilst there are examples of good practice, silence, embarrassment, avoidance, resistance and hostility are also frequently encountered responses. In some instances teachers would be taking an almost unacceptable risk in discussing the issue of sexualities with young people, as evidenced by the Polish government announcement in March 2007 that it is to ban discussions of homosexuality in all Polish schools with teachers facing dismissal, fines or imprisonment (BBC News Europe, 2007). Clearly, citizenship education does not always take place in a values-free zone; 'social and cultural space' means everything.

Global spaces, diverse responses

Although the evidence presented in the previous section suggests that there is a commonality of sexual experience which enables it to cross the boundaries of time and space, nationality or 'nationhood' is significant in determining the discourses of sexuality in any geographical location (Epstein and Johnson, 1998). Not only are nations geographically distinct, but they are culturally distinct in relation to sexuality, resulting in an extraordinary variety of responses. Culturally specific discourses about sexuality will not only be present within national boundaries, but variants will exist within regions, cities, districts, individual schools and social sub-groups within those school communities. What passes for the discussion of sexuality in any classroom will probably be a complex product of all of these influences. A key question to ask is what and who influences this debate? Although the concept of 'the state' has been brought into question (Cooper, 2002), what is more tangible are the laws and educational practices that exist within nations. Although in the twenty-first century the project of gay liberation appears to have brought a greater understanding and acceptance of gay identities, behaviours and lifestyles in some countries in the world, the pattern globally remains very mixed and even within supposedly liberal nations there is evidence that prejudice still exists. Ottoson (2010) identifies seventy-six countries in 2010 where homosexuality is not only illegal, but where governments are guilty of 'state-sponsored homophobia', exemplified by young men in their teens being executed in Iran because of their alleged homosexuality (BBC News Middle East, 2005), summary executions of lesbian, gay, bisexual or trans (LGBT) people undertaken by militia groups in Iraq (ILGA-Asia, 2009) and draft legislation in Uganda that if passed will impose severe penalties (including capital punishment in certain circumstances) against anyone found to be guilty of same sex sexual activity (BBC World Service, 2009). The credence given to homophobia by the laws in certain countries legitimizes prejudice, discrimination and violence, exemplified by the experiences of lesbians and bisexual women in South Africa who are being raped by gangs of men in an effort to 'correct' their sexuality (Martin *et al.*, 2009); high rates of transphobia (Turner *et al.*, 2009) within Europe and homophobic hate crime within the UK (Dick, 2009).

The core of the debate: the acceptability of same sex desire?

Central to the debate relating to inclusive models of sexuality is the question as to whether homosexuality is an acceptable behaviour, identity or lifestyle. In instances where it is seen as unacceptable the morality of exposing children and young people to 'contaminating knowledge' is frequently cited as a reason for avoiding the subject. On closer scrutiny there are some powerful dynamics at work here. Epstein and Johnson (1998) alert us to the fact that schooling and education about any form of sexuality are two elements that do not always sit easily together, discourses associated with children being characterized by notions of innocence and the need for protection. In educational contexts where knowledge of sexualities is withheld, the fact that homosexuality is 'against nature' is sometimes cited, suggesting that there is some kind of natural law when it comes to sexual behaviour. For this reason, in many educational spaces in the world what passes for the teaching of sexuality relies on a taken for granted assumption of heterosexuality. This is how sexuality 'should be', knowledge of which is helpful to the individual in negotiating the bigger sequential project of life's stages, involving the establishing of an opposite sex partnership, marriage and family. In this way heterosexuality becomes the privileged discourse in conversations with young people.

Gayle Rubin (1993) usefully reminds us that constructions of sexuality do not take place in neutral territory and are frequently bound up in larger systems of power in society that constitute a politics of sexuality. For this reason it seems legitimate to ask questions about the nature and distribution of power when it comes to sexuality and social groupings. Western twentieth century scholars (Butler, 1993; Mac an Ghaill, 1994; 1996; Connell, 2000; Harrison, 2000) identified the fact that gender and sexuality are inextricably linked and are instrumental in maintaining the hegemony of patriarchy. Subsequent research reveals the function of the primary school in developing pupils' understanding of gender roles used as a template for relationships later in life (Blaise, 2005; Renold, 2000; 2001a; 2001b; 2002; 2003; 2004; 2005). There are implications for both boys and girls here. For boys and young men, homophobia is used to police norms of masculinity to the point that one could be forgiven for thinking that the world is totally preoccupied with gay men and anal sex. Meanwhile, girls and young women run the risk of being pushed to the margins, young lesbians and bisexual women becoming invisible.

Another frequently deployed argument is that any discussion of homosexuality is against religious teachings relating to sexuality and therefore at odds with some of the dominant discourses in certain societies and countries in the world. This is a very complex issue although the assumption that homosexuality is incompatible with faith needs to be questioned, as evidenced by the ongoing current debate within Christianity. Halstead and Lewicka (1998) draw attention to some of the fundamental differences in understanding that exist between the western concept of sexualities and Islamic perspectives on homosexuality which conceptualize it only as a behaviour and not as an identity. These are very real and significant differences that affect the possibility of discussing this subject and I return to the issues of educator strategies later in the discussion.

An entitlement: why we should discuss the issue of sexualities

Although there may be strong resistance in certain spaces in the world, there are also potent educational reasons as to why an inclusive model of sexualities should be part of a citizenship agenda. The primary one is the fact that young people should have an entitlement to knowledge and understanding relating to the plurality of sexuality. This is not just for young people who may be questioning their sexuality and/or gender identity, but because there is a wider constituency of individuals who have other family members who may identify as LGBT, e.g. siblings, parents, aunts/uncles. More importantly, such knowledge should be an entitlement for *all* young people for fundamental humanitarian and compassionate reasons, enabling them to gain insights into difference, prejudice, discrimination and social justice.

Counter to the assertion that homosexuality should not be discussed on moral grounds is the argument that there is no morality in ignorance and silence. To position young people in a state of sexual ignorance is to place them in a profoundly vulnerable position which is very questionable from a 'moral' point of view.

Effective teaching about sexuality, far from being corrupting or contaminating, equips young people with knowledge, skills, values and emotional awareness that is much more likely to prove an asset than a liability (Sex Education Forum, 2005). Moreover, as educators, we should have a duty of care for the young people in our charge which responds to important health imperatives relating to mental and physical well being. These responsibilities include protecting children and young people from violence and homophobic bullying which, in the case of the UK, is currently seen as being endemic in schools (Rivers, 2000; 2001; Rivers and Duncan, 2002; Ellis and High, 2004; Hunt and Jensen, 2006; Hunt and Dick, 2008).

In a statement published in 2004, the World Health Organization (WHO) defined sexual health as:

> A state of physical, emotional, mental and social well being in relation to sexuality; it is not merely the absence of disease, dysfunction or infirmity. Sexual health requires a positive and respectful approach to sexuality and sexual relationships, as well as the possibility of having pleasurable and safe sexual experiences, free of coercion, discrimination and violence.
>
> (WHO, 2004: 3)

There is a clear agenda here for implementing sex and relationships education that both empowers and is inclusive, educating about safety and sexual behaviours. The urgency of this is underlined by the fact that in western countries, the prevalence of HIV infection amongst gay and bisexual men remains consistently high and that studies conducted across the world into the disproportionately high rates of suicidal thoughts and acts (Remafedi et al., 1998; Morrison and L'Heureux, 2001; Russell and Joyner, 2001) indicate that the mental well being of LGBT people is also very fragile.

Summary of the key issues raised in this section:

- The constitution of sexuality is complex, capable of producing a range of behaviours and identities that go beyond 'the heterosexual norm', hence the term sexualities;
- Geography and culture interact to determine the response in any nation, society and school. Again this is complex and unpredictable, apparently liberal spaces also showing hostility and vice versa;
- A growing body of evidence suggests that prejudice and discrimination are impacting on the metal well being of LGBT young people and that schools are well placed to challenge this in the context of citizenship education.

Assessing the potential contribution of an inclusive model of sexualities to critical citizenship

Given the very diverse range of social and political responses identified in the previous section to the concept of sexualities across the world, I now want to suggest three strategies for moving this work forward within citizenship contexts in schools. The first strategy, to initiate a search for a compassionate citizenship related to sexualities within the person of the educator, is available to all educators in the world, irrespective of culture and geographical location. This involves not only an opportunity to clarify personal values and attitudes but provides an opportunity to make a private appraisal of the context in which they are working. Given the assessment that is made, the second and third strategies not only provide an opportunity to learn about sexualities but also have the potential to cut into the work of critical citizenship, pushing the boundaries for teachers and young people.

Compassionate citizenship: developing empathy and understanding in the educator

In offering this first strategy I want to underline the importance of raising educator awareness and upgrading knowledge about sexualities. In my experience this is an intensely interesting and personally rewarding project and is central to the development of empathy, one of the core conditions for the development of relationships that facilitate personal development in young people in schools (Rogers and Freiburg, 1994). The range of sources cited in the suggested further reading section at the end of this chapter make a good starting point for developing this knowledge and awareness. They address not just the task of operationalizing learning about sexualities in schools, but also give an insight into the experiences of LGBT young people.

Based on their understanding of issues raised in the literature, educators are then in a position to move to the next stage which is to make an assessment of the feasibility of incorporating work on sexualities within citizenship. This is an important decision and one which needs to take account of the context at both a macro and micro scale. Ottoson's (2010) report into global homophobia quickly alerts the reader to the fact that to discuss sexualities in education contexts in certain countries is not an option at the present time. Extreme caution should be exercised and personal safety must take priority. Dramatic though it sounds, becoming a martyr is not a good strategy, whereas working to achieve social and political change via group activism may be safer and more productive in the long term. For educators working in more liberal contexts, attention to the micro scale of teaching this subject within a school may also be important. As sexualities education can conceivably be located within the wider area of sex and relationships education, consultation with school governors, parents and young people is accepted good practice (Sex Education Forum, 2005).

For educators who feel able to proceed, two further strategies are now offered. The first of these is aimed at younger children of primary school age using narrative as a trigger for wider discussion of sexualities and social justice.

Developing the insightful citizen

In this second strategy two projects are offered as examples of good practice and both focus on tackling homophobia and homophobic bullying in primary schools (children aged 5–11 years). In the Opening Hearts project, a writer was employed to produce a series of age specific and age appropriate materials using different genres, e.g. poetry, fictional text, drama/play text and non-fiction text such as reportage and storytelling theatre. These materials were used in the curriculum to explore sexuality as a dimension of difference and to examine prejudicial attitudes towards it. In the evaluation of this project, contrary to the belief that young people had little knowledge of the concept of sexualities, teachers reported that children as young as six were informed by elder siblings and information from the media and possess a surprising level of knowledge as a result. Other key findings to emerge from this work are that professional development for educators is an essential precursor to work in the classroom and the strategy has most impact when the work is part of a much bigger whole school approach that also addresses pupil behaviour, pastoral issues and school ethos (Biddulph, 2008). The materials from the project are available in published format:

Healthy Schools Derbyshire (2009) *Opening Hearts: Challenging homophobia and homophobic bullying in the primary school* – teachers resource available from Healthy Schools, Derbyshire. Derby: Healthy Schools.

The No Outsiders project also provides a wealth of materials and examples of good practice (DePalma and Atkinson, 2008, 2009). In addition to teaching materials, lesson plans and schemes of work, a wide overview is taken of the broader challenge of implementing this work in a primary school context. Central to both projects is the strategy of challenging homophobia at its source and the full write up of the project is provided in the following publication:

No Outsiders Project Team (2010) *Undoing Homophobia in Primary Schools.* Stoke on Trent: Trentham Books.

Supporting the work of both projects is UK government guidance for teachers which can be located as follows:

Department for Children, Schools and Families (DCSF) (2007) *Preventing and Responding to Homophobic Bullying in Schools.* London: DCSF. Available at: www.teachernet.gov.uk/wholeschool/behaviour/tacklingbullying/homophobic bullying (accessed 1st July 2010).

Department for Children, Schools and Families (DCSF) (2009) 'Sexist, sexual and transphobic bullying', *Guidance for Schools on Preventing and Responding to Sexist, Sexual and Transphobic Bullying – Safe to Learn: Embedding Anti-bullying Work in Schools* DCSF–01136-2009. London: DCSF.

Available at: www.teachernet.gov.uk/wholeschool/behaviour/tacklingbullying/
sexistsexualandtransphobicbullying/ (accessed on 1st July 2010).

For older young people of secondary school age a third strategy is now offered.

Healthy democracy: nurturing participation and activism

The concept of sexualities not only provides children and young people with
an opportunity to clarify values and beliefs in relation to sexuality, it also
provides a model of how a social and political movement can move towards
emancipation. A number of moments in LGBT history provide examples of how
a struggle has triggered activism: the Women's Movement, Gay Liberation in the
1960s and 70s, Queer politics and HIV activism in the 1990s and the push for
Trans rights in the twenty-first century are examples of this. Each of these provides a model for activism that not only reveals issues of inequality but also raises
questions about the role of the citizen and participation in the democratic process. Two excellent web sites, LGBT History Month and GLSEN, provide a
wealth of materials and resources that could support a school-based examination
of activism. In the UK, LGBT History Month is now celebrated in February
every year and the web site provides materials ranging from materials for professional development and teaching resources to profiles of famous LGBT people
in history and the unique contributions they have made to society. This can be
located at:

Lesbian, Gay, Bisexual, Trans (LGBT) History Month Resources for Schools.
London: LGBT History Month. Available at: www.lgbthistorymonth.org.uk/
schools/main.htm (accessed 1st July 2010).

Similarly, an LGBT History Month is also celebrated in the United States
(October of every year) and the Gay, Lesbian & Straight Education Network
(GLSEN) web site is a valuable resource for this. The network has produced a
documentary film *Gay Pioneers* which is the story of the first organized annual
'homosexual' civil rights demonstrations held in Philadelphia, New York and
Washington, DC from 1965–69. The web site describes this resource as:

> Directed by PBS award-winning documentary filmmaker Glenn Holsten and
> produced by PBS affiliate WHYY and Equality Forum. *Gay Pioneers*
> braids archival footage from these seminal demonstrations, FBI investigative
> files obtained under the Freedom of Information Act, gay pioneer interviews
> about the homophobia of that era, the protocol for the demonstrations and
> how those demonstrations impacted the movement.

GLSEN have produced a teaching guide to accompany the documentary which
can be downloaded from: Gay, Lesbian & Straight Education Network [online].

Available at: www.glsen.org/cgi-bin/iowa/all/home/index.html (accessed 1st July 2010).

Summary of the key considerations raised in this section:

- The range of responses to sexualities globally at the macro scale needs sensitive and careful consideration before any work with young people can be undertaken. Similarly an assessment at the micro level of the school should be undertaken. Consultation is key – ideally, it's important to have colleagues, parents and young people on board;
- Sexualities within citizenship education has the potential to provide a rich seam of investigation – this should be participatory, involving children and young people in a way that is age-appropriate. The upgrading of educator knowledge and awareness is an important precursor to this process.

Conclusion

Sexuality is a key dimension of humanity. It is also a moral and political arena and therefore it is prime material for citizenship education. Mead (2010) raises the question about how participation within citizenship is achieved and I agree with his view of the limitations of the 'liberal project of citizenship', where arguably tolerance is not enough. To be tolerant could imply that some concession is being made; it is a position of distance, of being a bystander which can be questioned from a moral point of view. But what about our response to the some of the evidence presented in this chapter? To the murders, the rapes, the hangings, twenty-first century condemnation from some religious leaders and the many other forms of non-violent discrimination that many LGBT people still face in a large number of countries of the world? Surely this requires more than passive observation?

In conclusion I want to share a quotation from the late Eric Rofes, a gay man, educator and activist who has left a legacy of radical ideas that still have the potential to challenge our thinking and push boundaries in terms of what might be possible. Writing in the early part of this decade, Rofes explains how the constituent parts of his identity fuse to inform his practice:

> While life may split down the middle to me, intellectually I know that my work in education and gay liberation emerges from the same source: a commitment to creating sites that resist, undermine and throw off institutionalized forms of oppression that have become endemic ... ultimately I believe my work as a teacher is about supporting students as they become agents of transgression and activists for social and political change.
>
> (Rofes, 2000: 441)

The challenge is to provide the debate about the plurality of sexuality in an inclusive and sensitive way that pushes students to really interrogate their values and understanding. I genuinely think this would make a fairer and more understanding world.

Questions for further investigation

1 What are my personal values, knowledge and experiences relating to the concept of sexualit*ies*? How do these elements shape my positioning as an educator? How does this currently influence my professional practice?
2 Looking around my professional context, what visible acknowledgement is there of sexualities? What is the physical/social/emotional response to these issues in the professional setting and in the wider culture?
3 What does a risk assessment of the professional environment reveal about the possibility of teaching about sexualities? How might this impact on you personally and professionally?
4 What strategies can be engaged to gain support for teaching about sexualities within citizenship? How might school policies and government initiatives support this endeavour? How can other stakeholders in the education process be engaged and consulted?
5 How might the rich mass of material relating to sexualities be mobilized within the citizenship curriculum? Which teaching and learning strategies will engage young people and have the greatest impact?

Suggested further reading

Blake, S. and Katrak, Z. (2002) *Faith, Values and Sex and Relationships Education*. London: National Children's Bureau. This book examines the intersection of faith, values and SRE and is the result of extensive consultation with religious communities, professionals working in, and supporting, schools and young people. It is aimed at teachers and all those who support teachers and educators in other settings, e.g. youth service and pupil referral units.
Garden, N. (1982) *Annie on My Mind*. New York, NY: Farrar, Straus & Giroux. *Annie on My Mind* is a novel about the evolving romantic relationship between two 17-year-old New York City girls, Annie and Liza. Although true love eventually wins through, the journey is sometimes rocky due to the response in the education environment around them. Interestingly, the presence of this book on some school library shelves was still causing controversy in some parts of the USA in the 1990s.
Rashid, N. and Hoy, J. (Eds.) (2000) *Girl2girl – the Lives of Young Lesbian and Bisexual Women*. London: Diva. A comprehensive collection of personal testimonies, stories and experiences documenting the lives of young lesbian and bisexual women.
Sex Education Forum (2005) *Effective Learning Methods: Approaches to Teaching about Sex and Relationships within PSHE and Citizenship*. London: National Children's Bureau. An excellent free downloadable fact sheet from the Sex

Education Forum that identifies issues, examples of good practice and resources relating to effective teaching and learning strategies within PSHE and citizenship.

Walsh, M. (2010) *Gypsy Boy: One Boy's Struggle to Escape from a Secret World.* London: Hodder. An autobiographical, compelling coming-out story of a young man, set in the context of a UK traveller community. The book recounts the experience of being marginalized within a marginalized community – very powerful and illuminating. Fascinating insights into the experiences of being in the school system.

References

American Psychological Association (APA) (2009) 'Sexual orientation and homosexuality: What is sexual orientation?' [online]. Available at: http://www.apa.org/topics/sexuality/orientation.aspx (accessed on 28th June 2010).

BBC News Middle East (2005) 'Iran must stop youth executions'. London: BBC [online]. Available at: http://news.bbc.co.uk/1/hi/world/middle_east/4725959.stm (accessed on 1st July 2010).

BBC News Europe (2007) 'Polish 'anti-gay' bill criticised'. London: BBC [online]. Available at: http://news.bbc.co.uk/1/hi/world/europe/6466205.stm (accessed on 1st July 2010).

BBC World Service (2009) 'Uganda considers new anti-gay law' [online]. Available at: http://www.bbc.co.uk/worldservice/news/2009/10/091016_uganda_aggravated_homosexuality_wt_sl.shtml (accessed on 1st July 2010).

Bhattacharyya, G. (2002) *Sexuality and Society.* London: Routledge.

Biddulph, M. (2008) *Opening Hearts: Challenging Homophobia and Homophobic Bullying in the Primary School. An Evaluation of the Pilot Study in North Derbyshire.* Chesterfield: Derbyshire Healthy Schools.

Blaise, M. (2005) *Playing It Straight: Uncovering Gender Discourses in the Early Childhood Classroom.* London: Routledge.

Butler, J. (1993) *Excitable Speech: A Politics of the Performative.* London: Routledge.

Connell, R. (2000) *The Men and the Boys.* London: Polity.

Cooper, D. (2002) 'Imagining the place of the state: where governance and social power meet', in Richardson, D. and Seidman, S. (Eds.) *Handbook of Lesbian and Gay Studies.* London: Sage.

DePalma, R. and Atkinson, E. (Eds.) (2008) *Invisible Boundaries. Addressing Sexuality Equality in Children's Worlds.* Stoke on Trent: Trentham Books.

——(2009) *Interrogating Heteronormativty in Primary Schools.* Stoke on Trent: Trentham Books.

Department for Children, Schools and Families (DCSF) (2007) *Preventing and Responding to Homophobic Bullying in Schools.* London: DCSF [online]. Available at: www.education.gov.uk/publications/eOrderingDownload/HOMOPHOBIC%20BULLYING.pdf (accessed 14th September 2011).

——(2009) 'Sexist, sexual and transphobic bullying', *Guidance for Schools on Preventing and Responding to Sexist, Sexual and Transphobic Bullying – Safe to Learn: Embedding Anti-bullying Work in Schools.* DCSF-01136-2009. Available at: www.anti-bullyingalliance.org.uk/pdf/SST%20Quick%20Guide.pdf (accessed on 14th September 2011).

Dick, S. (2009) *Homophobic Hate Crime: The Gay British Crime Survey.* London: Stonewall.

Dover, K. (1989) *Greek Homosexuality*. Cambridge, MA: Harvard University Press.

Ellis, V. and High, S. (2004) 'Something more to tell you: gay, lesbian or bisexual young people's experiences of secondary schooling', British Educational Research Journal, *30*, 2, pp. 213–25.

Epstein, D. and Johnson, R. (1998) *Schooling Sexualities*. Buckingham: Open University Press.

Foucault, M. (1981) 'The order of discourse', in Young, R. (Ed.) *Untying the Text: A Poststructuralist Reader*. London: Routledge.

——(1986) *The History of Sexuality, Volume 3: The Care of the Self*. London: Penguin.

Halstead, J.M. and Lewicka, K. (1998) 'Should homosexuality be taught as an acceptable alternative lifestyle? A Muslim perspective', *Cambridge Journal of Education*, *28*, 1, pp. 49–64.

Harrison, L. (2000) 'Gender relations and the production of school-based sexuality and HIV/AIDS education in Australia', *Gender and Education*, *12*, 1, pp. 5–19.

Hickson, F., Reid, D., Weatherburn, P., Stephens, M., Nutland, W. and Boakye, P. (2004) 'HIV, sexual risk and ethnicity among men in England who have sex with men', *Sexually Transmitted Infections*, *80*, 6, pp. 443–50.

Horowitz, J. and Newcomb, M. (2002) 'A multidimensional approach to homosexual identity', *Journal of Homosexuality*, *42*, 2, pp. 1–19.

Hunt, R. and Dick, S. (2008) *Serves You Right: Lesbian and Gay People's Expectations of Discrimination*. London: Stonewall.

Hunt, R. and Jensen, J. (2006) *The School Report*. London: Stonewall/Schools Health Education Unit.

ILGA-Asia (2009) '720 brutally murdered as "gay cleansing" continues unchecked in Iraq' [online]. Available at: http://ilga.org/ilga/en/article/m9EUjJn1eo (accessed on 1st July 2010).

Kinsey, A., Pomeroy, W. and Martin, C., (1948) *Sexual Behaviour in the Human Male*. Philadelphia: W.B. Saunders.

Kinsey, A., Pomeroy, W., Martin, C. and Gebhard, P. (1953) *Sexual Behaviour in the Human Female*. Philadelphia: W.B. Saunders.

LGBT History month (2011) GLSEN. Available at http://lgbthistorymonth.org.uk/schools/schools-resources/glsen/ (accessed 14th September 2011).

Mac an Ghaill, M. (1994) *The Making of Men: Masculinities, Sexualities and Schooling*. Buckingham: Open University Press.

——(1996) *Understanding Masculinities*. Buckingham: Open University Press.

Martin, A., Kelly, A., Turquet, L. and Ross, S. (2009) *Hate Crimes: The Rise of 'Corrective' Rape in South Africa*. London: ActionAid.

Mead, N. (2010) 'Conflicting concepts of participation in secondary school citizenship', *Pastoral Care in Education*, *28*, 1, pp. 45–57.

Morrison, L. and L'Heureux, J. (2001) 'Suicide and gay, lesbian, bisexual youth: implications for clinicians', *Journal of Adolescence*, *24*, 1, pp. 39–49.

No Outsiders Project Team (2010) *Undoing Homophobia in Primary Schools*. Stoke on Trent: Trentham Books.

Norton, R. (1997) *The Myth of the Modern Homosexual*. London: Cassell.

Ottoson, D. (2010) *State-sponsored Homophobia: A World Survey of Laws Prohibiting Same Sex Activity between Consenting Adults*. Brussels: ILGA (International Lesbian, Gay, Bisexual, Trans and Intersex Association).

Phillips, A., Lowndes, C.M., Boiley, M.C., Garrett, G.P., Gurav K., Ramesh, B.M., Anthony, J., Moses, S. and Alary, M. (2010) 'Men who have sex with men and women in Bangalore, South India, and potential impact on the HIV epidemic', *Sexually Transmitted Infections, 86*, 3, pp. 187–92.

Remafedi, G., French, S., Story, M., Resnick, M. and Blum, R. (1998) 'The relationship between suicide risk and sexual orientation: results of a population-based study', *American Journal of Public Health, 88*, 1, pp. 57–60.

Renold, E. (2000) '"Coming out": gender, (hetero) sexuality and the primary school', *Gender and Education, 12*, 3, pp. 309–26.

——(2001a) '"Square-girls", femininity and the negotiation of academic success in the primary school', *British Education Research Journal, 27*, 5, pp. 577–88.

——(2001b) 'Learning the "hard" way: boys, hegemonic masculinity and the negotiation of learner identities in the primary school', *British Journal of Sociology of Education, 22*, 3, pp. 369–85.

——(2002) 'Presumed innocence: (hetero)sexual, heterosexist and homophobic harassment among primary school boys and girls', *Childhood, 9*, 4, pp. 415–34.

——(2003) '"If you don't kiss me you're dumped": boys, boyfriends and heterosexualised masculinities in the primary school', *Education Review, 55*, 2, pp. 179–94.

——(2004) '"Other" boys: negotiating non-hegemonic masculinities in the primary school', *Gender and Education, 16*, 2, pp. 247–67.

——(2005) *Girls, Boys and Junior Sexualities: Exploring Children's Gender and Sexual Relations in the Primary School.* London: RoutledgeFalmer.

Rivers, I. (2000) 'Social exclusion, absenteeism and sexual minority youth', *Support for Learning, 15*, 1, pp. 13–18.

——(2001) 'The bullying of sexual minorities at school: its nature and long-term correlates', *Educational and Child Psychology, 18*, 1, pp. 32–46.

Rivers, I. and Duncan, N. (2002) 'Understanding homophobic bullying in schools: building a safe learning environment for all pupils', *Youth and Policy, 75*, pp. 30–41.

Rofes, E. (2000) 'Bound and gagged: sexual silences, gender and conformity and the gay male teacher', *Sexualities, 3*, 4, pp. 439–62.

Rogers, C. and Freiberg, H. J. (1994) *Freedom to Learn.* New York: Maxwell Macmillan International.

Rubin, G. (1993) 'Thinking sex: notes for a radical theory of the politics of sexuality', in Abelove, H., Barale, M. and Halperin, D. (Eds.) *The Lesbian and Gay Studies Reader.* London: Routledge.

Russell, S. and Joyner, K. (2001) 'Adolescent sexual orientation and suicide risk: evidence from a national study', *American Journal of Public Health, 91*, 8, pp. 1276–81.

Saxton, P., and Hughes, A. (2009) 'Comparison of HIV diagnoses among MSM in three jurisdictions 1984–2007', Research, Analysis and Information Unit Analysis Paper. Auckland: New Zealand AIDS Foundation.

Sex Education Forum (2005) *Effective Learning Methods: Approaches to Teaching about Sex and Relationships within PSHE and Citizenship.* London: National Children's Bureau.

Smith, A.D., Tapsdoa, P., Peshur, N., Sundars, E. J. and Juffe, H.W. (2009) 'Men who have sex with men and HIV/AIDS in sub-Saharan Africa', *The Lancet, 374*, 9687, pp. 416–22.

Turner, L., Whittle, S. and Combs, R. (2009) *Transphobic Hate Crime in the European Union*. Brussels: ILGA-Europe/Press for Change.

Weeks, J. (1981) 'Discourse, desire and sexual deviance: some problems in the history of homosexuality', in Plummer, K. (Ed.) *The Making of the Modern Homosexual*. London: Longman. pp. 76–111.

World Health Organisation (WHO) (2004) *Sexual Health: A New Focus for WHO: Progress in Reproductive Health Research*. Geneva: Department of Reproductive and Health Research, World Health Organisation.

Chapter 10

Peacebuilding dialogue as democratic education

Conflictual issues, restorative problem-solving, and student diversity in classrooms

Kathy Bickmore

OISE, UNIVERSITY OF TORONTO

Introduction

How should citizenship education be addressing conflict to build peace? State-funded schools are key locations for diverse young people to have guided opportunities to practise roles, skills, understandings and relationships for participation in democratic dialogue about the inevitable conflicts of social life. Yet constructive conflict learning opportunities in schools are often quite limited – for students in general, and especially for marginalized students. Teachers seem to have little institutional support, and few opportunities to develop skills and confidence, as conflict dialogue facilitators. Based on review of scholarly literature, this chapter examines diverse ways in which facilitated dialogue on difficult issues may be implemented in schools in various cultural and social contexts, and the implications of such learning opportunities for diverse student participants. The chapter juxtaposes different types of school-based conflict dialogue emerging from different roots in research and practice, arranged on a continuum from post-incident restorative justice problem-solving to pro-active critical discussion of contentious issues.

Conflict, democracy and education

Conflict – (perceived) opposition or struggle among interests, ideas, or demands – is omnipresent in social life. *Violence* is 'the use of force to establish or maintain otherwise dysfunctional relations of power and authority' (Franklin, 2006: 260). *Nonviolence,* in contrast, is resourcefulness: creation of options and relationships to address conflicts constructively, even in the face of long odds (ibid.: 261). 'The widely held and seldom expressed but implicit viewpoint of most cultures is that violence is real and nonviolence is unreal. But when non-violence becomes a reality it is a powerful force' (Kurlansky, 2006: 6). Thus conflict does not necessarily imply violence: it may be handled in ways that create learning, movement towards justice and other positive change. What kinds of implicit and explicit citizenship education might have these constructive, educative consequences?

Like other unheralded and taken-for-granted aspects of nonviolent action, conflict talk is all around us, greasing the wheels of society, often unnoticed unless it provokes offence or violence. Norwegian peace researcher Johan Galtung (1969) describes 'negative peace' as the (temporary) cessation or *absence* of overt, physical violence. 'Positive peace', in contrast, refers to the *presence* of social justice, embedded in democratic conflict management processes and structures – continually addressing conflict and violence in their systemic as well as surface manifestations. Positive peace requires, among other things, institutional spaces and learned habits for conflict dialogue across difference.

In plural and unequal societies, those inside and outside the culture of power (Delpit, 1995) have unequal opportunities to learn to communicate persuasively, and to be heard, across difference. What Brazilian educational theorist Paulo Freire (1970) called 'banking' education – traditional top-down delivery of ostensibly-uncontestable knowledge – is apparently reinforced by prevailing policies of curriculum standardization and high-stakes testing. Freire argued that such education reinforced passive acceptance of social injustice. In response, he argued for broad, inclusive implementation of 'problem-posing education' – critical dialogue about social conflicts – and 'praxis' – on-going cycles of reflection and action on those problems – as education for democratization. Thus, constructive conflict talk is foundational for democracy and democratic education, as well as peacebuilding (also see Curle, Freire and Galtung, 1974).

Given the *status quo* of inequality in imperfectly-democratic systems, Davies advocates 'interruptive democracy' practices that introduce and include conflicting voices and viewpoints to address injustices and support democratic learning (Davies, 2004). Like Freire and Galtung, Davies argues that conflict avoidance, or adopting a so-called neutral stance, legitimates the dominant system (also Apple, 1979). In contrast, inviting critical thinking, confrontation and talk about conflict – 'interrupting' the *status quo* – contributes to democratic peacebuilding. State-funded schools, as key institutions where diverse populations meet to prepare for a collective future, are the logical places to facilitate learning and practice of thoughtful, inclusive, interruptively democratic conflict dialogue.

Conflict learning opportunities (implicit citizenship education) in schools

Since conflict is inevitable in social life, it's not a matter of *whether* schools address conflict, but rather *how* they do so (silences and negative sanctions, as well as positive experiences of inclusion, shape learning experiences). Clearly, the regularized activities of schooling – discipline and classroom pedagogies – may address contentious social and political problems, as well as interpersonal disputes, in ways that offer (or deny) constructive guided opportunities to learn.

Peace and conflict theory distinguishes three overlapping goals for managing conflict: peace*keeping* (monitoring and control to temporarily prevent or stop violence), peace*making* (problem-solving dialogue to resolve disputes) and peace*building* (democratizing and nurturing healthy social relationships to address the underlying sources of violence) (Galtung, 1996; Harris and Morrison, 2003). In schools, students may learn from models and practices in every phase of the conflict cycle:

Before harm is done: do schools focus on enhancing security to prevent or minimize violence (peace*keeping*), and/or on teaching dialogic conflict management and anti-discriminatory practices to develop strong community relationships (peace*building* education)?

During management of conflicts: do schools focus on reasserting control through punishment and exclusion (peace*keeping*), and/or on guiding thoughtful, respectful dialogue for self-governing conflict resolution (peace*making*)?

After harm is done: do schools avoid facing divisive conflicts whenever possible, or facilitate restorative justice dialogue to (re-)build mutual understanding and cross-cutting social ties and redress underlying injustices (peace*building*)?

The lived 'citizenship' curriculum of conflict management in a peace*keeping*-heavy system would emphasize surveillance and restriction, especially for lower-status and non-compliant students. Alternatively, peace*making* and peace*building* systems would emphasize development of autonomous, equitable democratic skills and relationships. Conflict dialogue is one important component of peacemaking and peacebuilding.

Citizenship education theory and rhetoric often advocates conflict communication goals *in principle*; for example, school mission statements and curriculum documents invoke critical thinking, inclusion and mutual respect (e.g. Bickmore, 2006; 2008). Unfortunately, such opportunities seem to be rare *in practice* (e.g. Hahn, 1998; Sears, Clark and Hughes, 1999), especially in contexts of high-stakes accountability (Noguera and Cohen, 2006) and in classrooms of predominantly non-affluent and visible minority students (Dull and Murrow, 2008; Hess and Avery, 2008). On one hand, alternate perspectives and disrupting the *status quo* are essential for democratic peacebuilding: from this perspective, marginalized students' perspectives are best heard in, and resources for, conflict pedagogies. On the other hand, marginalized students' perspectives are, by definition, under-valued and often disrespected: from this perspective, they face disproportionate risk from conflict pedagogies.

Conflict dialogue in schools

Dialogue is a communication process that aims to build relationships between people as they share experiences, ideas, and information about a common concern. It also aims to help people take in more information and perspectives than they previously had, as they attempt to forge a new and broader understanding of a situation.

(Schirch and Campt, 2007: 6)

There are many kinds of conflict talk, such as debate, constructive controversy, issues discussion, conflict resolution and deliberation. I define the term *dialogue* broadly, to foreground facilitated communication for understanding in the context of interpersonal and intergroup conflict. Dialogue processes may be just as heated as debate, but are not focused on competing or winning. The goals of dialogue may emphasize developing understanding, or decision-making, as in deliberation or conflict resolution (Parker, 2003).

The conflicts addressed in dialogue need not be 'controversial issues', in the sense of continuing public disagreement among defensible opposing views (Hess, 2004; Hess and Ganzler, 2007). For example, justice problems (such as anti-Semitism, Islamophobia or gender-based violence), in which the teacher does *not* accept all viewpoints as legitimate, can provoke highly-conflictual and educative conversations, when participants examine the ways their own actions may perpetuate or resist those problems (e.g. Avery, Sullivan and Wood, 1997; Boler, 1997; Ellsworth, 1989). Even where teachers attempt to take an unbiased stance, their choices of what to talk about and how inevitably embody non-neutral values and ideologies (e.g. Apple, 1979; Freire, 1998). All contemporary conflict dialogue (like any citizenship education) takes place in the context of dynamic and unequal social power. Dialogue can be democratizing if such power differentials are explicitly acknowledged and addressed in both content and procedures.

Thus, while the typical hidden curriculum in Western public schooling is standardized, avoids conflict and (at least implicitly) teaches deference to hierarchy, it is entirely possible for implicit and explicit citizenship education to cut against this grain, and instead to encourage critical, inclusive engagement through constructive conflict dialogue. School-based opportunities for conflict dialogue learning and practice range from restorative problem-solving that addresses inescapable conflicts *after* they erupt into visible incidents of harm, to democratization initiatives that intentionally *bring to the surface* previously silenced underlying conflicts and unpopular viewpoints to create openings for conscientization and building positive peace (Freire 1970; Galtung, 1969).

Interpersonal peacemaking, restorative justice and student self-governance

School-based peacemaking dialogue initiatives include peer mediation, in which trained students facilitate negotiation to help peers autonomously resolve interpersonal disputes. Peer mediation can be implemented in classrooms, giving all enrolled an opportunity to participate (Johnson and Johnson, 1996). However, it is more commonly implemented as a co-curricular 'cadre' leadership initiative, in which selected students mediate on call or in the school yard. Quality peer mediation programmes reduce aggressive behaviour, and develop mediators' and peer participants' reasoning, social skills and openness to handle conflict constructively (Bickmore, 2002; Burrell, Zirbel and Allen, 2003; Cunningham, 1998;

Harris, 2005; Heydenberk and Heydenberk, 2005; Jones, 2004). Inclusive programmes with diverse peer mediators are the most sustainable and effective
(Bickmore, 2001; Day-Vines *et al.*, 1996). However, recent research in Canadian
schools (Bickmore, 2010) suggests that many peer peacemaking programmes are
not being sustained in the current educational policy climate, or do not offer
inclusive learning opportunities to diverse students.

Restorative and transformative justice circle dialogue processes, derived from
aboriginal traditions, are also emerging as effective alternatives to punitive systems in many contexts. Circle processes include victims, offenders and community members in problem-solving dialogue, to address underlying causes of
complex conflicts and aggression (also Consadine, 1999; Pranis, Stuart and Wedge,
2003).

> Transformative processes enable the wider community to participate
> [and] ... to take responsibility for the underlying causes of crime: poverty,
> abused children, unemployment, discrimination, and other deep social pro-
> blems. ... It does not need to solve the whole unemployment or poverty
> problem at once, but each case dealt with transformatively enables the com-
> munity to work on a portion of it, contribute to its healing, and understand
> and address better the larger issues that lie behind it.
>
> (Morris, 2000: 254)

In schools, circles are particularly appropriate for addressing seriously harmful
situations, and conflicts that are too complex or power-imbalanced for mediation.
However, like peer mediation, they are also appropriate for less acute conflict
situations and for proactive educational activities (Ashworth *et al.*, 2008; Blood
and Thorsborne, 2005; Claassen and Claassen, 2004). Brenda Morrison's (2007)
and Gillean McCluskey and colleagues' (2008) research show positive early
results of conferencing and other circle initiatives, in Australian, British, US and
Canadian schools. They explain that well-facilitated, inclusive, thoughtful conflict
dialogue can be transformational because it engages hearts as well as minds, and
supports development of skills and healthy relationships.

Dialogic peacemaking such as peer mediation and restorative circles are
instances of self-governance, in that students participate in making autonomous decisions to help resolve problems that affect them (Bickmore and
MacDonald, 2010). Other kinds of student governance, though not typically
recognized as peacemaking, are also opportunities to practice conflict dialogue.
Surveys associate such participation with young people's development of
commitment and skills for democratic participation (Kahne and Sporte, 2008;
Torney-Purta and Barber, 2005). Clearly student governance participation
constitutes a *potential* opportunity for conflict dialogue, but there is little
evidence that this occurs often, nor is it clear how such dialogic participation may
be most inclusively, equitably and effectively facilitated (Wyness, 2009; Wyse,
2001).

Conflict education infused in the academic curriculum

Contrasting ideologies, perspectives, and problems – conflicts – are embedded in any subject matter, and may be brought out into the light, probed and discussed in classroom pedagogy (e.g. Claire and Holden, 2007; Deng and Luke, 2008; Elbow, 1986; Kumashiro, 2000). Learning opportunities addressing such conflicts need not involve public issues. David and Roger Johnson, for example, propose a pedagogical strategy they call 'structured academic controversy', but explain it as 'a procedure for learning, not for addressing controversial issues or controversial subject matter' (2009: 39). At the same time, they argue that addressing conflict is what makes subject matter engaging:

> Conflict is to student learning what the internal combustion engine is to the automobile. The internal combustion engine ignites the fuel and the air with a spark to create the energy for movement and acceleration. Just as the fuel and the air are inert without the spark, so, ideas in the classroom are inert without the spark of intellectual conflict. Intellectual conflict is the spark that energizes students to seek out new information and study harder and longer.
>
> (Johnson and Johnson, 2009: 37)

Conflict dialogue practices integrated into subject-matter curriculum may focus, for example, on interpersonal communication skills, and/or questions of global justice, and/or characters' perspectives in literature or historical narratives, and/or discipline-based approaches to analysing problems (e.g. Bickmore, 1999a and b; Ibrahim, 2005; Jones and Sanford, 2003). Such pedagogies can facilitate engagement and skill-building in technical subjects such as math and science (Crumbaugh, 1996; Frankenstein, 1987; Settlage and Sabik, 1996), as well as in humanities subjects such as arts, literature and social studies (Barton and Levstik, 2004; Catterall, 2007; Luke and Myers, 1994; Sandmann, 2004; Wasson, Anderson and Suriani, 1999). Clearly, not all conflict skills curriculum offers opportunities for students to actually apply those skills in dialogue, or explicitly supports students' development of skills and understandings for talking about conflict.

Controversial and sensitive issues pedagogies in classrooms

To prepare for democratic citizenship in this conflictual world, young people evidently benefit from guided practice – not merely with generic conflict or discussion skills, but with actually addressing sensitive, controversial issues (e.g. Hess and Avery, 2008). Guided classroom lessons may be relatively safe environments (compared with the political world outside) in which students and teachers can learn to address such uncertain, emotional issues (e.g. Crocco and Cramer, 2005; McCully, O'Doherty and Smyth, 1999; Morishita, 1991; Otoya-Knapp, 2004; Wood, 2007). For example, Neil Houser (1996) argues that too often elementary teachers, in the name of safe and caring classrooms, over-emphasize conflict avoidance and under-emphasize the challenges and conflictive viewpoints that are equally essential to provoke learning.

Inclusive, thoughtful discussion of controversial political issues in citizenship education classrooms can effectively develop students' respect for alternative points of view, sensitivity to inequity, skills and inclinations to participate in democratic processes (Hahn, 1998; Hess and Ganzler, 2007; Hess and Posselt, 2002; Torney-Purta, Lehmann, Oswald and Schultz, 2001). Some research, including a study of newspaper-based pedagogies in grade 5–6 classrooms across Argentina (Chaffee *et al.*, 1997) and a survey of over 4000 non-affluent visible minority students in Chicago (Kahne and Sporte, 2008), suggests that these positive impacts of conflict discussion pedagogies may be especially pronounced among students of lower socio-economic status, who often have fewer opportunities for such learning outside of school. However valuable, implementation of con-flictual pedagogies is not common, at least in Canadian schools (Sears, Clark and Hughes, 1999; Sears and Hughes, 2006). A US observational study also found open, sustained classroom discussions of controversial or justice issues to be extremely rare, even though these were described by students as their most meaningful educational experiences (Simon, 2001).

At the same time, even the most well-intended, inclusive discussion of conflicts may not mitigate social inequalities (Ellsworth, 1989; 1997). When conflict surfaces, it is often the lowest-status and most marginalized participants who are exposed to the most risk, because it is their ways of being and thinking that are most likely to be unfamiliar or unpopular. Observational studies on teachers' strategies for facilitating conflict dialogue suggest that poor and visible minority students often have fewer opportunities to participate in sustained, inclusive dis-cussions in academic classrooms compared to more privileged peers (Dull and Murrow, 2008), and that when those discussions do occur, those students are disproportionately marginalized or stigmatized (Hemmings, 2000; Subedi, 2008). 'Just as diversity can be a deliberative strength, it can also re-inscribe social divi-sions if students feel they are being silenced or do not want to voice opinions that differ from the majority' (Hess and Avery, 2008: 514). However, pedagogical approaches do make a difference. For example, in comparing two classrooms in the same school, Hemmings (2000) found that a competitive debate approach marginalized less-confident and lower-status students more than a cooperative, open discussion approach.

Gender and sexual identities also may influence students' engagement and experiences in conflictual discussions. For example, a study of psychosocial development in a ten-week Holocaust/genocide and citizenship education grade 8 course found that girls on average reduced their degree of racism more than boys (Schultz, Barr and Selman, 2001). Another study (Larson, 2003) showed that some high school students who were quiet in in-person class discussions gained a voice in online discussions. Further research is needed on how teachers open curriculum-linked opportunities for dialogue and make it constructive in mixed groups, and the consequences of these experiences for diverse students.

Anti-oppression, human rights, inter-group bias and equity pedagogies

A different kind of controversial issues curriculum – anti-discriminatory and justice education – emerges from different communities of scholars than the above controversial issues work (e.g. Boler and Zembylas, 2003; Bolgatz, 2005; Cípolle, 2004; Day, 2002; Roberts, Bell and Murphy, 2008). For example, discussions may compare dominant texts with alternative narratives that reflect the experiences of racialized or otherwise oppressed peoples (e.g. Dei, 2000; Howard, 2004). Even very young children are capable of engaging in thoughtful, respectful discussions of oppression and other issues, for example in literature circles (Fain, 2008). Feminist dialogue and consciousness-raising approaches often focus on recognizing exclusions and facilitating inclusive opportunities for voice (e.g. Bell, 1996; Bickmore, 1996; Ellsworth, 1997; Tyson and Hinton-Johnson, 2003; Weikel, 1995; Wells, 1996). Again, discussion-based pedagogies that foreground identity-related injustice issues may be experienced differently by diverse student participants (see also Bajaj, 2004; Bekerman, Zembylas and McGlynn, 2009; Schultz, Buck and Niesz, 2000). Further theory and research is needed to understand the ways various approaches to dialogue pedagogies may offer diverse students equitable opportunities to participate in naming, speaking out and being heard on conflictual questions.

Some anti-bias education is organized around encounters: bringing together members of adversary groups, face-to-face or online, for facilitated cooperative activity and dialogue about current and historical conflicts between their groups. 'Contact' theory (Allport, 1954) argues that inter-group contact can reduce prejudice and increase openness to the other side's perspectives *if*: process and participant selection equalize status between the groups, contact is close and prolonged, groups cooperate towards common goals and institutional environments support such cooperation and prejudice reduction (Stephan, 1999; Tal-Or, Boninger and Gleicher, 2002). Unfortunately, these conditions are not often met in actual programmes. However, this literature often offers nuanced descriptions of facilitation strategies applicable to a range of dialogue on difficult issues, in the context of social difference and inequalities (e.g. King, 2009; Nagda, McCoy and Barrett, 2006; Schirch and Campt, 2007). Evaluations of such programming often indicate positive effects (at least in the short-term) on participants' awareness, empathy for the Other, and thinking skills for addressing diversity and equity (Dessel and Rogge, 2008; DeTurk, 2006; Maoz, 2002). Curriculum that recognizes both individual difference and multiple (hybrid, cross-cutting) group identities may facilitate de-escalation of destructive conflict between groups (Freedman, Weinstein, Murphy and Longman, 2008; Ross, 2007). Like restorative peacemaking approaches, critical anti-bias education initiatives, especially inter-group dialogue, often invite powerful emotions, including anger, that may provoke profound, transformative (though risky) learning experiences.

Contact dialogue initiatives in schools, in practice, are often of short duration, based on individualistic psychological assumptions and monological notions of identity and culture, and inadequately address inequality and power (Bekerman, 2007). Notable exceptions are a small but growing number of integrated schools attended by students from former enemy groups over extended periods (Bekerman and McGlynn, 2007; Zembylas, Bekerman, McGlynn and Ferreira, 2009). However, integrated schools may address inter-group conflicts in remarkably different ways: Caitlyn Donnelly and Joanne Hughes (2006) show how teachers in some Northern Ireland integrated schools tended to emphasize inter-group commonalities and avoid discussion of controversial issues, whereas teachers in some Israel-Palestine integrated schools tended to encourage expression and discussion of identity differences. On one hand, inter-group contact may disrupt the *status quo* by bringing representatives from different groups into dialogue about their experiences of oppression, mutual distrust, and conflict. Yet on the other hand, inter-group (and other anti-bias) initiatives may emphasize commonalities and individual attitudes rather than political and structural issues, and thus avoid fully confronting difficult conflicts or disrupting existing social hierarchies.

Discussion: cross-cutting issues

The above review of literature suggests clear agreement, among a wide range of citizenship education, justice education and restorative peacemaking scholars, that young people are only likely to develop nonviolent democratic engagement skills and inclinations when they have regular opportunities to practise voicing and discussing contentious questions. Some of this literature also demonstrates how such conflict dialogue may be feasibly and effectively implemented in public school settings. Yet, neither interpersonal conflict dialogue for restorative peacemaking nor critical citizenship conflict issues dialogue pedagogies are widely implemented in most state-funded schools in the West. While conflictual *topics* may be mentioned, evidently there is little *sustained, inquisitive, carefully-facilitated communicative talk* about difficult issues, especially in classrooms populated by working class and ethnocultural minority students. Despite the importance of social and democratic engagement, learning activities that risk provoking strong emotions are often avoided or prematurely curtailed in schools. Thus educators are not necessarily facilitating the democratic conflict and peacebuilding learning that research indicates is both possible and necessary.

Two cross-cutting issues, in particular, emerge from the above literature review and indicate where research is needed: how student diversity and inequality may be addressed in various kinds of conflict dialogue, and how teachers may receive opportunities and support to learn how to confidently, equitably and effectively facilitate such dialogue. Comparisons among contrasting cases of conflict dialogue – from post-incident restorative peacemaking through pro-active democratic and peacebuilding issues discussion – should shed light on different options and elements of addressing these challenges:

Student diversity: how are diverse, unequal-status students included in various kinds of conflict dialogue in schools, and how are they enabled (or not) to develop their distinct voices and democratic agency? Agency is 'the ongoing process of (un)making ourselves through explorations of our positioning within [multiple and contrasting] discourse' (McKenzie, 2006: 203). How are such explorations in schools facilitated to make them safe (respectful) enough, and yet challenging (dissonant) enough, to enable diverse and marginalized young participants' relational engagement and talk across differences? What dialogue formats, and what skills and strategies (performance), facilitate constructive, respectful expressions of diverse identities, ideologies and emotions by the widest possible range of participants?

Teacher preparation and support: what kinds of professional learning opportunities may best encourage and support teachers to take reasonable risks to facilitate effective conflict dialogue? Teachers very often teach 'defensively' (McNeil, 1986), avoiding both conflictual subject matter and open dialogue about complex issues. This problem is likely exacerbated by current policies of high-stakes accountability for narrowly-defined, standardized academic outcomes (Ladwig, 2010). Many teachers have had little opportunity to gain confidence or skills for handling complex, sensitive, social and political subject matter, either in their own student years or in typical teacher education (Boler and Zembylas, 2003; Kelly and Brandes, 2001; Tupper, 2005). Despite this context and the uncertainty, risks and time/energy costs of facilitating sustained, emotional conflict dialogue, a few teachers do persistently find ways to teach in ways that invite conflict dialogue learning opportunities (e.g. Blood and Thorsborne, 2005; Wolpow, Johnson and Wognild, 2002; Yamashita, 2006).

Conclusion

There is already much theory and research about what 'could' or 'should' be done to improve the democratic and peacebuilding learning opportunities of students in public school, and it's clear that conflict dialogue is an important part of that picture. What is missing and sorely needed is a well-grounded theoretical framework for understanding *why* those promising democratic peacebuilding pedagogies are so rare, especially in under-resourced public schools serving diverse populations, and *what can be done about it*. Such research has immense significance for addressing core goals in citizenship education and peace/conflict education theory, as well as practical utility for educators.

Acknowledgement

The Peace-Building Dialogue in Schools research project, emerging from the above literature review, is funded by the Social Sciences and Humanities Council of Canada.

Questions for further investigation

1 How valuable (worth the risks) do you believe it is to engage students in discussing sensitive, identity-linked social conflict issues in classrooms, and why?

2 How can contrasting voices and unpopular viewpoints be truly included? (E.g. 'relevant' justice topics, delegate authority to the group, pair-share, journaling, opinion spectrum, 4 corners, etc.)

3 How can the most vulnerable participants be protected? (E.g. roles, opportunities for all to speak, teach communication norms and skills, normalize conflict and dissent, non-competitive, etc.)

Suggested further reading

Bickmore, K. (2008) 'Social studies for social justice: learning/navigating power and conflict', in Levstik, L. and Tyson, C. (Eds.) *Handbook of Research in Social Studies Education.* New York, NY: Routledge. pp. 155–71. My chapter in this handbook, which outlines the state of research in Social Studies Education. A key text for researchers.

Claire, H. and Holden, C (Eds.) (2007) *The Challenge of Teaching Controversial Issues.* London: Trentham Books. A relevant and practical text, spanning early years to higher education, which tackles key dilemmas and offers possible approaches in teaching controversial issues. See also Dr Paul Warwick's chapter in this book.

Pranis, K. (2005) *The Little Book of Circle Processes: A New/Old Approach to Peacemaking.* Intercourse, PA: Good Books. Important book introducing peacemaking circles, which provide support for those affected by crime and conflict.

References

Allport, G. (1954) *The Nature of Prejudice.* Cambridge, MA: Addison Wesley.

Apple, M. (1979) *Ideology and Curriculum.* London: Routledge.

Ashworth, J., Van Bockern, S., Ailts, J., Donnelly, J., Erickson, K. and Woltermann, J. (2008) 'The restorative justice center: An alternative to school detention', *Reclaiming Children and Youth, 17,* 3, pp. 22–6.

Avery, P., Sullivan, J. and Wood, S. (1997) 'Teaching for tolerance of diverse beliefs', *Theory Into Practice, 36,* 1, pp. 32–38.

Bajaj, M. (2004) 'Human rights education and student self-conception in the Dominican Republic', *Journal of Peace Education, 1,* 1, pp. 21–36.

Barton, K. and Levstik, L. (2004). *Teaching History for the Common Good.* Mahwah, NJ: Lawrence Erlbaum Associates.

Bekerman, Z. (2007) 'Rethinking intergroup encounters: Rescuing praxis from theory, activity from education, and peace/co-existence from identity and culture', *Journal of Peace Education, 4,* 1, pp. 21–37.

Bekerman, Z. and McGlynn, C. (Eds.) (2007) *Addressing Ethnic Conflict through Peace Education: International Perspectives.* New York and Basingstoke: Palgrave Macmillan.

Bekerman, Z., Zembylas, M. and McGlynn, C. (2009) 'Working toward the de-essentialization of identity categories in conflict and postconflict societies: Israel, Cyprus, and Northern Ireland', *Comparative Education Review, 53,* 2, pp. 213–34.

Bell, L.-A. (1996) 'In danger of winning: Consciousness raising strategies for empowering girls in the United States', *Women's Studies International Forum, 19*, 4, pp. 419–27.

Bickmore, K. (1996) 'Women in the world, women in the classroom: Gender equity in the social studies', *High School Journal, 79*, 3, pp. 231–41.

——(1999a) 'Elementary curriculum about conflict resolution: Can children handle global politics?', *Theory and Research in Social Education, 27*, 1, pp. 45–69.

——(1999b) 'Teaching conflict and conflict resolution in school: (Extra-)curricular considerations', in Raviv, A., Oppenheimer, L. and Bar-Tal, D. (Eds.) *How Children Understand War and Peace*. San Francisco: Jossey-Bass. pp. 233–59.

——(2001) 'Student conflict resolution, power "sharing" in schools, and citizenship education', *Curriculum Inquiry, 31*, 2, pp. 137–62.

——(2002) 'How might social education resist (hetero)sexism? Facing the impact of gender and sexual ideology on citizenship', *Theory and Research in Social Education, 30*, 2, pp. 198–216.

——(2006) 'Democratic social cohesion? Assimilation? Representations of social conflict in Canadian public school curricula', *Canadian Journal of Education, 29*, 2, pp. 359–86.

——(2008) 'Peace and conflict', in Arthur, J., Davies, I. and Hahn, C. (Eds.) *Sage Handbook of Education for Citizenship and Democracy*. London: Sage Publications. pp. 438–54.

——(2010) 'Policies and programming for safer schools: Are "anti-bullying" approaches impeding education for peacebuilding?', *Journal of Educational Policy, 25*, 4 (July), pp. 648–87.

Bickmore, K. and MacDonald, A. (2010) 'Student leadership opportunities for making "peace" in Canada's urban schools: Contradictions in practice', *Interamerican Journal of Education for Democracy/Revista Interamericana de Educación para la Democracia, 3*, 2, pp. 125–52.

Blood, P. and Thorsborne, M. (2005). 'The challenge of culture change: Embedding restorative practice in schools', paper presented at the Sixth International Conference on Conferencing, Circles and other Restorative Practices, Sydney, Australia, March 3–5.

Boler, M. (1997) 'The risks of empathy: Interrogating multiculturalism's gaze', *Cultural Studies, 11*, 2, pp. 253–73.

Boler, M. and Zembylas, M. (2003) 'Discomforting truths: The emotional terrain of understanding difference', in Trifonas, P. (Ed.) *Pedagogies of Difference: Rethinking Education for Social Change*. Halifax: Fernwood. pp. 110–36.

Bolgatz, J. (2005) 'Teachers initiating conversations about race and racism in a high school class', *Multicultural Perspectives, 7*, 3, pp. 28–35.

Burrell, N., Zirbel, C. and Allen, M. (2003) 'Evaluating peer mediation outcomes in educational settings: A meta-analytic review', *Conflict Resolution Quarterly, 21*, 1, pp. 7–26.

Catterall, J. (2007) 'Enhancing peer conflict resolution skills through drama: An experimental study', *Research in Drama Education: The Journal of Applied Theatre and Performance, 12*, 2, pp. 163–78.

Chaffee, S.H. and others (1997) *Political Socialization via a Newspaper-in-Schools Program in Argentina: Effects of Variations in Teaching Methods* (Final Report). Stanford, CT: Spencer Foundation.

Cípolle, S. (2004) 'Service learning as a counter-hegemonic practice: Evidence pro and con', *Multicultural Education, 11*, 3, pp. 12–23.

Claassen, R. and Claassen, R. (2004) 'Creating a restorative discipline system: Restorative justice in schools', *The Fourth R*, Winter, pp. 9–12.

Claire, H. and Holden, C. (Eds.) (2007) *The Challenge of Teaching Controversial Issues.* London: Trentham Books.

Consadine, J. (1999) *Restorative Justice: Healing the Effects of Crime* (2nd Ed.). Lyttelton, NZ: Ploughshares Press.

Crocco, M.S. and Cramer, J. (2005) 'Women, WebQuests, and controversial issues in the social studies', *Social Education, 69*, 4, pp. 143–8.

Crumbaugh, C. (1996) 'From harmony to cacophony: A study of student disagreement in a fourth grade math classroom', paper presented at the American Educational Research Association, New York City.

Cunningham, C. (1998) 'The effects of primary division, student-mediated conflict resolution programs on playground aggression', *Journal of Child Psychology and Psychiatry, 39*, 5, pp. 653–62.

Curle, A., Freire, P. and Galtung, J. (1974) 'What can education contribute towards peace and social justice? Curle, Freire, Galtung panel', in Haavelsrud, M. (Ed.) *Education for Peace: Reflection and Action.* Keele: University of Keele. pp. 64–97.

Davies, L. (2004) *Education and Conflict: Complexity and Chaos.* London: RoutledgeFalmer.

Day, L. (2002) 'Putting yourself in other people's shoes: The use of Forum Theatre to explore refugee and homeless issues in schools', *Journal of Moral Education, 31*, 1, pp. 21–34.

Day-Vines, N., Day-Hairston, B., Carruthers, W., Wall, J. and Lupton-Smith, H. (1996) 'Conflict resolution: The value of diversity in the recruitment, selection, and training of peer mediators', *School Counselor, 43*, pp. 392–410.

Dei, G.S. (2000) 'Towards an anti-racism discursive framework', in Dei, G.S. and Calliste, A. (Eds.) *Power, Knowledge, and Anti-racism Education.* Halifax: Fernwood.

Delpit, L. (1995) *Other People's Children: Cultural Conflict in the Classroom.* New York, NY: New Press.

Deng, Z. and Luke, A. (2008) 'Subject matter: Defining and theorizing school subjects', in Connelly, F.M., He, M.F. and Phillion, J. (Eds.), *The Handbook of Curriculum and Instruction.* Thousand Oaks, CA: Sage. pp. 66–87.

Dessel, A. and Rogge, M.E. (2008) 'Evaluation of intergroup dialogue: A review of the empirical literature', *Conflict Resolution Quarterly, 2*, 62, pp. 199–238.

DeTurk, S. (2006) 'The power of dialogue: Consequences of intergroup dialogue and their implications for agency and alliance building', *Communication Quarterly, 54*, 1, pp. 33–51.

Donnelly, C. and Hughes, J. (2006) 'Contact, culture and context: Evidence from mixed faith schools in Northern Ireland and Israel', *Comparative Education, 42*, 4, pp. 493–516.

Dull, L. and Murrow, S. (2008) 'Is dialogic questioning possible in social studies classrooms?', *Theory and Research in Social Education, 36*, 4, pp. 391–412.

Elbow, P. (1986) *Embracing Contraries: Explorations in Teaching and Learning.* New York: Oxford University Press.

Ellsworth, E. (1989) 'Why doesn't this feel empowering? Working through the repressive myths of critical pedagogy', *Harvard Educational Review, 59,* 3, pp. 297–322.
——(1997) *Teaching Positions: Difference, Pedagogy, and the Power of Address.* New York, NY: Teachers College Press.
Fain, J.G. (2008) 'Um, they weren't thinking about their thinking: Children's talk about issues of oppression', *Multicultural Perspectives, 10,* 4, pp. 201–8.
Frankenstein, M. (1987) 'Critical mathematics education: An application of Paulo Freire's epistemology', in Shor, I. (Ed.), *Freire for the Classroom: A Sourcebook for Liberatory Teaching.* Portsmouth, NH: Boynton-Cook. pp. 180–210.
Franklin, U. (2006) 'Stormy weather: Reflections on violence as an environment', in Franklin, U. and Swenarchuk, M. *The Ursula Franklin Reader: Pacifism as a Map.* Toronto, ON: Between the Lines. pp. 257–62.
Freedman, S.W., Weinstein, H., Murphy, K. and Longman, T. (2008) 'Teaching history after identity-based conflicts: The Rwanda experience', *Comparative Education Review, 52,* 4, pp. 663–90.
Freire, P. (1970) *Pedagogy of the Oppressed.* New York, NY: Seabury Press.
——(1998) *Pedagogy of Freedom: Ethics, Democracy, and Civic Courage.* Lanham, MD: Rowman & Littlefield.
Galtung, J. (1969) 'Violence, peace, and peace research', *Journal of Peace Research, 6,* 3, pp. 167–92.
——(1996) *Peace by Peaceful Means: Peace and Conflict, Development and Civilization.* London: Sage Publications and International Peace Research Assn.
Hahn, C. (1998) *Becoming Political: Comparative Perspectives on Citizenship Education.* Albany, NY: State University of New York Press.
Harris, I. and Morrison, M. (2003) *Peace Education* (2nd Ed.). Jefferson, NC: McFarland.
Harris, R. (2005) 'Unlocking the learning potential in peer mediation: An evaluation of peer mediator modeling and disputant learning', *Conflict Resolution Quarterly, 23,* 2, pp. 141–64.
Hemmings, A. (2000) 'High school democratic dialogues: Possibilities for praxis', *American Educational Research Journal, 37,* 1, pp. 67–91.
Hess, D. (2004) 'Controversies about controversial issues in democratic education', *PS: Political Science and Politics, 37,* 2, pp. 253–5.
Hess, D. and Avery, P. (2008) 'Discussion of controversial issues as a form and goal of democratic education', in Arthur, J., Davies, I. and Hahn, C. (Eds.) *Sage Handbook of Education for Citizenship and Democracy.* London: Sage Publications. pp. 508–18.
Hess, D. and Ganzler, L. (2007) 'Patriotism and ideological diversity in the classroom', in Westheimer, J. (Ed.) *Pledging Allegiance: The Politics of Patriotism in America's Schools.* New York, NY: Teachers College Press. pp. 131–8.
Hess, D. and Posselt, J. (2002) 'How high school students experience and learn from the discussion of controversial public issues', *Journal of Curriculum and Supervision, 17,* 4, pp. 283–314.
Heydenberk, R. and Heydenberk, W. (2005) 'Increasing meta-cognitive competence through conflict resolution', *Education and Urban Society, 37,* 4, pp. 431–52.
Houser, N. (1996) 'Negotiating dissonance and safety for the common good: Social education in the elementary classroom', *Theory and Research in Social Education, 24,* 3, pp. 294–312.

Howard, T. (2004) 'Does race really matter? Secondary students' construction of racial dialogue in the social studies', *Theory and Research in Social Education*, 32, 4, pp. 484–502.

Ibrahim, T. (2005) 'Global citizenship education: Mainstreaming the curriculum?', *Cambridge Journal of Education*, 35, 2, pp. 177–94.

Johnson, D. and Johnson, R. (1996) 'Conflict resolution and peer mediation programs in elementary and secondary schools: a review of the research', *Review of Educational Research*, 66, 4, pp. 459–506.

——(2009) 'Energizing learning: The instructional power of conflict', *Educational Researcher*, 38, 1, pp. 37–51.

Jones, T. (2004) 'Conflict resolution education: the field, the findings, and the future', *Conflict Resolution Quarterly*, 22, 1–2, pp. 233–67.

Jones, T. and Sanford, R. (2003) 'Building the container: Curriculum infusion and classroom climate', *Conflict Resolution Quarterly*, 21, 1, pp. 115–30.

Kahne, J. and Sporte, S. (2008) 'Developing citizens: The impact of civic learning opportunities on students' commitment to civic participation', *American Educational Research Journal*, 45, 3, pp. 738–66.

Kelly, D. and Brandes, G.M. (2001) 'Shifting out of "neutral": Beginning teachers' struggles with teaching for social justice', *Canadian Journal of Education*, 26, 4, pp. 437–54.

King, J. (2009) 'Teaching and learning about controversial issues: Lessons from Northern Ireland', *Theory and Research in Social Education*, 37, 2, pp. 215–46.

Kumashiro, K. (2000) 'Toward a theory of anti-oppressive education', *Review of Educational Research*, 70, 1, pp. 25–53.

Kurlansky, M. (2006) *Nonviolence*. New York, NY: The Modern Library.

Ladwig, J.G. (2010) 'Beyond academic outcomes', *Review of Research in Education*, 34, pp. 113–41.

Larson, B. (2003) 'Comparing face-to-face discussion and electronic discussion: A case study from high school social studies', *Theory and Research in Social Education*, 31, 3, pp. 347–54.

Luke, J. and Myers, C. (1994) 'Toward peace: Using literature to aid conflict resolution', *Childhood Education*, 71, 2, Winter, pp. 66–9.

McCluskey, G., Lloyd, G., Kane, J., Riddel, S., Stead, J. and Weedon, E. (2008) 'Can restorative practices in schools make a difference?', *Educational Review*, 60, 4, pp. 405–17.

McCully, A., O'Doherty, M. and Smyth, P. (1999) 'The speak your piece project: Exploring controversial issues in Northern Ireland', in Forcey, L. and Harris, I. (Eds.) *Peacebuilding for adolescents*. New York: Peter Lang. pp. 119–38.

McKenzie, M. (2006) 'Three portraits of resistance: The (un)making of Canadian students', *Canadian Journal of Education*, 29, 1, pp. 199–222.

McNeil, L. (1986) *Contradictions of Control: School Structure and School Knowledge*. New York, NY: Routledge.

Maoz, I. (2002) 'Conceptual mapping and evaluation of peace education programs: The case of education for coexistence through intergroup encounters between Jews and Arabs in Israel', in Salomon, G. and Nevo, B. (Eds.) *Peace Education: Concepts, Principles and Practices around the World*. Mahwah, NJ: Lawrence Erlbaum Associates. pp. 259–70.

Morishita, F. (1991) 'Teaching about controversial issues: Resolving conflict between creationism and evolution through law-related education', *American Biology Teacher*, 53, 2, pp. 91–3.

Morris, R. (2000) *Stories of Transformative Justice*. Toronto, ON: Canadian Scholars Press.

Morrison, B. (2007) *Restoring Safe School Communities: A Whole School Response to Bullying, Violence and Alienation*. Leichhardt, NSW: Federation Press.

Nagda, B.R., McCoy, M.L. and Barrett, M.H. (2006) 'Mix it up: Crossing social boundaries as a pathway to youth civic engagement', *National Civic Review*, 95, 1, pp. 47–56.

Noguera, P. and Cohen, R. (2006) 'Patriotism and accountability', *Phi Delta Kappan*, 87, pp. 573–8.

Otoya-Knapp, K. (2004) 'When Central City high school students speak: Doing critical inquiry for democracy', *Urban Education*, 39, 2, pp. 149–71.

Parker, W. (2003) *Teaching Democracy: Unity and Diversity in Public Life*. New York, NY: Teachers College Press.

Pranis, K., Stuart, B. and Wedge, M. (2003) *Peacemaking Circles: From Crime to Community*. St Paul, MN: Living Justice Press.

Roberts, R., Bell, L.A. and Murphy, B. (2008) 'Flipping the script: Analyzing youth talk about race and racism', *Anthropology & Education Quarterly*, 39, 3, pp. 334–54.

Ross, A. (2007) 'Multiple identities and education for active citizenship', *British Journal of Educational Studies*, 55, 3, pp. 286–303.

Sandmann, A. (2004) 'Literature that promotes justice for all', *Social Education*, 68, 4, pp. 254–9.

Schirch, L. and Campt, D. (2007) *The Little Book of Dialogue for Difficult Subjects*. Intercourse, PA: Good Books, Inc.

Schultz, L., Barr, D. and Selman, R. (2001) 'The value of a developmental approach to evaluating character development programs: An outcome study of Facing History and Ourselves', *Journal of Moral Education*, 30, 1, pp. 3–27.

Schultz, K., Buck, P. and Niesz, T. (2000) 'Democratizing conversations: Racialized talk in a post-desegregated middle school', *American Educational Research Journal*, 37, 1, pp. 33–65.

Sears, A., Clark, G. and Hughes, A. (1999) 'Canadian citizenship education: The pluralist ideal and citizenship education for a post-modern state', in Torney-Purta, J., Schwille, J. and Amadeo, J. (Eds.) *Civic Education across Countries: Twenty-Four National Case Studies from the IEA Civic Education Project*. Amsterdam: IEA (International Association for the Evaluation of Educational Achievement), pp. 111–35.

Sears, A. and Hughes, A. (2006) 'Citizenship: Education and indoctrination', *Citizenship Teaching and Learning*, 2, 1, pp. 3–17.

Settlage, J. and Sabik, C.M. (1996) 'Harnessing the positive energy of conflict in science teaching', *Theory Into Practice*, 36, 1, pp. 39–45.

Simon, K. (2001) *Moral Questions in the Classroom*. New Haven, CT: Yale University Press.

Stephan, W. (1999) *Reducing Prejudice and Stereotyping in Schools*. New York, NY: Teachers College Press.

Subedi, B. (2008) 'Fostering critical dialogue across cultural differences: A study of immigrant teachers' interventions in diverse schools', *Theory and Research in Social Education*, 35, 4, pp. 413–40.

Tal-Or, N., Boninger, D. and Gleicher, F. (2002) 'Understanding the conditions necessary for intergroup contact to reduce prejudice', in Salomon, G. and Nevo, B. (Eds.) *Peace Education: The Concept, Principles, and Practices around the World*. Mahwah, NJ: Lawrence Erlbaum Associates. pp. 89–107.

Torney-Purta, J. and Barber, C. (2005) 'Democratic school engagement and civic participation among European adolescents: Analysis of data from the IEA Civic Education Study', *Online Journal for Social Science Education, Special Edition*.

Torney-Purta, J., Lehmann, R., Oswald, H. and Schultz, W. (2001) *Citizenship and Education in 28 Countries: Civic Knowledge and Engagement at Age 14*. Amsterdam: IEA (International Association for the Evaluation of Educational Achievement).

Tupper, J. (2005). *Searching Citizenship: Social Studies and the Tensions of Teaching*. Edmonton: University of Alberta Press.

Tyson, C. and Hinton-Johnson, K.V. (2003) 'Once upon a time: Teaching about women and social justice', *Social Education, 67*, 1, pp. 54–7.

Wasson, R., Anderson, R. and Suriani, M. (1999) 'Integrating a multicultural peace-building strategy into a literacy curriculum', in Forcey, L. and Harris, I. (Eds.) *Peacebuilding for Adolescents*. New York: Peter Lang. pp. 119–38.

Weikel, B. (1995) '"Girlspeak" and "boyspeak": Gender differences in classroom discussion' in Kleinfeld, J. and Yerian, S. (Eds.) *Gender Tales: Tensions in the Schools*. New York: St. Martin's Press. pp. 7–11.

Wells, M. (1996) 'From margin to centre: Interventions supporting gender equity in the Toronto Board of Education', *Women's Studies International Forum, 19*, 4, pp. 371–80.

Wolpow, R., Johnson, N. and Wognild, K. (2002) 'Designing, implementing and evaluating a teacher inservice program enabling 6th–12th grade rural teachers to integrate Holocaust studies into their curriculum', *Theory and Research in Social Education, 30*, 4, pp. 563–88.

Wood, A.G. (2007) *What Do We Tell the Children? Confusion, Conflict and Complexity*. Stoke on Trent: Trentham Books.

Wyness, M. (2009) 'Children representing children: Participation and the problem of diversity in UK youth councils', *Childhood, 16*, p. 535.

Wyse, D. (2001) 'Felt tip pens and school councils: Children's participation rights in four English schools', *Children and Society, 15*, 4, pp. 209–18.

Yamashita, H. (2006) 'Global citizenship education and war: The needs of teachers and learners', *Educational Review, 58*, 1, pp. 27–39.

Zembylas, M., Bekerman, Z., McGlynn, C. and Ferreira, A. (2009) 'Teachers' understanding of reconciliation and inclusion in mixed schools of four troubled societies', *Research in Comparative and International Education, 4*, 4, pp. 406–22.

Chapter 11

Climate change and sustainable citizenship education

Paul Warwick

UNIVERSITY OF LEICESTER

Introduction

A central aspect of citizenship education (CE) in the 21st century is recognition of the need to equip learners with the resilience, skills and attributes to navigate the complexity of a rapidly changing and unpredictable world.

This chapter considers the phenomena that Martin (2007) refers to as 'mega-problems'; issues of manifold crisis that go beyond the space of international boundaries and time. With a particular focus on the issue of climate change, it presents the need for a conceptualisation of CE that brings to the fore the notion of sustainability, drawing in particular from the current United Nations agenda of Education for Sustainable Development (ESD). This raises debate over whether or not notions of national citizenship or even anthropocentric notions of global citizenship are adequate conceptual models for the challenges of life in the 21st century. An emerging framework of sustainable citizenship education is proposed here that raises the need for a consideration of socio-ecological relationships within a contemporary conceptualisation of citizenship. In so doing this chapter also raises the importance of CE being implemented through participatory peda-gogical approaches that are congruent with its overarching aims and objectives of empowerment and democratic engagement. Whilst relevant examples of such an approach are provided throughout this book, one further pedagogical innovation is briefly outlined here; the critical literacy methodology of Open Space for Dia-logue and Enquiry.

The changing climate of mega-problems

Increasingly it is being recognised that young people today are growing up in the midst of an array of complex global issues. Martin (2007) refers to this as the phenomenon of 'mega-problems', issues of crisis that cross international boundaries and time. Such issues of concern in the world today include:

- climate change;
- biodiversity loss;
- air pollution;

- terrestrial system weakening (e.g. deforestation, desertification, agricultural over-use);
- fresh water supplies;
- poverty;
- inequality;
- debt;
- conflict;
- pandemics such as AIDS.

To begin to understand the interconnected nature of such problems, and to develop the capacity to navigate the risks and unpredictable consequences of these issues, requires learning spaces that cross disciplinary knowledge boundaries as well as human and ecological spheres.

Climate change is widely accepted as the single most pressing global issue facing society today. According to the Intergovernmental Panel on Climate Change (IPCC) in 2007, eleven of the twelve years between 1995 and 2006 ranked amongst the twelve warmest years since the recording of global surface temperatures began in 1850. For young people today climate change represents a familiar reality, an issue that is increasingly a central area of study for science, prevalent in a variety of forms within the media and debated at length by politicians.

At the same time climate change is commonly attributed in large part to human activity. A rise in atmospheric greenhouse gases, particularly carbon dioxide released by the burning of fossil fuels, is seen to be a major contributing factor. Other greenhouse gases such as methane and nitrous oxide are also identified as playing a role. Sources of these include industrial processes, livestock and the increased use of nitrogen based fertilisers.

Computerised global climate models, such as those developed at the Meteorological Office Hadley Centre, create a range of scenarios of how the climate will continue to change over the coming century with some predicting up to a 6 degree centigrade rise in global temperatures (Lynas, 2007). These models are used to point towards humankind facing challenges on an unprecedented scale. Whilst predictions of global warming rates vary, rising temperatures are increasingly being causally linked to the rise in unpredictable events of devastating social and ecological impact. This includes occurrences of extreme weather events, precipitation increases in areas such as South America and Northern and Central Asia, increases in drought conditions in areas such as Northern Africa and Southern and Eastern Australia and shrinking levels of ice cover within the Earth's cryosphere.

Whilst theories of climate change are over a century old, our understanding of this problem is still partial, unfolding and consequently contested. Young citizens are therefore required, when facing issues such as climate change, to engage with controversy. Holden (2007) summarises a controversial issue as being one in which:

- the issue is considered to be important and topical;
- the issue is complex;

- the issue includes values dimensions resulting in considerable differences of opinion;
- there are conflicting priorities, interests and interpretations;
- the issue can be emotive.

Climate change remains an issue over which there is no fixed or universally held point of view and where a variety of perspectives are possible. Consequently those debating the nature and implications of climate change also include so-called 'climate sceptics' such as Lord Monckton and the former Shadow Home Secretary David Davis. These sceptics question the scientific evidence for climate change and challenge the scale of the issue through questioning key issues, such as climate sensitivity, and the potential impact of critical feedbacks, such as the warming of seawater and resulting sea level rises. These climate sceptics have been given increasing media attention in recent months in the light of an independent enquiry into allegations, made in October 2009, that climate scientists were manipulating data at the University of East Anglia to support the theory of human induced global warming. During the United Nations 16th Climate Change Conference in Cancun, Mexico in December 2010 strenuous protests were once again made by climate sceptics over the threat to civil liberties and economic well-being posed by state imposed legislative and taxation measures to curb carbon emissions.

So with regard to the problem of climate change there remain differences of scientific opinion as to the extent and precise nature of the problem, and differences of political opinion as to who is to blame, what policy changes need to be made and who should pay the price. Finally there remains considerable international debate as to how best to mitigate the impact of climate change in terms of technological responses or adaptation approaches. As a consequence some commentators argue international political efforts to reduce climate change that have continually stalled or been compromised represent an insufficient mitigating response to the potential scale of the problem. This is increasingly leading to calls for citizens to engage with the problem and to take action for themselves. For example the Chairman of the United Nations Intergovernmental Panel on Climate Change recently claimed:

> Scientific evidence on various aspects of climate change is now very strong, highlighting the need for urgent action not only for mitigating the emissions of greenhouse gases but also for implementing measures involving adaptation to the impact of climate change. These actions would only be successful if communities and people at large were to take action on their own, irrespective of whatever governments and international bodies might do.
>
> (Dr Rajendra K. Pachauri, quoted in Hutchins, 2009: 5)

The phenomenon of climate change and other mega-problems highlight that we are living in unprecedented times of global, social and environmental concern.

These controversial issues are prompting increasing numbers of people to con-sider transforming the ways in which they live as citizens in the 21st century, and subsequently to consider transforming the ways in which young people are edu-cated in order not only to be resilient in the midst of these changes, but also to be able to participate in creating more sustainable futures.

Sustainable citizenship education – an emerging paradigm

Exploring controversial global issues such as climate change is currently a key aspect of CE as outlined in the National Curriculum within England. The framework for Key Stage 3 CE states that young people need to be given opportunities to develop critical thinking and enquiry and 'engage with and reflect on different ideas, opinions, beliefs and values when exploring topical and controversial issues and problems' (QCA, 2007: 30). Similarly the British Government's advisory group on citizenship stated:

> Education should not attempt to shelter our nation's children from the harsh controversies of adult life, but should prepare them to deal with such controversies knowledgeably, sensibly, tolerantly and morally. Of course, educators must never set out to indoctrinate; but to be completely unbiased is simply not possible, and on some issues, such as those concerning human rights, it is not desirable. When dealing with controversial issues, teachers should adopt strategies that teach pupils how to recognise bias, how to evaluate evidence put before them and how to look for alternative inter-pretations, viewpoints and sources of evidence; above all to give good rea-sons for everything they say and do, and to expect good reasons to be given by others.
>
> (QCA, 1998: 56)

At an international level, providing educational opportunities for young people to engage with global issues is very much at the heart of the current United Nations Decade of Education for Sustainable Development (DESD). Sustainable devel-opment is commonly defined as 'Development which meets the needs of the present without compromising the ability of future generations to meet their own needs' (WCED, 1987), and the UNESCO-led DESD running from 2005–14 seeks to 'integrate the principles, values, and practices of sustainable development into all aspects of education and learning, in order to address the social, economic, cultural and environmental problems we face in the 21st century' (UNESCO, 2005). ESD represents a synthesis of environmental and development education and UNESCO have recognised the central role that CE can play within this transformative educational agenda:

> The role of formal education in building society is to help students to determine what is best to conserve in their cultural, economic and natural

heritage and to nurture values and strategies for attaining sustainability in their local communities while contributing at the same time to national and global goals.

To advance such goals, a curriculum reoriented towards sustainability would place the notion of citizenship among its primary objectives. This would require a revision of many existing curricula and the development of objectives and content themes, and teaching, learning and assessment processes that emphasize moral virtues, ethical motivation and ability to work with others to help build a sustainable future. Viewing education for sustainability as a contribution to a politically literate society is central to the reformulation of education.

(UNESCO, 1997: paragraphs 67–68)

Responding to this challenge by seeking to integrate a sustainable development mandate within CE leads to a socio-ecological model as shown in Figure 11.1.

This model of CE seeks to broaden and extend the acknowledgement of the interconnectivity of life within notions of citizenship. The butterfly model of sustainable citizenship education shown in Figure 11.1 consists of two wings: the first includes three elements concerned with content; and the second wing

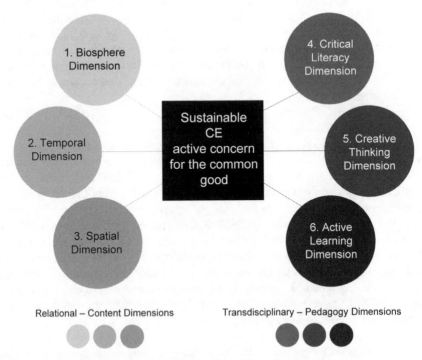

Figure 11.1 The core elements to sustainable citizenship education

includes three elements concerned with pedagogy. Considering each dimension in turn:

- *Biosphere dimension* – This recognises the interconnectivity between the well-being of people and the natural environment. It acknowledges that human problems and ecological problems are inextricably intertwined and need to be understood in relation to one another. This dimension gives greater emphasis within CE to ecological literacy (Stone and Barlow, 2005; Capra, 2002) and systems thinking approaches (Morris and Martin, 2009).
- *Temporal dimension* – This recognises the interconnectivity of life across time. It involves a consideration of the links between the past, present and future, and the connections across generations. It encourages consideration of the historical dimensions to the issues we currently face as well as consideration of the implications of our lifestyles on future generations and landscapes. It also advocates within civic decision making processes a long term view rather than short term gain or quick fix mentality. With regard to sustainability issues such as climate change this dimension raises the profile of the time lag that is present in many lifestyle and political decisions today. For example, Hutchins (2009) states that the effects of climate change being experienced today are a result of greenhouse gas emissions from 30 to 50 years ago. The emissions released today will similarly have an impact on the climate up to 2040 and beyond. Through such temporal connections the citizenship choices and decisions we make today will have an impact upon the lives of future generations and landscapes. Drawing from the work of Hicks (2001) this dimension can involve CE students in activities such as the consideration of probable and preferable futures.
- *Spatial dimension* – This dimension recognises the interconnectivity of life across place. It involves learners in a consideration of their local and global interdependency, recognising that through processes of globalisation, industrialisation and consumerism our lives today are very much caught up in a network of mutuality that goes beyond local neighbourhoods and nation states. This dimension involves citizens considering concepts such as the 'global village' and exploring their linkages to worldwide issues of justice, rights, equality and inclusiveness.
- *Critical literacy dimension* – This first of the pedagogical dimensions presents the need for learning spaces where pressing sustainable citizenship issues can be considered critically through engagement with multiple perspectives and where students are encouraged in reflexive awareness of their own worldviews. With regard to issues such as climate change this dimension requires learning opportunities for students to view the issue through the lenses of environmental, social, political or economic considerations and also through the viewpoints of non-mainstream value perspectives such as indigenous cultures. Within this dimension the aim is not simply to raise the student's awareness of 'the other' but to provide a consciousness raising opportunity to reflect upon their own perspectives; their sources, assumptions and implications.

- *Creative thinking dimension* – This dimension supports a re-conception of the importance of learning spaces that nurture people's creative capacities. It holds as a fundamental element to apt education for the 21st century the need to encourage young people in the process of generating and exploring what Robinson (2010) refers to as 'original ideas that are of value'. It is based upon the view that as educators we can have little idea about what is going to happen over the next 50 years (how multiple points of crisis are going to play out) and so it is hard to be definitive about what needs to be taught (Scott and Gough, 2004). Instead what is required, in the light of mega-problems such as climate change, is an education that gives explicit attention to developing young people's creative ability to problem-solve, imagine new scenarios and successfully navigate unpredictable change events.
- *Active learning dimension* – This dimension provides people with the learning space to explore experientially how sustainable citizenship issues interface with their own personal lives, their sense of identity and notions of community and belonging. Through the active learning process of conceptualising, planning, acting and reflecting it provides people with the space to develop what Wayman (2009) refers to as 'informed purposive action'; where critical thinking is combined with the creative act of interpreting images of the future. This dimension helps students to be prepared in the participatory and political skills necessary for democratic engagement with mega-problems such as climate change, whether that be at personal, grassroots movement or institutional levels.

Sustainable citizenship education is clearly a lifelong process in which schools can play an important role. A key challenge for schools seeking to engage and aid the progress of students as sustainable citizens is identified by Vare and Scott (2007) to be not simply about providing educational opportunities that promote sustainable behaviours. Instead they argue for learning spaces that support young people in thinking critically and that develop their capacity to deal with an uncertain future. Whilst research by Holden (2007) and Warwick (2008) has revealed that young people do hold an interest in a broad range of controversial global issues, it can be argued that exposure to mega-problems such as climate change can, in their scale, complexity and potentially devastating implications, all too easily create a sense of despair and powerlessness about the future. This presents a crucial challenge for educators as they consider how to best put SCE into practice.

Putting sustainable citizenship education into practice

There are a wide variety of approaches that educators can take to engage students with controversial sustainability issues such as climate change. For example, Oxfam (2006) identify different roles that a teacher can adopt when approaching controversial issues with students and these include:

- *Impartial chairperson* – Teacher seeks to ensure that a wide variety of viewpoints are represented either through students' statements or stimulus material. In this role the teacher refrains from stating their own opinion.
- *Objective* – Teacher seeks to offer a balanced approach where they present students with a wide range of alternative views without stating their own position.
- *Devil's advocate* – Teacher adopts provocative or oppositional position to the one expressed by students or the stimulus material. This helps to provide an atmosphere of challenge within the discussion and can prevent a sense of consensus quickly dominating the participants' exchanges.
- *Declared interest* – Teacher makes their position known within the discussion but presents or engages in considering a variety of positions as objectively as possible.

Much has already been written about the important professional requirements for citizenship educators to be sensitive and wise in their approach to controversial issues, and to avoid practice that amounts to indoctrination. Schools currently have a legal obligation to ensure that students do not only get presented with one side of a political or controversial issue. Key challenges for the CE teacher are therefore to firstly ensure that a variety of perspectives are always presented, and secondly to manage their own opinion on a given issue when working with their students, remaining critically aware and mindful of where and how they might be communicating their own personal bias.

A further challenge that has so far been given much less attention is how to engage students with mega-problems such as climate change in not only a critical way in terms of a healthy scepticism over the validity and evidence base of different perspectives, but also in terms of drawing out students' reflexivity. This is where they examine the origins of their perspectives, what the collective referents and underpinning assumptions are, as well as considering what the implications of this point of view are and where it is leading to.

As highlighted by the curriculum review led by Sir Keith Ajegbo (DfES, 2007), one pedagogical method that seeks to make inroads into this particular area is Open Space for Dialogue and Enquiry.

Open Space for Dialogue and Enquiry (OSDE)

OSDE is a method for engaging students with controversial issues in order to develop critical literacy and independent thinking. Developed by an international group of educationalists and researchers, the rationale behind such an approach is that learning to live together in a global, diverse and unequal context involves young people developing capacities that can support them to negotiate and cope with change, uncertainty and insecurity. Critical literacy helps learners analyse the relationships amongst language, power, social practices, identities and inequalities, to imagine 'otherwise', to engage ethically with difference and to understand the potential implications of their thoughts and actions.

Outlined below in Table 11.1 is the sequence of steps found to be an effective means for creating an open space for dialogue and enquiry.

Table 11.1 An open space for dialogue and enquiry methodology

Dialogue-based procedure for engaging students with sustainable citizenship issues such as climate change

Step 1: Establishing ground rules/principles of participation

It is important that educators firstly give attention to creating the open space in which students feel safe to participate, establishing the trusting conditions that are conducive to a community of enquiry being formed. The key issue is the educator cannot create this space on their own. They need the help of each student to make sure that no one is left out and that each young person feels able to share their own point of view. This involves challenges such as participants learning to listen attentively to each other, working as a team, and staying focused. One mechanism for helping to achieve the open space is to agree a set of basic principles that the students are required to adopt in order to take part, such as:

1. Every individual brings to the space valid and legitimate knowledge constructed in their own contexts.
2. All knowledge is partial and incomplete.
3. All knowledge can be questioned.

(OSDE, 2006)

Step 2: Critical engagement with different perspectives on a controversial global issue

Students are introduced to different and 'logical' perspectives on the chosen topic of climate change through stimulus material. These perspectives should present different angles on the issue, and can be taken from a variety of sources that represent alternative worldviews, knowledge bases and values systems. These perspectives can be presented in different formats such as web-based resources, documentary clips, newspaper articles, stories, photographs, etc.

Step 3: First thoughts and reflexive questioning

Students then need to be provided with the opportunity to consider for a moment what these different stimuli have presented. They can be encouraged to consider what might be the dominant views on this particular issue and why they are dominant and how they are constructed. Participants are also invited to consider reflexive questions where they identify what they themselves think about this issue, and how their perspectives have been shaped or influenced. Encouraging participants to consider what their personal responses to the different stimuli are can involve students working either by themselves or in pairs, and drawing, writing down or discussing their thoughts. When conducted within pairs this begins the process of students sharing their points of view and encountering the considered views of their peers; potentially beginning to identify aspects of commonality and difference in perspective.

Step 4: Group dialogue

Questions that critically explore the topic further can either be provided by the educator or generated by the students themselves to be explored within a dialogic setting. One participatory procedure is to invite each pair to negotiate a question that they would like to discuss, and then to organise a voting system where the whole group identifies one or two questions that they would prefer to explore. During the resulting dialogue the educator's role is to try and encourage the participants to engage in the challenge of exploring different angles and points of view on the issue, and to analyse assumptions, implications and contradictions. Questions that might be used to facilitate this reflexive critical thinking include:

Where is this perspective coming from? (How did you come to think like that?)
Where is this perspective leading to? (What are the implications of this idea?)
How could this issue be thought of otherwise? (What are other ways of thinking about this?)
Who decides what is good/bad, real/ideal? (What groups shape this understanding of the issue?)
In whose name is this decision made? (Who do these groups claim to represent? Is this representation fair?)
Who benefits from this decision and who does not? (What are the gains and losses for different groups of people, the environment, power relations, etc.?)

(OSDE, 2006)

Step 5: Dilemma-based learning

A dilemma-based scenario that is either real-world-based or a simulation exercise can then be presented to the students. This is in order to give them the opportunity to apply the skills and knowledge gained in the dialogue process to a situation of unpredictable change or mitigation that requires creative and collective decision making. The aim here is to engage the participants in considering what they might now do in a real-life situation in the light of their critical engagement with this issue.

Step 6: Debriefing
Last words – closing the open space

Students are invited to reflect on their participation and provide some feedback, either written or verbal, concerned with what they have learned about the topic, themselves, about others or about the learning process.

For further guidelines on these procedures visit www.osdemethodology.org.uk

The facilitatory role of the citizenship educator

Pedagogical innovations such as OSDE contribute to the current debate over the teaching and learning approaches that are apt for CE. This in turn has implications for the specific teacher training and professional development requirements of educators in this field. OSDE, it is argued, requires more of a 'facilitation' role as opposed to the conventional 'teaching' role within schools, as is framed in Table 11.2.

Huddleston and Kerr (2006) give specific attention to the professional development requirements of citizenship educators, and how schools and teachers can create a climate that facilitates students feeling they can risk expressing their opinions

Table 11.2 Comparison of the roles of the educator

Traditional 'teaching' role	OSDE 'facilitation' role
Focus on transmission or construction of content/knowledge pre-defined by the teacher or curriculum	Focus on building critical skills and ethical relationships within the group
The teacher is the holder of knowledge that is often considered 'universal'	The facilitator has partial knowledge that is always already culturally biased like everyone else in the group
The teacher decides what is right and what is wrong	The facilitator encourages participants to speak and to engage critically with what they say and what other people say
The teacher tries to get people to accept certain views as true	The facilitator tries to get people to question/examine assumptions and implications of any view
Conflicts and contradictions need to be 'resolved'	Dissonance, conflicts and contradictions are necessary components of the methodology
The teacher promotes consensus and agreement – students learn to avoid or solve conflict	The facilitator steers the group away from consensus – students learn: a) to think independently; b) to disagree and (still) respect one another; and c) to live with difference and uncertainty
The safety of the environment is based on the authority of the teacher	The safety of the environment is based on trust and respect for difference

Source: Andreotti and Warwick (2007).

freely. The citizenship educator through adopting a facilitatory role, that approaches such as OSDE require, has the difficult task of seeking to model and encourage specific behaviours that create an ethos of trust, that invite students to question and to analyse assumptions and implications (especially those of 'common sense'), and to establish a learning space where participants are allowed to 'disagree' with each other and with the teacher without being silenced or put down.

Conclusion

The current Education for Sustainable Development agenda is raising some important points of debate within citizenship education. It is asking questions with regard to the sense of duty and responsibilities of citizens to people across time and place, but it is also prompting questions over what constitutes a right relationship with nature (Bonnett, 2003).

A notion of sustainable citizenship education has been presented here as an example of current debate, with regard to the apt conceptualisations of CE for the 21st century. It has presented the case for notions of citizenship that go beyond anthropocentric considerations and that seek to embrace the relationships with, and responsibilities towards, the natural environment. It has supported the view presented by Selby (2006) that what is required within education is a change in attitude towards the biosphere, where we are able to learn from nature: 'lessons of cycles, flows, networks, partnerships, diversity and ... unpredictability, uncertainty and turbulence can, and should, infuse both the curriculum and process of our learning and teaching, as well as the way our learning institutions work' (Selby, 2006: 363).

Issues such as climate change raise the importance, within CE, of new forms of literacy that go beyond the political, social and economic. They prompt debate over the present need for citizens who are also ecologically literate, with an understanding of the basic principles of ecology and the ability to live accordingly:

> Thus ecological literacy or eco-literacy must become a critical skill for politicians, business leaders and professionals in all spheres, and should be the most important part of education at all levels – from primary to secondary schools to colleges, universities and continuing education ...
>
> (Capra, 2002: 201)

Current issues facing the global community, such as climate change, arguably represent in part a failure of schooling and academia in not giving priority to problems associated with living over problems associated with knowledge. CE is a trans-disciplinary initiative that has the potential to contribute towards addressing this failure. It can provide learning spaces for young people to critically and creatively read their world, and to engage with the complexity of the opportunities they currently face, and the unpredictability of change and challenge that such issues point towards for their future.

Questions for further investigation

1 Should the role of school be to protect young people from controversial issues such as climate change or to help them to learn how to navigate such problems, as an essential element of democratic life in the 21st century?
2 Does sustainable citizenship education represent a model that brings cohesiveness and universality to CE, or does it simply represent another attempt by a subgroup in society to promote their particularistic claims that ultimately brings division and incoherence to the notion of citizenship?
3 What do you consider to be the merits and weaknesses of the OSDE pedagogical approach to engaging students with mega-problems? What alternative teaching and learning approach would you consider to be an apt and vital response to the issue of climate change?

Suggested further reading

Hicks, D. and Holden, C. (Eds.) (2007) *Teaching the Global Dimension: Key Principles and Effective Practice*. London: Routledge. This book exploring the theory and practice of 'global education' specifically considers how to teach about controversial issues such as climate change in the classroom.

Qualifications and Curriculum Authority (QCA)(2009) *Sustainable Development in Action: A Curriculum Planning Guide for Schools*. London: QCA. A practical guide on how to develop the sustainable development dimension of the curriculum within schools, with specific sections looking at the links to CE and how to tackle the issue of learning about climate change.

Scott, W. and Gough, S. (Eds.) (2003) *Sustainable Development and Learning: Framing the Issues*. London: RoutledgeFalmer. This text provides an overview of the sustainable development movement, and considers how educators can support students in bringing about change through engaging critically with sustainability issues.

References

Andreotti, V. and Warwick, P. (2007) *Engaging Students with Controversial Issues through a Dialogue Based Approach*. Available at: http://www.citized.info/pdf/commarticles/Post-16%20Paul%20Warwick.doc (accessed 12th January 2011).

Bonnett, M. (2003) 'Education for sustainable development: sustainability as a frame of mind', *Journal of Philosophy of Education*, 37, 4, pp. 675–90.

Capra, F. (2002) *The Hidden Connections: A Science for Sustainable Living*. London: Harper.

DfES (2007) *Curriculum Review: Diversity and Citizenship*. Nottingham: DfES.

Hicks, D. (2001) *Citizenship for the Future*. Godalming: WWF.

Holden, C. (2007) 'Teaching controversial issues', in Hicks, D. and Holden, C. (Eds.) *Teaching the Global Dimension: Key Principles and Effective Practice*. London: Routledge.

Huddleston, T. and Kerr, D. (Eds.) (2006) *Making Sense of Citizenship: A Continuing Professional Development Handbook*. London: Hodder Murray.

Hutchins, C. (2009) *Climate Change: Our Warming World*. Bristol: Alistair Sawday Publishing.

Intergovernmental Panel on Climate Change (IPCC) (2007) *Climate Change 2007: Synthesis Report. Report of the Intergovernmental Panel on Climate Change*. Geneva: IPCC.

Lynas, M. (2007) *Six Degrees: Our Future on a Hotter Planet*. London: HarperCollins.

Martin, J. (2007) *The Meaning of the 21st Century*. London: Transworld Publishers.

Morris, D. and Martin, S. (2009) 'Complexity, systems thinking and practice', in Stibbe, A. (Ed.) *The Handbook of Sustainability Literacy*. Dartington: Green Books.

Open Spaces for Dialogue and Enquiry (OSDE) (2006) *Critical Literacy in Global Citizenship Education: Professional Development Resource Pack*. Derby: Global Education Derby.

Oxfam (2006) *Global Citizenship Guides: Teaching Controversial Issues*. Oxford: Oxfam.

Qualifications and Curriculum Authority (QCA) (1998) *Education for Citizenship and the Teaching of Democracy in Schools: Final Report of the Advisory Group on Citizenship*. London: QCA.

——(2007) *Citizenship. Programme of Study for Key Stage 3 and Attainment Target*. London: QCA.

Robinson, K. (2010) *The Element*. London: Penguin.

Scott, W. and Gough, S. (2004) *Key Issues in Sustainable Development and Learning.* London: RoutledgeFalmer.

Selby, D. (2006) 'The firm and shaky ground of education for sustainable development', *Journal of Geography in Higher Education, 30,* 2, pp. 351–65.

Stone, M. and Barlow, Z. (Eds.) (2005) *Ecological Literacy: Educating Our Children for a Sustainable World.* San Francisco, CA: Sierra Club Books.

UNESCO (1997) *Educating for a Sustainable Future: A Transdisciplinary Vision for Concerted Action.* Available at: http://www.desd.org/About%20ESD.htm (accessed 4th September 2011).

——(2005) 'Decade of education for sustainable development'. Available at: http://www.unesco.org/en/esd (accessed 12th January 2011).

Vare, P. and Scott, W. (2007) 'Learning for a change: exploring the relationship between education and sustainable development', *Journal of Education for Sustainable Development, 1,* 2, pp. 191–8.

Warwick, P. (2008) 'The development of apt citizenship education through listening to young people's voices', *Education Action Research Journal, 16,* 3. pp. 321–33.

Wayman, S. (2009) 'Futures thinking', in Stibbe, A. (Ed.) *The handbook of sustainability literacy.* Dartington: Green Books.

World Commission on Environment and Development (WCED) (1987) *Our Common Future: The Report of the Brundtland Commission.* Oxford: Oxford University Press.

Part III

Key debates in teaching, learning and curriculum

Chapter 12

Assessing citizenship education

Challenges and opportunities

Tom Harrison

UNIVERSITY OF BIRMINGHAM

Introduction

It will soon be the tenth anniversary of citizenship education being taught in schools in England and recently Ofsted have made suggestions that they feel the subject is now 'established' (Ofsted, 2010). However, the theory and practice of how best to assess citizenship education are still massively under-developed. This is perhaps to be expected given that it is not hard to find theorists who believe the subject should not be assessed and practitioners who believe the subject cannot be assessed. Even amongst those who agree that citizenship education should and can be assessed, it seems the arguments are not straight-forward. There are disagreements about how best to go about it, who should undertake it, what methods should be used and when it should take place. Publications offering advice as well as official policy documents often seem to ask more questions than they answer. It is therefore not surprising that many teachers seem confused about how best to assess citizenship education and have chosen to simply ignore it. This chapter will consider what it is about the nature of citizenship education that makes assessing it so contentious and challenging.

The English schools inspectorate, Ofsted, have regularly regarded assessment as one of the weakest aspects of citizenship education. Ofsted concluded bluntly in their 2003 report that, 'assessment is currently a weak aspect of citizenship and few schools have progressed very far with it' (Ofsted, 2003: 17). An Ofsted report a few years later showed that the picture had improved slightly, but that assessment still presented many difficulties for schools and teachers. The 2006 report, *Towards Consensus?*, stated that '[a]ssessment in citizenship is at a very early stage and teachers currently hav[e] only a very tentative view of standards and progression in citizenship. Indeed, the whole notion of assessment in citizenship remains controversial' (Ofsted, 2006: 42), whilst the latest Ofsted report in 2010, *Citizenship Established?* commented:

> Despite the steady improvements in standards at Key Stage 4 and gains in teachers' confidence in establishing standards at Key Stage 3, many schools

identified the accurate assessment of standards and achievement as a challenge, particularly those where examination courses were not in place.

(Ofsted, 2010: 11)

This report went on to say that in 50 per cent of the schools that they looked at either no assessment was taking place or that it was being undertaken to an inadequate standard (Ofsted, 2010: 22). The difficulties schools face in implementing appropriate citizenship assessment procedures is also highlighted in the CELS longitudinal study (Kerr *et al.*, 2009). This study has looked at the development of citizenship education in England between 2003 and 2009. The latest report is based on a survey of 317 schools and colleges as well as a more in-depth analysis of 12 case study schools and states that 'the assessment of citizenship is one of the greatest challenges for the subject' (Kerr *et al*, 2009: 10). The 2008 survey found that just 54 per cent of schools at Key Stage 3 and 51 per cent at Key Stage 4 had an agreed assessment policy for citizenship education (Kerr *et al.*, 2009: 25). This means that nearly 50 per cent of schools had not put in place any formal assessment procedures six years after the subject had become statutory. It seems that teachers and schools are either reticent about implementing assessment or unsure how to go about it.

In 2008 the then Qualifications and Curriculum Authority (QCA) introduced a new eight level scale, similar to those used in other curriculum subjects, for citizenship education. Alongside this framework the QCA and other organisations published supporting materials to help schools assess the subject better. However, despite this increased emphasis on assessment and the introduction of new supporting materials, it seems schools and teachers are still struggling to implement the citizenship assessment procedures as outlined in the orders. So what is making it so hard for teachers to develop and then implement a coherent assessment policy in their schools?

To assess or not to assess?

The role and place of assessment in citizenship education has been contentious from the birth of the subject. The *Towards Consensus?* report stated that the 'tentative grasp that teachers had about the standards expected in citizenship, was partly due to the fact that even the idea of assessment in citizenship was controversial for many' (Ofsted, 2006: 22).

This controversy corresponds to wider debates about the place of assessment in education generally. Recent governments have argued that in order to obtain world class standards in education, we must have rigorous assessment frameworks that help focus young people's minds on developing knowledge and learning skills. To this end, assessment in schools has traditionally been based on summative approaches and often reliant on tests and exams. However, there has been a backlash against this stance by those who believe that education has a wider responsibility than simply to teach academic knowledge and skills. There is a growing argument that education should also play a part in helping to develop caring and responsible young people who are able to play a full part as active citizens in wider society (Arthur, 2003; Layard and Dunn, 2009). These same arguments are being played out in citizenship education and bring the challenges associated with assessing the subject into even sharper focus.

The group that was originally tasked with developing the subject for the National Curriculum struggled to come to terms with the place of assessment in citizenship education. Brockington comments that 'there was a spectrum of views on assessment in the Crick Citizenship advisory group' and that 'the group agonized over whether citizenship, as a statutory subject like any other, should be assessed in the same way as any other' (Potter, 2002: 194). The group eventually elected to use a 'light touch' assessment framework, which consisted of students being assessed on whether they were working towards, achieving or working beyond pre-defined expectations. Brockington believes that the group shied away from recommending a more formal assessment framework for the subject as those at the heart of the group, such as Bernard Crick and David Blunkett, had social and political agendas for the subject. They felt the vision for the subject should be to help restore community, responsibility and collective care, and should be based on an 'agenda of social inclusion and social justice' (Potter, 2002: 194). Therefore the group felt it would not be acceptable to adopt a pass and fail approach to assessment.

It seems that the Crick group were keen to look at more formative assessment techniques, ones that allow for a greater focus on personal as well as academic development. They were worried that too much of a focus on formal assessment of skills and knowledge could effectively kill off the subject. As Brett commented at the time 'a sense of realism is important. If citizenship education is to move forward it is important not to scare away potential allies with the scale of the assessment enterprise' (Brett, 2004: 27). Brett argued that many citizenship teachers traditionally dislike assessment and that ultimately it will be passionate teachers that will help citizenship education become a fully established subject. Brockington agreed and commented, 'we must get on with the real business, which is difficult enough, of developing a caring and just community with involved, committed, caring and educated citizens, and leave behind us the business of passing and failing people' (Potter, 2002: 198).

Another concern that many had about assessment and citizenship education is that it could lead to some students leaving school being labelled as 'failed citizens'. Potter warned that 'if children and young people are put in a position where they fail citizenship the whole endeavour will become counterproductive. We'll simply alienate young people still further from school and society' (Potter, 2002: 188).

Recently there has been a growing body of individuals and organisations who have argued that citizenship education can and must be assessed. In 2006 Ofsted commented that 'the lack of a robust system for assessment contributed to its uncertain start' (Ofsted, 2006: 8). They believed that the decision to implement a lighter touch assessment framework meant that it was not taken seriously by some schools. At the time, some believed that had citizenship education adopted a more formal assessment model at the start, its status as a National Curriculum subject would have been raised. Students might also have taken the subject more seriously if they felt they were being properly assessed. If more rigorous assessment procedures had been adopted to begin with, this might have provided a bigger carrot, or stick, to encourage students to do well in the subject, which in turn might have driven up standards.

The *Pupil Assessment in Citizenship Education: Purposes, Practices and Possibilities* study (Kerr *et al.*, 2009), which included data from eight European countries, showed that in the majority of the countries studied some form of assessment of citizenship learning was being undertaken. The study showed overwhelmingly that 'participants emphasised not only that you can assess pupils in citizenship education' but that 'you should assess citizenship learning' (Kerr *et al.*, 2009: 2). Furthermore this study showed that the participants in most of these countries thought that the assessment of pupils' learning in citizenship education would actually become more prevalent and widespread.

Assessing what we value in citizenship education

The assessment system in education tends to determine what is of value. The prevailing discourse is that if something is assessed then it is likely to be considered more important and valuable than things that are not assessed. Therefore it is imperative to consider what elements of citizenship education are important and are of value before any attempt can be made to draw up coherent assessment models. The challenge for practitioners, it seems, is to measure what they value about citizenship education and not only value the aspects that are easy to measure.

It is often said that a citizenship teacher's task is to educate young people through, about and for citizenship. Educating young people about citizenship is perhaps easiest to assess. Educating young people through citizenship is a little harder. Whilst educating young people for citizenship presents practitioners with a real assessment challenge. Citizenship education requires teachers to not simply assess civic knowledge but also civic competency. Deakin Crick argues that 'since the goals of citizenship education include personal development, and active engagement in the community, assessment practices need to be formative and to focus on the process of learning itself, as well as on the processes of personal development' (Deakin Crick, 2003: 1).

If assessment is to have a place in citizenship education it seems it must focus on evidence of civic achievement as well as focus on the ability of young people to remember civic facts and information. As Brown argues:

> this means a lesser concentration on traditional written assessments, particularly time constrained unseen exams, and a greater emphasis on assessment instruments that measure not just the recall of facts, but also the students' abilities to use the material they have learned in live situations.
>
> (Brown, 2004: 82)

The many faces of citizenship education

It is clear that the assessment of citizenship education is regarded by many as one of the weakest aspects of an already weak subject. Those tasked with coordinating citizenship education in schools have often struggled to get the subject recognised by senior managers, colleagues and students, let alone to formulate robust assessment models. In many schools assessment has simply been forgotten. Up till now the authorities seemed to have taken a fairly 'light touch' approach to assessment, with very few if any inspection reports pulling schools up for poor assessment procedures.

It is not uncommon to hear teachers say that they are not entirely sure what citizenship education is. Some might be able to describe elements of the subject, but few can give a coherent definition. It would be hard to give a clear definition of citizenship education, as you could perhaps for subjects like history or biology or many other subjects. This is perhaps due to the fact that Crick and his team adopted what McLaughlin (2000) has called a 'maximal' approach to developing the breadth and the scope of the subject.

This 'maximal' approach presents a challenge for those tasked with creating a rigorous assessment framework for the subject, a fact pointed out by Kerr: 'The competing definitions and models of citizenship and citizenship education are important precisely because they point towards the potential for an incoherent vision and varied practice of citizenship education to develop in English schools' (Kerr, 2003: 5). How can teachers be expected to undertake assessment of citizenship education if they are unsure about what they are actually assessing? As Brett comments, 'A fundamental prerequisite of assessment is to identify very clearly what is being assessed. Yet there are many different ways in which citizenship education can be interpreted and approached' (Brett, 2004: 5). Uncertainties about what exactly citizenship education is have not helped those arguing for it to be more rigorously assessed. It seems that some big questions need to be answered first, such as: How can you best assess all the forms that citizenship education comes in? How can you best assess the vast range of key concepts, key processes and content that make up the subject? How can you successfully assess all the teaching formats it adopts and what is an appropriate methodology to use?

Currently citizenship education is delivered in a number of different ways across schools; perhaps during discrete timetable slots, perhaps across the curricula, perhaps through drop-down or suspended timetable days or, sadly still today, perhaps not at all. It is generally agreed that the subject is easiest to assess when it is taught discretely, where an assessment framework can be developed for each learning activity. However the situation gets more complicated when we consider the other possible methods of delivery. As Ofsted notes, 'the schools where assessment was at its weakest were those without core citizenship programmes and, more broadly, where they did not recognise or understand the high standards implied by the National Curriculum and its assessment requirements' (Ofsted, 2010: 22).

A lot of time, as well as excellent communication, between all subject leads would be required to build a coherent plan for assessment, if citizenship is to be delivered across the curricula. A cross-curricula approach to delivering citizenship education presents some real challenges for practitioners. There is a requirement to communicate assessment procedures across all the personnel involved to ensure standards remain rigorous. As Kerr *et al.* argue:

> It is easier to assess pupil learning in citizenship where that learning is delivered through discrete blocks. It is much more difficult to assess pupil learning where citizenship is delivered through cross-curricular approaches where the tendency is for a mixed learning approach and where citizenship learning is transmitted through a range of subjects that have a number of competing assessment practices.
>
> (Kerr *et al.*, 2009: 2)

It seems that assessment of suspended timetable days is also currently poor. Ofsted commented that 'it was very rare to find effective assessment of achievement and progress where suspended timetable days were in operation' (Ofsted, 2010: 27).

Emerging opportunities

The eight level scale, introduced in 2008, presented an opportunity to move away from the uncertain start that surrounded citizenship education and the assessment of it. The scale provided a challenge to practitioners to consider new ways to tackle some of the bigger questions that citizenship education assessment had raised. In their 2010 report, Ofsted argued that the eight level scale was improving assessment practice in schools, whilst the 2009 CELS study report stated that 'where assessment policies were in place they have become much clearer, more visible, and more rigorous' (Kerr *et al.*, 2009: 81). However, the challenge remains for all schools and teachers to develop commensurate assessment arrangements based on the eight level scale.

The introduction of the eight level scale brought with it a new focus on assessment and citizenship education and an opportunity to consider other current, wider developments in assessment. The debates about assessment in education have been shifting in recent years. Despite the fact there is seemingly more summative testing than ever before, work undertaken by authors such as Black and William on formative assessment approaches is becoming more influential with both teachers and policy makers. In the citizenship community formative assessment techniques seem to resonate with many and there is a particular interest in the assessment *for* learning movement. The Assessment Reform Group (Assessment Reform Group, 1999) developed a distinction between assessment *of* learning, for grading and reporting purposes, and assessment *for* learning, which is assessment designed to develop learning.

Increasingly theorists (Kerr *et al.*, 2009; Deakin Crick, 2003) have seen the assessment for learning movement as a good vehicle to move forward the debate on citizenship education assessment. Kerr comments that the assessment for learning debate is 'creating exciting opportunities to assess not only the more traditional cognitive dimension (knowledge and understanding) of citizenship but also the active dimension (skills and behaviours) and affective dimension (values and attitudes)' (Kerr *et al.*, 2009: 3). The report *Pupil Assessment in Citizenship Education* recommends using assessment for learning strategies to develop effective assessment frameworks for citizenship which are not only true to the aims and purposes of citizenship education but can also be comparable in rigour and standards to that of other curriculum subjects and areas (Kerr *et al.*, 2009).

Another debate that is currently prevalent, and pertinent to citizenship education, is the adoption, by many teachers, of peer and self assessment techniques. For many, a core element of citizenship education is about developing student voice and therefore approaches that enable students to become more instrumental to their own learning, which includes the assessment of it. Peer and self assessment is also something that is recommended by advocates of the assessment *for* learning movement. The movement suggests that those that are responsible for developing assessment frameworks for citizenship education should focus on how teachers and students can work better in partnership. Evidence used to make assessment judgements can be based on the verdicts of teachers, peers and the learner. The eight level scale could help make such an approach possible, as both teachers and learners are able to clearly see what they are aspiring towards.

Conclusion

The manner in which citizenship education was introduced into the curriculum led to a great deal of confusion, for both the theorists and practitioners, who were tasked with developing models to assess the subject. For several years this led to a hiatus and the assessment of citizenship education, if it was carried out at all, was generally undertaken to a poor standard in schools and by teachers.

However, the introduction of an eight level scale for citizenship as well as other initiatives in assessment, such as the assessment *for* learning movement and an increased focus on peer and self assessment techniques, has recently presented new opportunities. These opportunities could become realties if citizenship education continues to be accepted by schools and is better understood by teachers and students. As we draw towards the tenth anniversary of citizenship education being taught in schools, and as Ofsted has indicated that citizenship education is perhaps now established, it is a good time for schools and teachers to reconsider the assessment challenge. It is, therefore, important to develop assessment practices that not only benefit the subject but also new assessment methods that help support its core aims and purposes.

Questions for further investigation

1 Suggest three potential methods for assessing citizenship education in schools and list the strengths and weaknesses of each method.
2 Why is it important to assess citizenship education within the school context?
3 Discuss the importance of the distinction between assessment *of* learning and assessment *for* learning, and the benefits that each brings.

Suggested further reading

Arthur, J. (2003) *Education with Character: The Moral Economy of Schooling*. London: RoutledgeFalmer. This book provides an introduction to character education within the British context by exploring its meanings, understandings and rationale through the perspective of a number of academic disciplines, and adopts a cross-disciplinary approach in its investigation and exploration into the imprecise meanings often attributed to character education.

Crick, B. (2000) *Essays on Citizenship*. London: Continuum. A selection of essays by Bernard Crick on the subject of citizenship. The first half of the book presents essays outlining the basic theory of political education, while the latter half of the text comprises essays which reflect Crick's later thinking.

Bibliography

Arthur, J. (2003) *Education with Character: The Moral Economy of Schooling*. London: RoutledgeFalmer.

Assessment Reform Group (1999) *Assessment for Learning: Beyond the Black Box*. Cambridge: University of Cambridge, School of Education.

Black, P., Harrison, C., Lee, C., Marshall, B. and Wiliam, D. (2003) *Assessment for Learning: Putting It into Practice*. Maidenhead: Open University Press.

Black, P. and Williams, D. (1998) *Inside the Black Box: Raising Standards through Classroom Assessment*. London: Kings College London, School of Education.

Brett, P. (2004) *The Assessment of Pupils in Citizenship*. Available at: www.citized.info (accessed 17th November 2010).

Brown, S. (2004) 'Assessment for Learning', *Learning and Teaching in Higher Education*, *1*, pp. 81–9.

Brown, S., Race, P. and Smith, B. (1996) *500 Tips on Assessment*. London: Kogan Page.

Crick, B. (2000) *Essays on Citizenship*. London: Continuum.

Deakin Crick, R. (2003) *Citizenship, Lifelong Learning and Assessment*. Bristol: University of Bristol.

Harrison, T. (2008) *Assessing Citizenship*. London: ACT.

Jerome, L. (2008) 'Assessing Citizenship Education', in Arthur, J., Davies, I. and Hahn, C. (Eds.) *Sage Handbook of Education for Citizenship and Democracy*. London: Sage.

Keating, A., Kerr, D., Lopes J. *et al.* (2009) *Embedding Citizenship Education in Secondary Schools in England (2002–08): Citizenship Education Longitudinal Study Seventh Annual Report*. Slough: NFER.

Kerr, D. (2003) *Changing the Political Culture: Reviewing the Progress of the Citizenship Education Initiative in England.* Slough: NFER.

Kerr, D., Cleaver, E. and Ireland, E. (2003) *Citizenship Education Longitudinal Study: First Year Findings – Establishing a Baseline for Developing Citizenship Education.* Slough: NFER.

Kerr, D., Ireland, E., Lopes, J., Craig, R. with Cleaver, E. (2004) *Making Citizenship Education Real.* Slough: NFER.

Kerr, D., Keating, A. and Ireland, E. (2009) *Pupil Assessment in Citizenship Education: Purposes, Practices and Possibilities. Report of a CIDREE Collaborative Project.* Slough: NFER/CIDREE.

Knight, P. (1995) *Assessment for Learning in Higher Education.* London: Kogan Page.

Layard, L. and Dunn, J. (2009) *A Good Childhood: Searching for Values in a Competitive Age.* London: Penguin.

McLaughlin, T. (2000) 'Citizenship Education in England: The Crick Report and Beyond', *Journal of Philosophy of Education, 34,* pp. 541–70.

Ofsted (2003) *National Curriculum Citizenship: Planning and Implementation.* London: HMI.

——(2004) *Subject Reports 2002/03: Citizenship in Secondary Schools.* London: HMI.

——(2006) *Towards Consensus? Citizenship in Secondary Schools.* London: HMI.

——(2010) *Citizenship Established? Citizenship in Schools 2006/09.* London: HMI.

Potter, J. (2002) *Active Citizenship in Schools.* London: Kogan Page.

Qualifications and Curriculum Authority (QCA) (1998) *Education for Citizenship and the Teaching of Democracy in Schools: Final Report of the Advisory Group on Citizenship.* London: QCA.

Chapter 13

Governing citizenship education

Hilary Cremin and Moira V. Faul

UNIVERSITY OF CAMBRIDGE

Introduction

In all formal education systems someone, somewhere, decides what is to be taught, and how. This, however, is just the beginning. What happens in classrooms is influenced by the informal as well as the formal, the global as well as the national and the local. It is these processes of governance that are the subject of this chapter. In 2002, the government in England decided that citizenship should be taught in schools. Yet decisions about what may be taught and in what ways were not fixed in stone, particularly given the 'light touch' approach that was adopted (QCA, 1998). Who governs the 'what' and 'how' of citizenship education continues to be open to debate, and – given the nature and content of the subject – is open to even more political influence than other subjects.

Why is it relevant to consider the governance of citizenship education in a book such as this? We argue here that the debate about who governs citizenship education links to a wider debate about who governs our societies, economies, environment and our education systems. This is the very stuff of citizenship education. In this chapter, we propose that patterns of rule in citizenship education create at least two challenges for practitioners. The first relates to how teachers conceptualise their own role in governing citizenship education, since it is they who decide (at least in part) what and how they teach, and who else they involve in such decisions. The second relates to how practitioners support young people to develop as 'active citizens, willing, able and equipped to have an influence in public life' (QCA, 1998: 7). We propose that the critical and mindful application of concepts of govern*ance* and govern*ing* can support practitioners and young people in recognising and engaging in new public spaces for democratic engagement beyond national govern*ment*, including in their own classrooms.

Who governs?

In many ways, it could be argued that national governments can and should govern what happens in citizenship education, and indeed education more generally. After all, they are democratically elected to do so, and finance the not-inconsiderable costs of mass public education: in 2010, for example, England's education budget was £89bn (UK Treasury, 2010: 5). Some have contended that the purpose of mass public education is to build and define nations (Marshall, 1948), particularly since mass education 'directly expands the definition of what citizenship and the nation mean and what obligations and rights are involved' (Meyer, 2007: 124). Indeed, the very concept of 'citizenship' implies 'citizen *of*' (in contemporary times, at least) a nation-state. Given this national financing, national purpose and national citizenship, should it then be the nation-state's prerogative (through inspection or curriculum regimes, for example) to govern education, and citizenship education in particular?

Certainly, this was the dominant view in the 1940s and 1950s, when a statist idea of governing education reigned (for example, the Norwood Report, 1943). In the 1980s, however, public sector reform was carried out under the banner of reducing the involvement of national government. Reducing the role of the state in education was linked to a policy narrative of local control and accountability of schools, and school improvement driven by market-like competition between schools. More broadly, in the related 'neoliberal' policy narrative, the role of government would be to steer the course of public sector policy and provision, rather than rowing the public sector 'boat' (Osborne and Gaebler, 1992).[1] Regardless of whether or not this public sector reform (and the neoliberal policy narrative underwriting it) is to be desired, it is worthwhile to enquire as to whether the reform has delivered what was expected of it. Are the democratically elected national government and associated governmental organisations (such as the Office for Standards in Education (Ofsted) inspection regime) now steering, rather than rowing, the public sector boat?

Ball's (2008) research enumerates the large number and variety of non-state actors in the network governing education in England, and their mutually entwined relationships with the government and with each other (see Figure 13.1). These include unelected quasi-autonomous non-governmental organisations (quangos), business and financial actors and non-governmental organisations (NGOs), educational institutions and interested individuals. Even after the pruning of quangos in 2010, new quango-type organisations are emerging,[2] whilst existing business interests continue to wield the influence they enjoyed under the previous government.

In this way, national government[3] no longer governs education alone, if indeed it ever did. The many unelected actors in this network are not only delivering services; they are also influencing policy directions and the distribution of resources – that is, they are governing. Therefore, as well as rowing the boat of public service delivery, non-state actors are also involved, alongside the state, in steering public policy and resource allocation.

Beyond Education, a review of social research into broader UK public sector reforms of the 1980s and 1990s concludes that the result has been 'fragmented service delivery and weakened [state] control without establishing markets' (cited in Bevir, 2007: 6). Thus the unintended consequences of these reforms are more in evidence than the intended consequences (as elaborated in the policy narrative

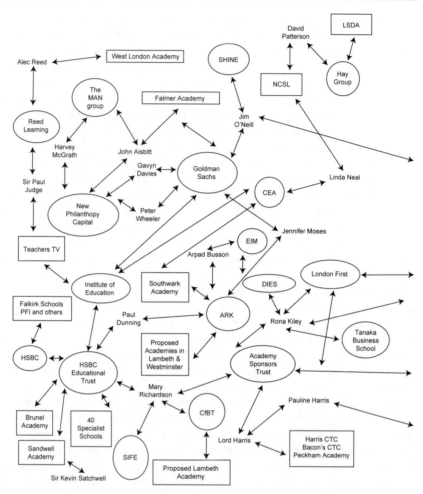

Figure 13.1 Example education policy network
Source: Ball, 2008: 750

or policy documents). This may have positive as well as negative consequences for the teaching of citizenship in schools, however. Is there an opportunity to be seized as a result of less governmental control? The involvement of non-state organisations and individuals in networks of governance can be regarded as 'filling-in' (rather than 'hollowing-out') the governing function of the state (Taylor, 2000). If we consider this and other policy networks as bodies that govern with the state, and as new public spaces, what are the consequences for teachers of citizenship? How may they be made more democratic and accountable? How might practitioners prepare their pupils for citizenship in a context that includes such networks?

First we will consider other influences on education policy, before returning to these challenges for teachers. Within the European Union (EU), for example, the Europe 2020 agenda focuses on the role of education in strengthening the economic performance of the EU.[4] Further afield, the UK participates in (and is influenced by) international testing comparisons such as PISA (Programme of International Student Assessment) which is administered by the Organisation of Economic Cooperation and Development (OECD). PISA prioritises the testing and international comparison of student scores in literacy, numeracy and scientific reasoning and makes no reference to other subject areas (OECD, 2010). Each of these international agendas carries implicit and explicit assumptions about the purposes of education, and therefore may constrain or enable particular policy decisions, thus privileging the development of certain skills, knowledge and values over others. These international agendas also privilege certain understandings of the purposes of education over others (see Table 13.1).

Table 13.1 Some purposes of education

The EU's Europe 2020 agenda defines the purpose of education as improving the economic performance of the EU. Here are some contrasting views on the purposes of education:

Education should 'meet society's economic, technological and labour needs, to enable the child to adapt to changes in these and preserve the existing social order.' (Alexander, 1995: 310)

'Education should seek to transmit skills that enable individuals to fulfil work roles.' (Fien, 1993: 16)

'Send him somewhere they will teach him to think for himself.' Mrs Shelley replied, 'Teach him to think for himself! Certainly not! Teach him to think like other people.' (Arnold, 1888: 169)

In education, the 'intellectual, emotional, physical, spiritual and moral development of students is developed to their full potential'. (Lynch, 1992)

'Education should seek to create critics willing and able to participate in the transformation of society.' (Fien, 1993: 16)

'[Education] creates a generation which has a highly developed sense of ethics and of global as well as national citizenship.' (Barber, 1997: 191)

Beyond these international policy constraints on state behaviour, schooling is now carried out within a hyper-dynamic context of globalisation (Held *et al.*, 1999) which affects schools, classrooms, pupils and the teaching profession (Bottery, 2006). Technological innovations are changing classrooms (Becta, 2011); increased migration (within and across borders) is changing who we teach; and pupils may be linked into networks of family and friends that extend across national borders (Schattle, 2007). Moreover, what is considered appropriate to teach and learn is changing (for example, the growing importance of global citizenship and sustainability, Davies *et al.*, 2005). Whilst these relationships occur outside school, they also affect relationships and curriculum choices inside school.

In this context of national public sector reform alongside international, global and transnational constraints and opportunities, what are the challenges for citizenship educators? First, national government is no longer the only space in which the education agenda – and the citizenship education agenda in particular – is decided. Practitioners need to remain mindful of their power to decide who they allow to participate in setting the citizenship education agenda in their classrooms. Second, a central purpose of citizenship education is 'to create active and responsible citizens' (Crick, 2002: 501). However, when 'public life' changes (that is, when how we are governed changes), changes are necessary in citizenship education in order to support young people in learning how to access and participate in new public spaces.

Teachers governing

The first challenge that the governance debate in citizenship education raises is remembering, in the face of stringent govern*ment* demands, that teachers are govern*ing* too. Practitioners ultimately decide what and how they teach, and who else they allow to participate in setting the citizenship education agenda in their classrooms. The recognition of competing local, national, regional and global forms and arenas of governance need not be paralysing. Rather, it can be liberating. No longer is citizenship education solely governed by national curricula and inspections; rather, the central role of practitioners in deciding what should be taught and how, and who should be involved in making those decisions, can be acknowledged.

Where citizenship teachers recognise and reveal contemporary 'patterns of rule' (Bevir, 2007), they can become more critically aware of their own ability to co-govern. From this awareness, teachers can then involve their pupils in actively participating in governing citizenship education in their school. The concepts of govern*ance* and govern*ing* (rather than govern*ment*) bring to the fore practitioners' role in governing citizenship education in their schools, and in a way that can be essentially grounded in the voices and preferences of young people.

Pupils governing

The second challenge engendered by the governance debate is that when 'public life' changes (that is, when how we are governed changes), we need to change the ways we support young people to become 'willing, able and equipped to have an influence in public life' (QCA, 1998: 7). In the contemporary political and social context, teaching about government and voting is no longer sufficient if we claim to support the development of knowledge and skills of participation and responsible action (QCA, 2000). That is not to say that learning how to participate in processes of government is unnecessary, merely that in the 21st century it is not sufficient: pupils need to learn skills of democratic participation in new arenas and processes of governance.

Given changes in what may be considered 'public life', citizenship education has an important role in supporting young people to learn how to access and participate in new public spaces. Teachers can support their pupils in developing an awareness of contemporary forms of governance beyond formal national government. In this way, young people may be better able to learn how to access and democratise the new public spaces opened by contemporary govern*ance* (rather than govern*ment*). The concept of govern*ance* helps us to recognise contemporary public spaces and strategies for political action that do not necessarily involve national govern*ment*.

One way of supporting young people to become involved in governing schools at the same time as practising democratic skills is through schools councils. School Councils UK (the umbrella organisation for schools councils) defines schools councils as, 'a representative group of students who have been proposed and elected by their peers to represent their views and raise issues with the Senior Managers and Governors of their school'.[5] Schools councils can enable young people to feel that their views and feelings matter, and are taken into account. They can lead to feelings of empowerment and affirmation, and can develop skills of communication, negotiation and participation. Adults can learn more about young people's perspectives, and can ensure that their views are taken into account in matters that affect them. These matters are not simple, however. Some have argued that in revitalising the public sphere, teachers and pupils need to take into account the embedded power relations that constitute formal and informal governance (Arnot and Reay, 2007).

Case study

The following case study illustrates some of the issues raised above. It is taken from research that was carried out in 2008 in a secondary school in the Midlands, which is reported in more detail in Cremin, Mason and Busher (2010). The school was in an area of social disadvantage, and data were collected from interviews with young people and teachers and from photographs that young people took to represent their identity in school. The research was particularly interested in student voice.

Official discourses of the school stated that pupils were consulted and that their views helped to shape practice. The Student Council was felt to be effective. Senior teachers noted the importance of the student council in enabling pupil voices to be heard:

> Senior teacher one: There's a student voice level where, you know, we get youngsters who represent the school, who give their ideas, and so on and so forth, and we see them growing up and gaining confidence.
> Senior teacher two: You can see the student council working.

Some pupils also helped to form the school anti-bullying policy. They were offered examples of wording and pictures and the final version was an amalgam of all of these, guided by staff.

Pupils were also consulted about their learning. In the English department, for example, there was a document called 'Voices from Below' where pupils commented on what they had done in English and what they had enjoyed. This way of conceptualising pupil voice frames young people as ideal pupils and as 'expert witnesses' (Rudduck and Flutter, 2004) able to comment on the business of teaching and learning as insiders.

> Senior teacher one: Because they [pupils] have been in classrooms all their lives, and they see staff, and they know what a strong member of staff is and they know what a weak member of staff is.

Evidence from both adults and pupils suggests, however, that official discourses are at variance with unofficial discourses. In relation to pupils as good citizens, for example, although the citizenship teacher felt that 'Students are as important as the Principal in helping the school to be healthy and work as a community', she also acknowledged that some teachers in school do not allow pupils out of their lessons to attend student council, and others simply select a class representative rather than organising voting by peers. Worse, only around 50 per cent of the achievable things that pupils had asked for had been actioned by the Principal and other teachers with whom they had held meetings, with more challenging and complex issues ignored. This, she felt, had consequences for the ways in which the pupils felt valued:

> I think that sometimes they don't think that we are putting them first, and that means we are not putting them first.

There were thus several barriers that prevented individual pupil voices being both articulated and heard. At times, the potential of pupil voice to make a difference to practice in school was mitigated by the vagaries of school life. For example, the citizenship teacher pointed out that although each department in school carries out extensive consultation with young people through surveys, questionnaires and interviews, the results of these are not always collated and passed on to staff and pupils.

> If staff don't know the outcomes of what students are saying, how are the students going to know? So that maybe needs to be addressed. But again, in the hurly-burly of the school life, that gets pushed to one side unfortunately.

She expressed concern that a 'tick box' culture in the school was having the effect of disenfranchising the pupils. This she put down to lack of time, and people who are just too busy 'doing their day job'.

> Because I truly think that students are used to … tick boxes, and they are not really consulted about things a lot of the time. As much as we try and

include students I think it is done as a last minute thing rather than being involved with something right from the start.

This results in pupils merely responding to an adult-led agenda. Even the voices of pupils who follow the rules, volunteer their time as good citizens and provide constructive feed-back on teaching and learning are not always given the support to make a genuine contribution. According to the senior teacher who has responsibility for developing policy in this area, school policy on pupil voice is 'not coordinated fully'. He contrasted some policies which are something 'you have to do' with policy on pupil voice, which is recommended by government, but not a statutory obligation.

Discussion

Who governs citizenship education, then, has changed. We no longer live in a world – if we ever did – where national government and its associated institutional technologies, such as inspection regimes, absolutely define what is possible in classrooms. Recent national public sector reforms have empowered national and sub-national non-state actors to govern, as well as deliver, public policy. Additionally, influences from beyond national borders shape public policy directions and service provision. What happens in classrooms is influenced by a range of influences, for good or ill, from the local to the national to the global, and teachers would do well to take this into account in reflection on their practice. Whilst new opportunities come from a decline in the role of govern*ment*, new challenges come from competing agendas at local and global level. Govern*ing* and govern*ance* can be no less challenging when it comes to setting priorities for what teachers and students do in Citizenship curriculum time. Whilst it remains imperative to educate young people as active and engaged citizens, barriers to this engagement at school level and beyond remain.

Conclusion

How then might the concepts of 'govern*ance*' or 'govern*ing*' (rather than govern*ment*) help with the twin challenges brought about by the governance debate in citizenship education? The first challenge for practitioners lies in the competing pressures they face from local, national, regional and global levels as to the curriculum and pedagogy in their classrooms. It is practitioners, however, who ultimately decide who they allow to be involved in deciding what and how to teach. Teachers can actively, and critically, co-govern citizenship education alongside government bodies, school management teams and pupils.

The second challenge pertains to the development of young people's skills of participation and critical thinking in citizenship education. We propose that effective, informed, democratic, accountable pupil participation might effectively develop these skills in schools. Teachers can – through their choices and practices – support or undermine their students' participation in governing what happens in their classrooms and schools. The case study above demonstrates the challenges of engaging with student participation. Are we paying lip service or truly engaging with pupils? What are they learning about representative democracy when things go wrong? When things don't work out at whole-school level what can be done to make a difference despite setbacks? Asking 'Who governs?' is particularly pertinent to professionals involved in citizenship education, since they ultimately 'govern' what happens in classrooms, forming young people's first experiences of citizenship.

Questions for further investigation

1 Look back at Table 13.1 'Some purposes of education'. Add two more to the list. Put them in a diamond rank, and write for five minutes on why you chose to rank them this way. Write for another five minutes on how you might adapt your teaching choices (curriculum and pedagogy) to better reflect your preferences as revealed in the ranking exercise.

2 Write for five minutes on why the concepts and reality of 'govern*ance*' and 'govern*ing*', rather than govern*ment*, could affect what you teach in your classroom. What changes could you make to your planning and teaching that reflect governance rather than government? What strategies and resources might support you in this?

3 What is the difference for you between education *through* citizenship, *for* citizenship, *as* citizenship, and *about* citizenship? We can meaningfully reverse the first three phrases (resulting in citizenship *through, for* and *as* education), but this is not possible with the last (citizenship *about* education means little). What might that indicate for your citizenship education curriculum and pedagogy? Look at one of your schemes of work: what might you do differently in your classroom to expand the way pupils experience each of these modes of citizenship education?

Notes

1 George (2000) summarised the neoliberal policy trinity of market liberalisation, deregulation and privatisation.

2 After the election of the Conservative-Liberal Democrat coalition government in the UK, many new, quango-type bodies have been set up. Examples include the Office of Tax Simplification (formed on 20th July 2010: http://www.hm-treasury. gov.uk/ots.htm); Office for Budget Responsibility (launched in May 2010: http://www.hm-treasury.gov.uk/data_obr_index.htm); or the International Aid Watchdog (announced in June 2010: http://www.dfid.gov.uk).

3 The England government Department for Education and Schools (DfES). The DfES was superseded by the Department for Children, Schools and Families (DCSF) in 2006 and by the Department for Education (DfE) in 2010.

4 Europe 2020 is the economic strategy in Europe launched in March 2010 as a successor to the Lisbon Agenda: http://ec.europa.eu/europe2020/index_en.

htm. It focuses on achieving economic growth that is smart, sustainable and inclusive. Education is considered critical to 'smart growth'.

5 www.schoolcouncils.org.uk.

Suggested further reading

Crick, B. (2002) 'Education for citizenship: the Citizenship Order', *Parliamentary Affairs*, 55, pp. 488–504. Important journal article by Sir Bernard Crick on citizenship education and the curriculum.

Organisation for Economic Cooperation and Development (OECD) (2010) 'Programme for International Student Assessment (PISA)' [online]. Available at: http://www.pisa.oecd.org (accessed 15th February 2011) OECD website which details ongoing assessments of how far students, near the end of their compulsory education, have acquired some of the knowledge and skills essential for full participation in society.

References

Alexander, R.J. (1995) *Versions of Primary Education*. London and New York: Routledge.

Arnold, M. (1888) *Essays in Criticism: Second Series*. London: Macmillan and Co.

Arnot, M., and Reay, D. (2007) 'A sociology of pedagogic voice: power, inequality and pupil consultation', *Discourse: Studies in the Cultural Politics of Education*, 28, 3, pp. 311–25.

Ball, S.J. (2008) 'New philanthropy, new networks and new governance in education', *Political Studies*, 56, 4, pp. 747–65.

Barber, M. (1997) *The Learning Game: Arguments for an Education Revolution*. London: Indigo.

Becta (2011) 'ICT procurement for schools' [online]. Available at: http://www.naht.org.uk/welcome/comment/key-topics/infrastructure/becta-ict-procurement.frameworks (accessed 14th September 2011).

Bevir, M. (2007) *Encyclopaedia of Governance*. London: Sage.

Bottery, M. (2006) 'Education and globalization: redefining the role of the educational professional', *Educational Review*, 58, 1, pp. 95–113.

Cremin, H., Mason, C. and Busher, H. (2011) 'Problematising pupil voice using visual methods: findings from a study of engaged and disaffected pupils in an urban secondary school', *British Educational Research Journal*, 37, 4, pp. 585–603.

Crick, B. (2002) 'Education for citizenship: the Citizenship Order', *Parliamentary Affairs*, 55, pp. 488–504.

Davies, L., Harber, C. and Yamashita, H. (2005) *Global Citizenship Education: The Needs of Teachers and Learners*. Birmingham: University of Birmingham.

Fien, J. (1993) *Education for the Environment: Critical Curriculum Theorising and an Environmental Education*. Geelong, Australia: Deakin University Press.

Held, D., McGrew, A., Goldblatt, D. and Perraton, J. (1999) *Global Transformations*. Oxford: Polity Press.

Lynch, J. (1992) *Education for Citizenship in a Multicultural Society*. London: Cassell.

Marshall, T.H. (1948) *Citizenship and Social Class*. New York, NY: Doubleday.

Meyer, J. (2007) 'The effects of education as an institution', in Sadovnik, A.R. (Ed.) *Sociology of Education: A Critical Reader*. London: Routledge. pp. 115–30.

Norwood Report (1943) *Report of the Committee of the Secondary Schools Examination Council, Curriculum and Examinations in Secondary Schools.* (Board of Education). London: HMSO.

Organisation for Economic Cooperation and Development (OECD) (2010) 'Programme for International Student Assessment (PISA)' [online]. Available at: http://www.pisa.oecd.org (accessed 15th February 2011).

Osborne, D. and Gaebler, T. (1992) *Reinventing Government.* Reading, MA: Addison-Wesley.

Qualifications and Curriculum Authority (QCA) (1998) *Education for Citizenship and the Teaching of Democracy in Schools: Final Report of the Advisory Group on Citizenship*. London: QCA.

——(2000) *Programmes of Study* [online]. Available at: http://curriculum.qcda.gov.uk (accessed 10th February 2011).

Rudduck, J. and Flutter, J. (2004) *How to Improve Your School: Giving Pupils a Voice.* London: Continuum Books.

Schattle, H. (2007) *The Practices of Global Citizenship.* Lanham, MD: Rowman & Littlefield.

Taylor, A. (2000) 'Hollowing out or filling in? Taskforces and the management of cross-cutting issues in British government', *British Journal of Politics and International Relations*, 2, 1, pp. 46–71.

UK Treasury (2010) 'Budget 2010' [online]. Available at: http://hm-treasury.gov.uk/junebudget_easyread.htm (accessed 15th February 2011).

Chapter 14

ICT and citizenship education

Terry Haydn

UNIVERSITY OF EAST ANGLIA

Introduction

Given the possibilities afforded by developments in a wide range of new technology applications, in terms of accessing information, communicating with a wide range of other people and groups, discussing and debating issues with others and presenting information in a variety of forms, it would be surprising if ICT was not of interest to those involved in citizenship education. Given the ubiquity of ICT both inside schools and colleges and outside them, new technology has major implications for teachers of all subjects, but perhaps particularly for those involved with citizenship education, given the importance attached to issues such as information, media and democratic literacy, community cohesion and global citizenship. As Selwyn (2007: 11) points out, there is increasing acknowledgement of the extent to which new media are 'substantively altering the ways in which individual citizens interact with the contemporary political, democratic and civic landscape'. Concern has also been expressed about 'the digital divide' – the fact that there are still some young people who do not have access to computers and the internet, and that they are therefore severely disadvantaged as citizens living in a digital society (see, for example, Warschauer, 2004).

However, there are radically different views about the ways in which new technology might contribute to citizenship education, and important misconceptions about the impact of ICT on teaching and learning. This chapter explores the implications of recent developments in ICT for citizenship education and considers how both teachers and students might explore the ways in which ICT can make a positive contribution to citizenship education. It also raises questions about what it means to be 'a good citizen' in relation to the use of new technology.

Different ideas about citizenship education

There have been different ideas about the attributes required to be 'a good citizen'. Victorian and early 20th century pronouncements placed an emphasis on virtues such as duty, obedience and 'serviceability' (see Aldrich, 1989), and this conception of citizenship education was reiterated more recently by the then Secretary of State for Education John Patten, arguing that 'public education systems contribute to a willingness of persons to define themselves as citizens, to make personal sacrifices for the community and to accept the legitimate decisions of public officials' (quoted in Porter, 1994). Another strand of this model of citizenship education has been the idea that a positive and celebratory transmission of the history, institutions and culture of the nation state and celebration of 'British values' (Brown, 2006) would help to secure a shared appreciation of and common loyalty to the state, and contribute to 'community cohesion'. The potential of new media to provide access to alternative meta-narratives about the history, politics and culture of the state obviously has implications for this version of citizenship education.

Another vision of education for citizenship has emerged in more recent years, which has placed more emphasis on information literacy and intellectual autonomy and Tosh's idea (2008) of 'the critical citizen' (as against Patten's idea of 'the loyal and obedient citizen'). This idea of citizenship education is articulated more fully in this extract from Letwin's call for all students to leave school with what Letwin terms 'a grounding':

> An understanding of all those things which it is necessary to understand in order to take a properly independent role in the life of our society. To be such an independent actor, people must be able to read and comprehend information of diverse sorts, otherwise, they are unable to make properly independent choices about their jobs, their houses, their everyday purposes, their travel and so forth. They must be able to make sense of the newspapers, and the spoken words of public life, since how else can they hold independent, informed attitudes about their governors, and the political system?
>
> (Letwin, 1989: 70)

Selwyn (2007: 10) also makes the useful distinction between what he terms 'active' and 'passive' modes of citizenship education, arguing that in the UK, citizenship has to at least some extent taken the 'passive' option of 'privileging delivery of information rather than attempting to concentrate on the "lived experiences" of citizenship-as-practice.' In terms of the role of ICT, this means using the powers of ICT primarily to provide access to information about citizenship, the constitution, the political system, democracy, etc., as if citizenship education were 'no more than learners acquiring knowledge, understanding and relevant behaviours' (Longman et al., 2004: 2).

This is in spite of the fact that both the Crick Report on Citizenship (QCA, 1998) and the National Curriculum for Citizenship (QCA, 2007a) place explicit emphasis on citizenship education in terms of 'process' rather than simply as a body of knowledge to be assimilated, with clear implications for *how* citizenship education should be taught, as well as *what* should be taught. Crick placed considerable emphasis on the importance of citizenship education developing values and dispositions and skills and aptitudes. The National Curriculum for

Citizenship, with its emphasis on the development of 'skills of enquiry and communication' and 'developing skills of participation and responsible action' (QCA, 2007a), also mandated what Selwyn (2007) would term 'active' citizenship, in the sense of requiring learners to *do things, as well as receive and assimilate information about citizenship.*

These distinctions, between an education for citizenship founded principally on the transmission and dissemination of a body of knowledge about citizenship and one emphasising the development of skills, aptitudes, values and dispositions, have profound implications for the ways in which ICT might be of use in supporting education for citizenship. They are also particularly pertinent given the pronouncements of education ministers in the recently elected coalition government in the UK. Schools Minister Nick Gibb has spoken of the need to ensure 'greater net concentration on academic rigour and the passing on of a core of knowledge' and his belief that 'education is about the transfer of knowledge from one generation to the next'. In the same speech he was critical of the recent emphasis which has been placed on 'the processes of learning rather than the content of knowledge that has to be learned' (Gibb, 2010). Similar sentiments have been expressed by Secretary of State for Education Michael Gove, who has called for a return to 'a traditional education, with children sitting in rows, learning the kings and queens of England' (Gove quoted in Thomson and Sylvester, 2010: 3). It is important to keep in mind that not all commentators and policymakers are in favour of 'active learning' or the importance of student involvement and engagement. In the words of former Chief Inspector for Schools Chris Woodhead (2010: 9), 'Pupils should not be encouraged to express their opinions … Who cares what they think or feel?', echoing Lawlor's earlier critique of recent emphasis on collaborative enquiry and discussion based approaches to learning: 'There is no reason to imagine that pupils learn from talking. Indeed they may not want to talk. They may have nothing to say' (Lawlor, 1989: 89). These moves towards seeing citizenship education (and the school curriculum in general) as being about the transmission of an established body of knowledge have profound implications for the ways in which ICT might be used to support (or perhaps 'deliver'?) citizenship education.

In terms of providing a 'warrant' for active modes of citizenship education which involve learners in 'doing things', demonstrating commitment and initiative and working collaboratively with others, the 'aims, values and purposes' of the National Curriculum contain the following statements which argue for 'active' rather than transmissive modes of citizenship education. Amongst other statements the aims, values and purposes section suggests that the curriculum should enable all young people to be responsible citizens who make a positive contribution to society, as well as having the essential learning skills in information and communications technology. It also suggests that young people be creative, resourceful and able to identify and solve problems, have enquiring minds and think for themselves to process information, reason, question and evaluate and communicate well in a range of ways. Young people should be equipped to learn independently as well as with others, relate well to others and form good relationships, and become increasingly independent, taking the initiative and organising themselves. The curriculum should allow young people to take managed risks, stay safe, work co-operatively with others, respect others and act with integrity. Young people are also encouraged to challenge injustice, be committed to human rights, strive to live peaceably with others and to sustain and improve the environment both locally and globally (QCA, 2007b).

In my work with student teachers in recent years, I have found that this facet of the National Curriculum is often neglected, and yet these statements have obvious implications for how ICT might be used in citizenship education, and they might form a useful agenda for considering how ICT might contribute to effective and meaningful citizenship education.

Different ideas (and misconceptions) about ICT

The enthusiasm that nearly all UK politicians have shown for the use of ICT in education (see Haydn, 2003 for further development of this point), has been based in part on a tendency to underestimate the complexity of processes influencing teaching and learning. The belief that learning results from the transfer of information from teacher to learner, in a fairly straightforward way, and the facility to exponentially increase the volume of information which could be transmitted across all elements of the educational system through the use of ICT was seen as a way of increasing educational productivity. As Naughton was to point out, 'It's not every day that you encounter a member of the government who appears to understand the net. Most politicians … see it as a kind of pipe for pumping information into schools and schoolchildren' (Naughton, 1998).

The role of ICT in citizenship education in this 'engineering model' of ICT use (Elliott, 2007) was one of transmission and 'delivery', with the idea of 'the absorbent citizen' who would assimilate the messages and desirable attributes transmitted from the centre. However, the vision outlined in *Connecting the Learning Society* (DfEE, 1997) has not been realised as 'official' portals such as the National Grid for Learning (NGfL) have failed to flourish, and the ways in which young people use new technology have failed to conform to predicted patterns (Haydn, 2003; JISC, 2008). Research into the views of young people and where they acquired these views show that young minds are not *tabula rasa* to be inscribed on, and that many of their views about society, the state and citizenship are formed outside school rather than within it (Ofcom, 2010; Wineburg, 2001). Moreover, there is emerging evidence to suggest that young people are either resistant or indifferent to attempts to use social studies education to fashion a positive rendering of the national past which might serve as 'social cement' (Grever *et al.*, 2008).

Whereas politicians have generally adopted a very positive attitude to the educational uses of ICT (Haydn, 2003), research into teachers' and young people's use of ICT has revealed negative as well as positive effects on learning. The idea that ICT will act as a form of 'sugar coating' to make the nasty business of learning difficult things palatable has led to what Kay (1995) has termed 'junk learning', with meretricious quiz games, facile activities and the avoidance of difficulty, or a need for extended reading or concentration (Greenfield, 2010). The idea that ICT would make possible more genuinely 'interactive learning' has been questioned by Walsh (2006), Heppell (2010) and others, who have pointed out that the use of PowerPoint and interactive whiteboards has led to an increase in didactic teacher-talk lessons.

It has become apparent that although new technology offers the potential for young people to learn about (and practise) citizenship outside the classroom, the majority of them do not use 'out of school' ICT for educational purposes (JISC, 2008; Englander *et al.*, 2010).

The past decade has seen increasing acknowledgement that new technology can have negative as well as positive impacts on learners:

> These risks ... include encountering pornographic, self-harming, violent, racist or hateful comments online, inappropriate or potentially harmful contact via grooming or harassment and, attracting recent attention, problematic conduct among peers such as bullying, 'happy slapping', or privacy invasions of one kind or another.
>
> (Livingstone and Helsper, 2010: 2)

In addition to these concerns, a recent report by Kakabadse *et al.* (2009) found that 26 per cent of young people admitted to spending over six hours a day on the internet, with over 60 per cent reporting that they felt either 'quite' or 'very' addicted to internet use, and 84 per cent admitting that they 'copied and pasted' from the internet to complete homework. Other negative facets of ICT use included the distracting effects of multimedia, 'pinball'-type unfocused and time-consuming browsing of hyperlinks, the foreshortening of learners' attention spans and the loss of sequential narrative provided by book-based learning (Tiffin and Rajasingham, 1995; Tufte, 2006; Greenfield, 2010).

ICT does provide access to a wider range of citizenship education resources than was available hitherto, but even apart from 'filtering' and quality control issues – the danger of learners accessing unsavoury, inflammatory and distorted information about citizenship issues – there are some disadvantages to this exponential increase in the volume of information available to learners. As Bonnet has pointed out:

> Volume of content does not equate with richness of experience. ... One of the chief dangers of information overload is that it can, at one and the same time, inhibit authentic thinking, and seduce us into believing that all we need to solve problems is yet more information.
>
> (Bonnet, 1997: 155)

In addition to what Walsh (1998) has termed 'Encarta Syndrome' (learners copying and pasting from the web without reading or understanding the content they have accessed), there is also the danger that learners waste inordinate amounts of time in simply accumulating more information, instead of using it for 'knowledge application' (see Desforges, 2004: 4, for further development of this concept/ problem).

Thus, far from being the unproblematic educational miracle envisioned by most politicians and policymakers in the 1990s (Haydn, 2003), ICT use turned out to be an uneasy mixture of potential benefits, possible risks and unfulfilled hopes. Used in 'the right ways' it could make an important contribution to the development of citizens who are well informed, critical and 'enabled' in terms of being able to communicate in a wide range of ways with various networks of people and groups. Used in 'the wrong ways' it could create 'screen-potato' citizens who use it in harmful, worthless and anti-social ways.

So, what does ICT offer citizenship education?

Access to high quality and 'impact' resources on citizenship

One of the most obvious attributes of the internet in terms of its potential use in citizenship education is the massive amount of information it makes available to teachers and learners about citizenship issues.

ICT provides access not just to 'more stuff', but to 'impact' resources, which can have a particularly powerful effect on learners, which can make points in a memorable way (Haydn, 2007), and help students to appreciate the importance and relevance of citizenship issues to their own lives (to give just one example, the archive of clips about citizenship on YouTube provides some intriguing and powerful messages about the use of citizenship tests). The range of moving image clips now available on the internet provides a rich source of stimulus material to problematise a wide range of citizenship issues, as an introduction to enquiries, discussions and debates on these issues. The easy availability of newspaper archives on the internet also provides access to high quality writing about citizenship by simply clicking on a URL which has been pasted into a VLE or electronic worksheet.

Resources which help to develop students' information literacy

The pressure to cover curriculum content often militates against letting pupils use the internet to find things out for themselves, given the amount of time which is often wasted. But in the longer term, we want pupils to become mature, efficient and autonomous users of the internet. Considering the importance of the internet in society generally, teaching pupils to make best use of the internet in their lives outside school and after they leave school ought to be a key aim of citizenship education for young people growing up in the 21st century. As *The National Curriculum for ICT* points out,

ICT capability encompasses not only the mastery of technical skills and techniques, but also the understanding to apply these skills purposefully, safely and responsibly in learning, everyday life and employment. ICT capability is fundamental to participation and engagement in modern society.

(QCA, 2007c)

This raises the question of how well pupils are prepared to make efficient and critically astute use of the internet, and social networking and Web 2.0 applications. Recent JISC surveys suggest that many teachers make little or no use of social networking and other Web 2.0 applications which play a major part in their pupils' lives outside the classroom (JISC, 2008), or of 'WebQuest' approaches to structuring internet enquiry (see 'WebQuest' in Wikipedia, 2010 for a succinct explanation of WebQuest approaches).

A recent study found that young people's information literacy has not improved with widening access to technology and that most young people spend little time in evaluating information either for relevance, accuracy or authority (Rowlands *et al.*, 2008). The Crick Report (QCA, 1998: 44) argued that by the end of their schooling, all young people should possess the ability 'to use modern media and technology to gather information, to assess information critically, and to recognise forms of manipulation and persuasion', and the proliferation of digital information sources which have developed over the past decade, with blogs, wikis and a range of other Web 2.0 tools, has provided a wide range of opportunities for young people to practise the development of these skills.

Ways of working, communicating and discussing citizenship issues with a wide range of other people and groups

The development of Virtual Learning Environments, Web 2.0 tools and social networking platforms also allows students to work collaboratively and to discuss and debate citizenship issues outside the classroom, and with students from other schools and in other countries. This has been particularly useful in addressing global citizenship issues (see, for example, *Global Dimension – Ideas and Resources for Teachers* [online]; *Classroom 2.0* [online]). The development of such sites has made it much easier for teachers who want to set up links with other institutions to do so. Wikis can also be used to sub-contract aspects of citizenship topics so that different groups within a class can address particular strands of the topic. As McFarlane (2009) has noted, there is still a danger that VLEs can be used mainly as repositories of information, where documents end up being copied and pasted rather than read, discussed and debated, and not for genuinely dialogic learning, where learners' ideas develop and change in the light of their exchanges. However, these Web 2.0 developments still offer a considerable resource to those involved with citizenship education, compared to the era of textbooks, worksheets and schools broadcasts. As Richardson (2006) points out, there is something very powerful about *easily* being able to share resources and ideas with a web audience that is willing to share back what they thought of those ideas.

Ways for learners to express themselves 'digitally' in a range of formats

Although there are still departments where students' work is expressed primarily in written form, there are increasing numbers of departments where learners can express themselves 'digitally', using digital cameras, camcorders, digital voice recorders and imaging software to produce podcasts, photo-stories and short films and animations. This is sometimes achieved at some cost in terms of content coverage but it does offer the opportunity for learners to communicate in a much more creative way, and a wider variety of ways. As Shirky (2010) has pointed out, the development of Web 2.0 tools, including blogs, wikis and podcasts, requires a degree of active thought and commitment to produce something that watching television does not require. Whilst acknowledging the time-wasting and 'trivial pursuits' that social networking activity can engender, Shirky also points to the citizenship-inspired campaigning and social activism which it also occasions, and which is being harnessed by an increasing number of schools to promote citizenship education.

The following list, compiled by QCA (2001), provides an *aide-mémoire* for teachers involved in citizenship education to consider the ways in which the use of ICT might help to improve the outcomes of their teaching. It might be interesting for those who are involved in citizenship to think about the extent to which they have explored these possibilities.

ICT contributes to citizenship by enabling pupils to:

- find, collate and combine information from different points of view;
- use e-mail (and now, other Web 2.0 applications) to communicate and collaborate with others, including those from different ethnic, religious and cultural backgrounds at a regional, national and international level;
- use electronic communication to participate in discussion forums and the activities of voluntary and community groups;
- publish information, including on the internet, for an authentic audience;
- use models to investigate options and alternatives when problem-solving;
- discuss the moral, ethical, environmental and social impact of ICT on society, including the impact on work and globalisation;
- consider issues of legal and human rights raised by the electronic collection, storage and use of personal information by commercial organisations and governments;
- understand that the collection, processing and presentation of data is not a neutral process and to consider the use and abuse of statistics.

Conclusion

What does it mean 'to be good at ICT' as a citizenship educator? In part, this entails teacher awareness and initiative in terms of being able to access and deploy high quality and 'impact' resources which will make citizenship education more powerful, meaningful and effective for learners. But it is also partly about being able to use ICT to get pupils actively involved in the *processes* of citizenship education: to collaborate with a wide range of 'others' in discussion, debate and argument, in order to develop learners' understandings and abilities in the field of citizenship. A recent OECD report on the educational uses of ICT made the point that Web 2.0 applications can be particularly helpful in this respect (OECD, 2010). It also involves being able to use ICT to develop the information literacy of young people, 'so that they know when they are being manipulated, by whom, and for what purpose' (Longworth, 1981: 19). It is also helpful if educators can develop learners' ability to express themselves, and make positive contributions digitally, as well as orally and in writing, so that they can develop 'skills of participation and responsible action' (BECTa, 2002).

And what does it mean 'to be good at ICT' as a learner or citizen? As Livingstone and Helsper (2010) have pointed out, using the communicative and networking powers of ICT presents a mixture of opportunities and risks for young people. Given that young people in the UK are spending on average over 12 hours a week online (Ofcom, 2010), helping students to make mature and constructive use of ICT is one of the central challenges facing citizenship educators. The philosopher of education Richard Peters defined education as 'induction into worthwhile activities' (Peters, 1967: 27). Many young people currently use ICT to avoid education rather than to engage with it, and to do meretricious or harmful things rather than worthwhile activities which will help to make them better informed, more discerning and more enabled citizens. In developed countries such as the UK, where the overwhelming majority of teachers and young people have access to the internet either at school, at home or both (Ofcom, 2010), the most significant digital divide is between citizens (and learners) who are able to use ICT discerningly and effectively in order to engage in 'worthwhile activities', and those who are either unable or unwilling to use ICT in ways which will help to make them better and more effective citizens. Given the enormous potential of ICT to do either great good or great harm (Shirky, 2010), this is an important challenge for citizenship education.

Questions for further investigation

1 To what extent do you exploit the potential of ICT to get pupils exploring citizenship issues *outside* the classroom?
2 In what ways can ICT be used to build up a collection of powerful 'impact' resources to engage pupils with citizenship issues and to problematise key debates in citizenship education?
3 What does it mean 'to be good at ICT' as a citizen?

Suggested further reading

Connolly, J. and Short, G. (2009) *Citizenship through ICT*. London: Folens. This book has the advantage of being comparatively up to date, and therefore inclusive of recent Web 2.0 developments. Section on 'Extending student voice' has guidance on setting up school council blogs and online surveys.

CitizEd website. Available at: http://www.citized.info One of the main portals for citizenship education, see in particular, 'Citizenship and ICT: beyond websites and PowerPoints', for a succinct (8 page) introduction to a range of possible uses of ICT, including photostories and dissemination of school council activities – http://www.citized.info/pdf/other/NQT_article_SC_and_RC.doc (accessed 20th January 2011).

Communicty. Available at: http://communicty.wikispaces.com/Global. A good example of a wiki devoted to supporting the teaching of global citizenship, see also, www.globaldimension.org.uk.

Selwyn, N. (2007) *Citizenship, technology and learning: a review of recent literature*. London: Futurelab. This book is useful as a broad overview of recent developments, including different conceptions of citizenship education, and the implications for the ways in which ICT might or might not be of use and relevance.

References

Aldrich, R. (1989) 'Class and gender in the study and teaching of history in England in the twentieth century', *Historical Studies in Education*, *1*, 1, pp. 119–35.

BECTa (2002) *How to use ICT in citizenship*. Coventry: BECTa.

Bonnet, M. (1997) 'Computers in the classroom: some values issues', in McFarlane, A. (Ed.) *Information technology and authentic learning*. London: Routledge. pp. 145–59.

Brown, G. (2006) 'Keynote address', *Fabian Society Conference on Britishness*, London: 14th January 2006.

Classroom 2.0 [online]. Available at: www.classroom20.com (accessed 1st August 2010).

Department for Education and Employment (DfEE) (1997) *Connecting the learning society*. London: DfEE.

Desforges, C. (2004) *On learning and teaching*. Nottingham: NCSL.

Elliott, J. (2007) *Reflecting where the action is: the selected works of John Elliott*. London: RoutledgeFalmer.

Englander, F., Terregrossa, R. and Wang, Z. (2010) 'Internet use among college students: tool or toy?', *Educational Review*, *62*, 1, pp. 85–96.

Gibb, N. (2010) 'Speech to the Reform Conference', 1st July 2010. Available at: http://www.education.gov.uk/inthenews/speeches/a00191704/nick-gibbs-speech-to-reform-aqa-conference (accessed 24th September 2011).

Global Dimension – Ideas and Resources for Teachers [online]. Available at: www.globaldimension.org.uk (accessed 2nd August 2010).

Gove, M. (2010) Quoted in 'Pupils to learn poetry by heart in Tory return to "traditional" school lessons', *The Times*, 6th March: p. 3.

Greenfield, S. (2010) 'Is the web changing our brains?', *The Virtual Revolution Blog*. Available at: http://www.bbc.co.uk/blogs/digitalrevolution/2009/09/susan-greenfield-is-the-web-ch.shtml (accessed 20th January 2011).

Grever, M., Haydn, T. and Ribbens, K. (2008) 'Identity and school history: the perspective of young people from the Netherlands and England', *British Journal of Educational Studies, 56*, 1, pp. 76–94.

Haydn, T. (2003) 'Computers and history: rhetoric, reality and the lessons of the past', in Haydn, T. and Counsell, C. (Eds.) *History, ICT and learning*. London: Routledge. pp. 11–37.

Haydn, T. (2007) 'ICT and impact learning'. Available at: http://www.youtube.com/watch?v=C5VIUMrnXIY (accessed 27th July 2010).

Heppell S. (2010) 'Address to BETT Conference'. London: January 2010.

JISC (Joint Information Systems Committee) (2008) *Great expectations of ICT: findings from the second phase of the report*. London: JISC. Available at: www.jisc.ac.uk/publications/documents/greatexpectations.aspx (accessed 22nd September 2009).

Kakabadse, A., Kakabadse, N., Bailey, S. and Myers, A. (2009) *Techno addicts: young persons addicted to technology*. Cambridge: Sigel Press.

Kay, A. (1995) 'Computers, networks and education', *Scientific American, special issue: The computer in the twenty first century*, pp. 148–55.

Lawlor, S. (1989) 'Correct core', in Moon, B., Murphy, P. and Raynor, J. (Eds.) *Policies for the Curriculum*. Buckingham: Open University Press.

Letwin, O. (1989) 'Grounding comes first', in Moon, B., Murphy, P. and Raynor, J. (Eds.) *Policies for the Curriculum*. London: Hodder and Stoughton. P. 70.

Livingstone, S. and Helsper, E. (2010) 'Balancing opportunities and risks in teenagers' use of the internet: the role of online skills and self-efficacy', *New Media and Society, 11*, 8, pp. 1–25.

Longman, D., Jones, L., and Clarke, R. (2004) *ICT and Citizenship education in initial teacher training*. Newport: University of Wales. Available at: http://www.ict-tutors.co.uk/documents/ICT%20and%20Citizenship%20Education%20in%20Initial%20Teacher%20Education.doc (accessed 17th July 2010).

Longworth, N. (1981) 'We're moving into the information age – what shall we teach the children?', *Computer Education*, June: pp. 17–19.

McFarlane, A. (2009) 'Thinking with content', paper presented at the CAL 09 Conference. Brighton: 24th March 2009.

Naughton, J. (1998) *The Observer*, 22nd March 1998.

OECD (2010) *ICT and initial teacher training*. Paris: OECD. Available at: http://www.oecd.org/document/13/0,3343,en_2649_35845581_41676365_1_1_1_1,00.html (accessed 2nd August 2010).

Ofcom (2010) *UK Adults' media literacy report*, May 2010. London: Ofcom.

Peters, R. (1967) *The concept of education*. London: Routledge and Kegan Paul.

Porter, J. (1994) *The Joseph Lauwerys Memorial Lecture*. London: Institute of Education, University of London, 12th May 1994.

Qualifications and Curriculum Authority (QCA) (1998) *Education for citizenship and the teaching of democracy in schools: final report of the Advisory Group on Citizenship*. London: QCA.

Qualifications and Curriculum Authority (QCA) (2001) *Citizenship through ICT at Key Stage 3*. London: QCA.

Qualifications and Curriculum Authority (QCA) (2007a) *The National Curriculum for Citizenship*. London: QCA.

Qualifications and Curriculum Authority (QCA) (2007b) *The National Curriculum: aims, values and purposes*. London: QCA.

Qualifications and Curriculum Authority (QCA) (2007c) *The National Curriculum for ICT*. London: QCA.

Richardson, W. (2006) *Blogs, wikis, podcasts and other powerful webtools for classrooms*. London: Sage.

Rowlands, I., Nicholas, D., Williams, P., Huntingdon, P and Fieldhouse, M. (2008) *The Google generation: the information behaviour of the researcher of the future*, CIBER, School of Library, Archive and Information Studies, University College London. Available at: http://www.jisc.ac.uk/media/documents/programmes/reppres/gg_final_keynote_11012008.pdf (accessed 27th July 2010).

Selwyn, N. (2007) *Citizenship, technology and learning: a review of recent literature*. London: Futurelab. Available at: http://www2.futurelab.org.uk/resources/documents/lit_reviews/Citizenship_Review_update.pdf (accessed 29th July 2010).

Shirky, C. (2010) 'Interview with Decca Aitkenhead', *Guardian 2*, 5th July 2010, pp. 7–9.

Tiffin, J. and Rajasingham, L. (1995) *In search of the virtual class*. London: Routledge.

Tosh, J. (2008) *Why history matters*. Basingstoke: Palgrave Macmillan.

Tufte, E. (2006) *The cognitive style of PowerPoint*. New York, NY: Graphis Press.

Walsh, B. (1998) 'Why Gerry likes history now: the power of the word processor', *Teaching History, 93*, pp. 6–15.

Walsh, B. (2006) *Beyond multiple choice*, seminar presentation at the e-help conference, Stockholm, 7th October 2006. Available at: http://www.e-help.eu/seminars/walsh2.htm (accessed 20th January 2011).

Warschauer, M. (2004) *Technology and social inclusion: rethinking the digital divide*. Cambridge, MA: MIT Press.

WebQuest Wikipedia (2010) [online]. Available at: http://en.wikipedia.org/wiki/WebQuest (accessed 3rd August 2010).

Wineburg, S. (2001) *Historical thinking and other unnatural acts*. Philadelphia, PA: Temple.

Woodhead, C. (2010) 'Children at school to learn, not to think critically', *Sunday Times, News Review*, 25th July 2010, p. 9.

Chapter 15

Values, ethics and citizenship education

Mark A. Pike

UNIVERSITY OF LEEDS

Ethics and citizenship education

In *Democracy and Education* John Dewey observed that 'democracy is more than a form of government; it is primarily a mode of associated living' (Dewey, 1966/ 2002: 101). On this view, citizenship education is not simply about politics, it concerns how we live our lives. It concerns ethics because it is not just about how we live our lives, but concerns how we *should* live our lives. The term 'Education for Democratic Citizenship' (EDC) describes how certain people believe we should live, it does not simply denote education *about* democracy but education *for* democracy. Such an educational project is committed to the inculcation of particular beliefs and seeks to instill certain values. It fosters loyalty to a particular way of living and promotes certain allegiances. The 'idea of citizenship-as-outcome reveals a strong instrumental orientation in the idea of citizenship education' (Biesta and Lawy, 2006: 72) and the 'transformative' aims of the citizenship curriculum might be regarded, in McLaughlin's (2000) terms, as 'maximal' not 'minimal'.

The research review of scholarly literature on EDC published between 1995 and 2005, conducted by Osler and Starkey (2005) on behalf of the British Educational Research Association (BERA), acknowledged that citizenship education 'provokes heated debate and controversy in schools' with 'certain critics even questioning whether schools should be engaged in this area of learning' (Osler and Starkey, 2005: 4). In this chapter I suggest that if citizenship is to be taught in school, teachers must be open with students about the beliefs and values upon which their citizenship education is based. Arguably, to seek to influence a child or young person's beliefs and values through a particular curriculum without sufficient transparency about the values underpinning that curriculum is to treat such a learner more like a 'subject' than a 'citizen' (Pike, 2007).

This is especially important if Education for Democratic Citizenship does not so much entail children and young people being encouraged to reflect critically on the different ways of living offered by different political systems as it seeks to induct them into one particular system. In *On Liberty*, John Stuart Mill points out that, 'He who does anything because it is the custom makes no choice' (Mill,

1909) and certain interpretations of democratic values have become so 'customary' in our society that they are rarely 'chosen' (Pike, 2009). Yet it is essential in a liberal, democratic society for students to gain sufficient critical distance from accustomed ways of living. If 'liberal values permeate the curriculum of the common school generally, and the subject of citizenship in particular' (Halstead and Pike, 2006: 23) then students should be helped to critically evaluate those values. In this way citizenship education can provide an opportunity for students to reflect on issues, on their own beliefs and values and on the society in which they wish to live.

When discussing the aims of citizenship education, Andrew Peterson, in Chapter 16, notes that young people are to learn certain values, attitudes and skills necessary for political participation and refers to liberal theorist Will Kymlicka (2003), who argues that this entails acquiring a range of dispositions, virtues and loyalties that are inseparable from the practice of democratic citizenship. Peterson's chapter shows how the 'civic republican' tradition, which privileges political participation, was far from declared, open and transparent at the time of the Crick Report even though it is the political philosophy underpinning the Citizenship curriculum. Ian Davies' chapter (Chapter 3) compares and contrasts the 'communitarian' and 'civic republican' roots of citizenship and cogently demonstrates that they are far from the 'either/or' option they are sometimes thought to be and that it would be a mistake to equate these with the Left or Right on the political spectrum. What is important to note, as far as the analysis in this chapter is concerned, is that curriculum models of education for citizenship derive from certain sets of beliefs (Arthur and Davison, 2002: 30).

Citizenship: the new RE?

There are twin emphases within Education for Democratic Citizenship: democratization and human rights. Arguably, these form the twin pillars of the brave new secular state 'religion' in democratic societies. A key emphasis of Education for Democratic Citizenship is the emphasis on human rights. Yet there are many citizens who may view the emphasis on individual rights and democratization as a cause for concern. While their secular compatriots are putting their faith in human rights legislation to offer them 'protection', some religious communities may not see this as something to be welcomed. At the very least there is 'a tension between cultural and religious tradition on the one hand and universal notions of rights' (Gearon and Brown, 2003: 205) on the other. We should not forget that 'dignity does not depend solely on individual *rights*' (Burtonwood, 2000: 281, my italics). When the 'ethic of contract becomes more and more the pervasive ethic of society' (Wolterstorff *et al.*, 2004: 91) we need to consider the implications for the choice citizens exercise and the freedom they enjoy. The same is true of the democratization of schools. A family with a pervasively religious rather than a secular worldview, who have firsthand experience of the injustices and inequalities that are possible within a secular liberal democratic society, may not see democratization as a panacea for all perceived injustice. Indeed if they privilege hierarchy and respect for authority above democratization, they may view the prospect of their children's schools becoming *more* democratic with dismay.

It has been suggested that Citizenship is the 'new RE' but there is one important difference between the two subjects beyond their content that should be noted. Since the 1960s RE (religious education), in most schools in England, has rejected a 'confessional' approach, which was designed to nurture children in the Christian faith, and adopted a 'phenomenological' approach, whereby religion is studied as a phenomenon. Conversely citizenship education might be regarded as 'confessional' rather than 'phenomenological' as it teaches children and young people to 'believe in' its doctrines (Pike, 2008). Citizenship is not *about* democracy, it is *for* democracy as it seeks to nurture children in the democratic faith. It has even been claimed that freedom can only be experienced when 'a nation state is unified around a set of democratic values' (Banks *et al.*, 2005: 7). Clearly, there is the 'danger of disintegration in societies that can no longer be forced into unity around a shared religious faith' that 'has haunted the liberal tradition since its inception', and comprehensive liberalism may be thought to exacerbate the danger by attempting to ground legitimacy in a 'divisive secular analogue to religious faith' (Rawls, 1993: 37–38). While it has been suggested that 'the liberal educator has to promote the values that are necessary to living in a liberal society' but should 'stop short of promoting a liberal set of moral beliefs or lifestyle' (Haydon 1997: 128), the task of distinguishing between *political* and *cultural* liberalism in the citizenship lesson is far from straightforward. Distinguishing between being a good *citizen* and being a good *person* presents the same sort of problem.

Education policy for civic and personal virtue: fostering good citizens

Support for liberal democracy (Pike, 2008) rather than support for moral or character education seems to have been the priority of government education policy in the UK between 1997 and 2010 under New Labour. However, Peterson in Chapter 16 suggests the emphasis may change under the Conservative-Liberal Democrat Coalition that took office in 2010 given two key policy intentions of the Coalition government: the Big Society and the National Citizen Service. Certainly, David Cameron sees the task of government being to 'help build responsible *character* in people' (cited in Arthur, 2010: 6, my italics).

The similarities and differences between character education and citizenship education have been discussed elsewhere (Davies *et al.*, 2005) and, put simply, the emphasis in citizenship is upon *political* knowledge and activity (the 'informed' and 'active' citizen) rather than *moral* knowledge and activity or the development of good character. The problem is that life is not as simple as that. Ian Davies, in Chapter 3 of this book, agrees with Derek Heater that being 'virtuous' is important in the fulfilment of both the civic republican and liberal aims of citizenship (Heater, 1999: 177) and Eamonn Callan (1997: 3) has promoted a 'politics of virtue' aimed at 'creating virtuous citizens'. But what do different people mean by 'virtue'? This is a good question because we live in a plural society. It certainly makes little sense to separate the *civic* virtues of the citizen from his or her *personal* virtue and character.

In a context where the emphasis in official policy has been more upon citizenship education (QCA, 1998; DFEE/QCA, 1999; Crick, 2000; Pike, 2006) than moral and character education (Arthur, 2003, 2010; Pike 2009, 2010) many teachers may feel decidedly uncomfortable when it comes to teaching children how to live. Character education, whereby children and young people are taught with the intention that they should acquire certain values and virtues, tends to be viewed with suspicion, and even alarm, by those who privilege autonomy as the aim of education. In some quarters, character education is even regarded as indoctrinatory. Gerald Grace points out that 'character education is compromised by its historical associations with various forms of religious and moral indoctrination' (Arthur, 2003: x). It is important to note, however, that many of those who have reservations about promoting character education and personal virtue have no qualms about inculcating democratic values. The paradox is that while accepting the legitimacy of instrumental citizenship education that seeks to inculcate certain loyalties and commitments, beliefs and values, many educationists have been sceptical about moral and character education.

The first point to make when there are concerns about schooling being 'indoctrinatory' is that education and schooling are deeply value-laden and it is impossible for schooling to be neutral as far as character and morality are concerned. As we saw at the opening of this chapter, this is especially true of citizenship education. No tool is neutral once it is in human hands and no curriculum is neutral in the hands of government or teachers. If one of the reasons for the reluctance to teach specific values is that teachers do not want to be accused of indoctrination, the sobering reality is that, taken literally, all teachers are 'indoctrinators' (although not in the pejorative sense) for a 'doctrine' is a 'teaching' and to 'in-doctrinate' is to lead others into that 'teaching'. The second point to make is that an occupational hazard of school teaching is that one usually leads learners into particular 'teachings' and this should not be considered to be wrong *per se*. For instance, schools in Western liberal democracies routinely 'indoctrinate' children in the value of 'tolerance' (although what we mean by this needs careful analysis and is explored towards the end of this chapter). Schooling in general, not just citizenship education, is an instrumental practice that seeks to change children in specific ways. Even if we do not focus on the more obviously value-laden areas of the curriculum, the lessons, processes and procedures of schools, as well as the attitudes and interactions of people within them, all communicate powerful messages to children and young people about what is of greater or lesser worth, what is more valuable and what is less valuable. The question is not *whether* schooling teaches children how to live but *how* it does so and *what* values it teaches. An even better question might be to ask how children and young people learn to live and the values they acquire.

Core values in citizenship and character education

This raises a number of ethical questions: In a diverse, plural society, whose values should we teach? If there is disagreement in society about matters of fundamental importance, is it not rather dangerous to bring such matters up in school? Might it not be especially dangerous in schools where children come from different communities that have different values? Would it not be better, and more conducive to community cohesion, to just pretend that we all agree? Would it not be safer to focus on skills and knowledge (and effectiveness and efficiency in numeracy and literacy) rather than becoming enmeshed with difficult and controversial areas such as the teaching of right and wrong that is part and parcel of character education?

The situation may not be as fraught as we might at first imagine. Teaching common core values in a diverse, plural society might after all be possible. Tom Lickona, one of the world's leading authorities on character education, notes that:

> Despite this diversity, we can identify basic, shared values that allow us to engage in public moral education in a pluralistic society. Indeed, pluralism itself is not possible without agreement on values such as justice, honesty, civility, democratic process, and a respect for truth.
>
> (Lickona, 1991: 20)

Certainly Lickona's 'Ten Essential Virtues' are 'found in cultures and religions around the world' (Lickona, 2004: 8) and a brief summary of each of these virtues will enable us to see what we can all agree on and what all schools could teach:

- Wisdom or Good Judgement: knowing when to act, how to act and how to balance the virtues when they conflict – like telling the truth when it will cause hurt;
- Justice: includes interpersonal virtues such as civility, honesty, respect, responsibility and tolerance – moral indignation in the face of injustice;
- Fortitude: courage, resilience, patience, perseverance, endurance and self-confidence are part of fortitude – we develop our character more through sufferings than successes – setbacks make us stronger so long as we don't feel sorry for ourselves;
- Temperance: self-control and the ability to govern ourselves, to regulate our sensual appetites – pursue legitimate pleasures even in moderation – the power to resist temptation;
- Love: goes beyond fairness and justice – love is selfless – willingness to sacrifice oneself for the sake of another – best summed up in 'love your neighbour as yourself';
- A Positive Attitude: our happiness or misery depends on our dispositions and not on our circumstances – we're as happy as we make up our minds to be;
- Hard Work: includes initiative, diligence, goal setting and resourcefulness – an old-fashioned virtue;

- Integrity: being faithful to moral conscience, keeping our word, standing up for what we believe – to have integrity is to be 'whole' so that what we say and do in different situations is consistent;
- Gratitude: choosing to be thankful is the secret of a happy life – we all drink from wells we did not dig – counting our everyday blessings;
- Humility: avoiding pride, taking responsibility, apologizing, making amends – not causing harm because we want to feel important.

Such a list will appear daunting even to the best of citizens. Yet according to Lickona, although we all fall short, we all possess these virtues to some degree. Many public (state) schools in the USA have been influenced by work such as Lickona's on character education although such explicitness about virtues or core values appears to be much less common in the UK. However, lest we were to think of 'character education' as an American invention (at least so far as the last sixty or seventy years are concerned) educators in England have no further to look than the University of Oxford at the time of the Second World War. C.S. Lewis, who lectured at Oxford in political philosophy as well as literature, draws a disturbing picture in the first chapter of *The Abolition of Man* (Lewis, 1978/1943: 19) that is entitled 'Men without Chests' to signify that the heads of people (that our education system has fostered) look so much bigger than their chests. In fact, the 'heads are no bigger than the ordinary: it is the atrophy of the chest beneath that makes them seem so' (ibid.: 19). In other words, the intellect has been nurtured but not the character for the chest is the seat 'of emotions organized by trained habit into stable sentiments' (ibid.). It is significant that Lewis refers to 'trained habit' because character education 'has long relied upon an Aristotelian principle that character is formed in large part through habitual behaviour that eventually becomes internalized into virtues (character)' (Berkowitz and Bier, 2004: 80).

For Lewis, the 'sentiments' are vital for it 'may even be said that it is by this middle element that man is man' (Lewis, 1978/1943: 19). By this he means that our character and 'just sentiments' are what make us fully human. By our moral sense we constitute more than an intellect (the head) and we are more than an animal with appetite (the stomach) for we have character (chests). For our 'sentiments' to be 'just', and in order to be of good character, our moral sense requires a true guide. Lewis, in common with character educators such as Lickona, has recourse to Natural Law which he terms the *Tao*. As an appendix to *The Abolition of Man*, he gives 'Illustrations of the *Tao*', eight examples drawn from different cultures and traditions such as the ancient Egyptian, Babylonian, Old Norse, Chinese, Indian, Jewish, Roman, Greek and Native American. Unsurprisingly the list is similar to Lickona's. According to the *Tao*, or Natural Law, certain actions '*merit*, our approval or disapproval' (ibid.: 14). Lewis uses terms such as 'righteousness', 'correctness', 'order' and 'truth' to denote the *Tao* and this has important implications for both character and citizenship education: 'Hence the educational problem is wholly different according as you stand within or without the *Tao*. For those within, the task is to train in the pupil those responses which are in themselves appropriate' (ibid.: 17). According to Lewis, the 'task of the modern educator is not to cut down jungles but to irrigate deserts' and by this he means that it is as teachers 'inculcate just sentiments' (ibid.: 13) that they are irrigating deserts and enabling good character to thrive and flourish. It is important for citizenship and character educators to understand what is meant by 'just sentiments' and it is not to the English or to the Americans but to the Greeks and the early Church Fathers that Lewis turns:

> St Augustine defines virtue as *ordo amoris*, the ordinate condition of the affections in which every object is accorded that kind and degree of love which is appropriate to it. Aristotle says that the aim of education is to make the pupil like and dislike what he ought. When the age for reflective thought comes, the pupil who has been thus trained in 'ordinate affections' or '*just sentiments*' will easily find the first principles in *Ethics*.
>
> (ibid.: 14–15, my italics)

Common core values and comprehensive moral education?

There will, however, be certain limitations to citizenship and character education if it relies exclusively on common core values derived from Natural Law. In discussing core values and how agreement can be reached in a diverse society, Arthur (2005) draws upon Sunstein's (1994) analysis of how law is possible in a heterogeneous society. Put simply, the idea is that people of different faiths and with different commitments are able to show respect for one another because outcomes are agreed upon and difference regarding basic or fundamental commitments is tolerated. Arguably, this is the way in which most schools operate; there is agreement on the need for particular results, behaviour or actions on the part of students, while the justification for the behaviour or action is often left unexplored. In other words, 'Teachers and pupils will have divergent rationales for guiding their actions, but these are deliberately left unexplained' so that 'not specifying the rationale for actions allows a community to live together and for its members to show each other mutual respect' (Arthur, 2005: 250–51). Yet if we have a process of 'agreeing rules without having a theory to justify such rules' (ibid.: 251), this 'may not be morally right as a guiding principle in education' (ibid.: 253). Ethically, this may be the weakness of many forms of citizenship and character education:

> Character educators who argue that we should develop moral characters without believing in the truth of morality do so from an impoverished position. They want the forms and outcomes of traditional character education without the substance of particular beliefs and sanctions.
>
> (Arthur, 2010: 86)

According to Glanzer, a 'limited' approach to moral and character education 'derived from a particular moral tradition based in the social contract narrative' is the cause of systemic failure in citizenship and character education because liberalism 'fundamentally does not endorse a particular comprehensive vision of the good for individuals or groups – even through its public education system' (Glanzer, 2003: 293). Glanzer focuses on the specific charge made in the *The Death of Character* (Hunter, 2000) that an ostensibly inclusive and non-partisan approach to moral and character education actually 'obliterates the differences of particular communities and creeds and empties morality of its substance and depth' in an effort 'to capitalize on what habitus remains by creating an inclusive moral vocabulary that is shared by all' (ibid.: 225). It has even been claimed that highly respected character educators, such as Lickona, 'take an approach that divorces conceptions of virtue from particular traditions' and that while teaching common virtues 'these approaches avoid narratives for defining, understanding and applying these virtues' (Glanzer, 2003: 300). Indeed, Glanzer pins the blame for the demise of moral and character education in public schools in the USA upon 'the current structure of American public education that encourages moral educators to provide forms of moral education divorced from particularity and acceptable to all' (ibid.: 294). According to Glanzer (2003), we are presented with a choice of *either* being able to provide core values that are particular and comprehensively meaningful for the child *or* being inclusive but lacking comprehensive vision and moral authority. I shall contend in the following section that the situation is more complex than the 'either-or' choice that Glanzer seems to give us; we are not, for instance, only given the choice of either secular or religious citizenship.

Christianity and citizenship education

Equally, in the UK and other Western nations, which are characterized by secularism and diversity but which also have an influential Christian heritage, we should not ignore the relation between Christianity and citizenship (Arthur, 2003; Freathy, 2007). Certainly, 'for a considerable proportion of English history and for a considerable proportion of the population, consideration of social and moral responsibilities and community involvement would have been inconceivable without reference to Christian beliefs and ethics' (Freathy, 2007: 372). For Arthur (2010), 'Christianity offers a religious narrative in order to access the virtues' and notes that according to traditional Christian teaching 'matters of right and wrong have an objective basis' so that 'values are not matters of opinion – they are not relative, and we can teach them to others' (ibid.: 87). The capacity of such Christian faith to inspire character and citizenship education in a plural twenty-first century Britain requires careful examination, especially when a third of the school age population attend schools with a Christian foundation.

A recent case study of a school with a Christian foundation (Pike, 2010) illustrates how core values can be agreed upon and embraced by a wide range of students while the perceived sources of those values differ. The core values of the school in question bear a striking resemblance to Lickona's 'essential virtues':

Honourable Purpose: We aim to be positive in everything, doing what is good and aiming to benefit others as well as ourselves;

Humility: We seek to do our personal best without bragging and to encourage others to achieve their best without being critical or jealous of their efforts;

Compassion: We care for those who are in difficulty and who are hurting, recognizing that the world does not exist for us alone;

Integrity: We can be trusted to be honest and truthful, to say what we mean and to do what we say;

Accountability: We recognize that having the freedom to express ourselves means we must also accept responsibility for our words, thoughts and actions;

Courage: We aim to do what is right, whatever the cost; we stand up for the weak, whatever the danger; we face our fears and find ways of defeating them;

Determination: We know that hard work and the refusal to give up are essential if we are to achieve anything worthwhile.

What is of particular interest in the light of the views of Arthur (2003, 2010) and Glanzer (2003) is that although the school's core values appear secular and are not in any way overtly 'religious', it was also open and transparent about its Christian foundation. It was clear from interviews with school leaders that although 'Jesus Christ is the model for human virtues within the Christian faith community' (Arthur, 2003: 56) and had inspired the school's core values, these values were accessible to a largely secular student body. Indeed, one might say that, in this respect, it reflects the situation in the country as a whole. During focus group work with 14-year-old students I was told, 'Whether you are a Christian or you aren't, the school's core values are good values to follow'. Subsequently, a survey of the 191 students in Year 9 and 101 staff at the school (all of whom completed and returned their anonymous questionnaires in my presence) showed that 99 per cent of staff and 96 per cent of students 'agreed' or 'strongly agreed' with this statement. The school's core values provide the basis for its character education but just as the school is inclusive and 'non-selective' being 'open to children of all faiths and none' so too, are its core values. This shows us that people may differ in their beliefs about the sources of, or justification for, the values they share. Nevertheless they can agree on core values such as 'kindness':

> A Christian could claim that treating people kindly is justified because the Bible or God says that it is justified. A Kantian might say that treating people kindly is justified because reason dictates that we should treat people as ends and not only as means. … We can imagine, then, a Catholic and a secular Kantian who endorse an identical set of liberal political values. But the Catholic believes that these values are justified (at least in part) because God and the Catholic Church have sanctioned them as moral truths. The secular Kantian, on the other hand, believes that the only possible normative source of moral values is our nature as autonomous human beings.
>
> (Dagowitz, 2004)

Herein lies the source, I suggest, of the consensual solution we seek. Rather than the usual *modus vivendi* of avoiding discussion of the *sources* of values or the ways in which values are justified, I contend that these are precisely what we should be discussing in schools. Indeed, genuine tolerance is only possible if disagreement is acknowledged and respected.

By acknowledging and respecting the Judaeo-Christian tradition as a source of shared values in a liberal democratic society the leadership of the case study school did not seek to impose the religious truth claims of Christianity on students but neither did they eschew the sources of values and the narratives in which those values are located. Students' autonomy can be supported by such transparency when they are encouraged to explore the sources of values promoted through the curriculum. The pressing challenge for character and citizenship educators is to find ways of enabling young people to engage ethically with the sources of the values underpinning their education.

Of course there are those who would rather the case study school limited itself to a promotion of its 'secular' core values and did not bother to declare its source or inspiration for them. Professor Brenda Almond, who is well known for her work in applied ethics, has observed 'the emergence of an increasingly powerful form of secularism' that is 'intolerant of religion' and asks 'How can this have happened in countries like Britain and the USA in which tolerance and liberty, especially freedom of religion and freedom of thought and of speech, are amongst their highest political ideals?' (Almond, 2010: 139). Of course Almond is right and schools with a pervasive secular ethos that 'maintain a deafening silence about spiritual or anti-materialist values' (Brighouse, 2005: 85) are not a neutral alternative to those that declare the religious inspiration for their values. As Almond (2010) demonstrates, tolerance and respect in a plural society is entirely compatible with disagreement and it is possible to behave respectfully, courteously and considerately to those with whom one profoundly disagrees about religious truth claims or sexual ethics. Toleration, rightly understood, is about respecting difference rather than being forced, in an entirely illiberal fashion, to celebrate beliefs or practices which one believes to be wrong. Yet the possibility of having a Christian foundation, for instance, while respecting diversity is sometimes doubted by those who are uneasy about referring to the Judaeo-Christian sources of much citizenship and character education.

If secularists have concerns about 'core values' or 'essential virtues' being seen by some people as 'Christian', they should be aware that while the life, work, ministry and teaching of Christ have influenced the values of many schools and societies, adopting those values cannot, according to the New Testament, make one a Christian; one comes to Christ not on the basis of good character but by faith (Ephesians, 2: 8–9). Further, young citizens should be helped to understand the importance of biblical 'source' texts for the tolerance, liberty and equality they experience in a liberal democracy (Pike, 2009). Lickona notes that 'we should help students appreciate that every person has intrinsic dignity and value – sacred value, if one believes that we are each created in the image of God' (Lickona, 2004: 140). The teacher of citizenship is not awarded more votes than the cleaner of his or her classroom (on the basis of superior knowledge) and the influence of the Christian tradition upon citizenship in our democratic society should not be ignored.

Conclusion

Although many liberal educators are suspicious of 'character education' it has recently re-emerged in educational policy in the UK (Arthur, 2005) and citizenship educators in particular should not fail to see its importance. There are important initiatives such as 'Learning for Life: Exploring Core Values' (Character Education, 2010), as well as examples of good practice in many schools such as the one referred to in this chapter (Pike, 2010). Yet character education, that enables young people to consider the sources of values, is much less common in Britain than one might hope. We need more not less discussion about the sources of our core values in character and citizenship education.

Questions for further investigation

1 Which values should all schools seek to inculcate in their students and why?
2 Why is it so important to discuss the sources of values in citizenship education?
3 Is citizenship the 'new RE'? What are the implications for teachers and students if it is?
4 Why is Christianity still important in citizenship education for our diverse society?
5 Why is encouraging 'tolerance as respect' a more justifiable ethical stance than requiring 'toleration as celebration' in a plural society?

Suggested further reading

Almond, B. (2010) 'Education for tolerance: cultural difference and family values', *Journal of Moral Education*, 39, 2, pp. 131–43. This is a seminal article on the new tolerance debate and essential reading.

Arthur, J. (2010) *Of Good Character: Exploring virtues and values in 3–25 year-olds*. Exeter: Imprint Academic. This short book reports findings from a major funded research project into the values of children and young people and succinctly discusses findings in context.

Arthur, J., Harrison, T. and Wilson, K. (2010) Character Education, *Learning for Life: Exploring core values* [online] available at: http://www.learningforlife.org.uk (accessed on 14th September 2011).

Halstead, J.M. and Pike, M.A. (2006) *Citizenship and Moral Education*. London: Routledge. This book provides the philosophical background to learning values and then gives practical pedagogic examples from citizenship lessons across the curriculum.

Lickona, T. (2004) *Character Matters*. London: Touchstone. This is one of the most important books on character education from a very well-respected, world-leading character educator.

References

Almond, B. (2010) 'Education for tolerance: cultural difference and family values', *Journal of Moral Education, 39*, 2, pp. 131–43.

Arthur, J. (2003) *Education with Character*. London: Routledge.

——(2005) 'The re-emergence of character education in British education policy', *British Journal of Educational Studies, 53*, 3, pp. 239–54.

——(2010) *Of Good Character: Exploring virtues and values in 3–25 year-olds*. Exeter: Imprint Academic.

Arthur, J. and Davison, J. (2002) 'Experiential learning, social literacy and the curriculum', in Scott, D. and Lawson, H. (Eds.) *Citizenship Education and the Curriculum* (Vol. 3). Westport, CA: Greenwood Publishing. pp. 27–44.

Banks, J.A., McGee Banks, C.A., Cortés, C.E., Hahn, C.L., Merryfield, M. M., Moodley, K.A., Murphy-Shigematsu, S., Osler, A., Park, C. and Parker, W.C. (2005) *Democracy and Diversity: Principles and concepts for educating citizens in a global age*. Seattle, WA: University of Washington. Available at: http://depts.washington.edu/centerme/DemDiv.pdf (accessed 31st October 2010).

Berkowitz, M. and Bier, M. (2004) 'Research-based character education', *The ANNALS of the American Academy of Political and Social Science, 591*, 1, pp. 72–85.

Biesta, G. and Lawy, R. (2006) 'From teaching citizenship to learning democracy: overcoming individualism in research, policy and practice', *Cambridge Journal of Education, 36*, 1, pp. 63–79.

Brighouse, H. (2005) 'Faith-based schools in the United Kingdom: an unenthusiastic defence of a slightly reformed status quo', in Gardner, R., Cairns, J. and Lawton, D. (Eds.) *Faith Schools: Consensus or Conflict*. London: RoutledgeFalmer. pp. 83–9.

Burtonwood, N. (2000) 'Must liberal support for separate schools be subject to a condition of individual autonomy?', *British Journal of Educational Studies, 48*, 3, pp. 269–84.

Callan, E. (1997) *Creating Citizens*. Oxford: Oxford University Press.

Crick, B. (2000) *Essays on Citizenship*. London: Continuum.

Dagowitz, A. (2004) 'When choice does not matter: political liberalism, religion and the faith school debate', *Journal of Philosophy of Education, 38*, 2, pp. 239–54.

Davies, I., Gorard, S. and McGuinn, N. (2005) 'Citizenship education and character education: similarities and contrasts', *British Journal of Educational Studies, 53*, 3, pp. 341–58.

Dewey, J. (1966/2002) *Democracy and Education*. New York, NY: Macmillan.

DfEE/QCA (1999) *Citizenship – The National Curriculum for England*. London: HMSO.

Freathy, R. (2007) 'Ecclesiastical and religious factors which preserved Christian and traditional forms of citizenship in English schools, 1934–44', *Oxford Review of Education, 33*, 3, pp. 367–77.

Gearon, L. and Brown, M. (Eds.) (2003) 'Active participation in citizenship', *Learning to Teach Citizenship in the Secondary School*. London: Routledge. pp. 203–24.

Glanzer, P. (2003) 'Did the moral education establishment kill character? An autopsy of *The Death of Character*', *Journal of Moral Education, 32*, 3, pp. 291–306.

Halstead, J.M. and Pike, M.A. (2006) *Citizenship and Moral Education*. London: Routledge.

Haydon, G. (1997) *Teaching about Values: A new approach*. London: Cassell.

Heater, D. (1999) *What is Citizenship?* Cambridge: Polity Press.

Hunter, J. (2000) *The Death of Character: Moral education in an age without good or evil*. New York, NY: Basic Books.

Kymlicka, W. (2003) 'Two dilemmas of citizenship education in pluralist societies', in Lockyer, A., Crick, B. and Annette, J. (Eds.) *Education for Democratic Citizenship: Issues of theory and practice*. Aldershot: Ashgate. pp. 47–63.

Learning for Life: Exploring Core Values (2010). Available at: http://www.learning forlife.org.uk.

Lewis, C.S. (1978/1943) *The Abolition of Man*. Glasgow/Oxford: Fount Paperbacks/ Oxford University Press.

Lickona, T. (1991) *Educating for Character: How our schools can teach respect and responsibility*. New York, NY: Bantam Books.

Lickona, T. (2004) *Character Matters*. London: Touchstone.

McLaughlin, T.H. (2000) 'Citizenship education in England: Crick Report and beyond', *Journal of Philosophy of Education*, 34, 4, pp. 541–70.

Mill, J.S. (1909) *On Liberty* (Vol. 25, Part 2). New York, NY: Collier.

Osler, A. and Starkey, H. (2005) *Education for Democratic Citizenship: A review of research, policy and practice 1995–2005*. London: BERA.

Pike, M.A. (2006) 'From beliefs to skills: the secularization of literacy and the moral education of citizens', *Journal of Beliefs and Values*, 27, 3, pp. 281–89.

Pike, M.A. (2007) 'The state and citizenship education in England: a curriculum for subjects or citizens?', *Journal of Curriculum Studies*, 39, 4, pp. 471–89.

Pike, M.A. (2008) 'Faith in citizenship? On teaching children to believe in liberal democracy', *British Journal of Religious Education*, 30, 2, pp. 113–22.

Pike, M.A. (2009) 'Religious freedom and rendering to Caesar: reading democratic and faith-based values in curriculum, pedagogy and policy', *Oxford Review of Education*, 35, 1, pp. 1–14.

Pike, M.A. (2010) 'Transaction and transformation at Trinity: private sponsorship, core values and Christian ethos at England's most improved academy', *Oxford Review of Education*, 36, 6, pp. 749–65.

QCA (1998) *Education for Citizenship and the Teaching of Democracy in Schools: Final report of the Advisory Group on Citizenship*. London: QCA.

Rawls, J. (1993) *Political Liberalism*. New York, NY: Columbia University Press.

Sunstein, C.R. (1994) 'Political conflict and legal argument', The Tanner Lectures on Human Values, Harvard University, 29th–30th November 1994.

Wolterstorff, N., Joldersma, C.W. and G. Stronks, G. (Eds.) (2004) *Educating For Shalom*. Grand Rapids, MI: Eerdmans.

Chapter 16

Where now for citizenship education?

Andrew Peterson

CANTERBURY CHRIST CHURCH UNIVERSITY

Introduction

A reflection on the future for citizenship education is both pertinent and challenging. It is now over a decade since the publication of the highly influential final report of the Advisory Group on *Education for Citizenship and the Teaching of Democracy in Schools* (QCA, 1998, hereafter referred to as the Crick Report), which not only led and shaped the introduction of citizenship education in schools, but also provided a blueprint for contemporary understandings of the subject. The Citizenship Order (Education (National Curriculum) (Attainment Target and Programmes of Study in Citizenship) (England) Order 2000), which established statutory programmes of study for Key Stage 3 and Key Stage 4 to be taught from August 2002, and was supplemented by non-statutory programmes of study for Citizenship and PSHE for Key Stage 1 and Key Stage 2, 'followed the reasoning of the Crick Report to a considerable extent' (Annette, 2005: 329). So too, the revised statutory programmes of study for citizenship education published in 2007 (for teaching from September 2008) were heavily informed by the Crick Report's delineation of three strands of citizenship education, namely social and moral responsibility, community involvement and political literacy. Whilst there is evidence of clear progress in the teaching of citizenship in schools (as the other chapters in this volume suggest) issues certainly remain for the teaching of citizenship in England.

The analysis offered here is challenging because of the complexity and dynamism of education and educational initiatives in England as well as the changing use of the term 'citizenship' in political and policy discourse (see Keating *et al.*, 2009, section 1.4.1) The results of the General Election of May 2010 and the establishment of a coalition government between the Conservative Party and the Liberal Democratic Party under the leadership of David Cameron has brought into sharp focus the question of how a change of government may impact upon the subject in schools. Whilst at the time of writing it is too early to know precisely what the new government's intentions concerning citizenship education are, there are reasons for both pessimism and optimism. On the one hand the coalition government has not explicitly committed its support for maintaining the statutory requirements for citizenship education (something which had caused much concern for the subject association for citizenship – the Association of Citizenship Teaching) and appears committed to reform of the National Curriculum in favour of the core curriculum subjects as well as a strengthening of the place of History. On the other hand, the aims of citizenship education are clearly commensurable with two key policy intentions of the coalition government – the Big Society and the National Citizen Service – and whilst key figures have not fully committed their support to the subject, there has been no explicit statement of intention to remove it from or radically change its place in the curriculum. So what next for citizenship education?

Before considering the question of where now for citizenship education, it is worthwhile briefly setting out a baseline. The 2009 report of the National Foundation for Educational Research's Citizenship Education Longitudinal Study (Keating *et al.*, 2009: 1) provides a detailed analysis of provision in England based around the central research question 'How far has citizenship education become embedded in schools in England since 2002, and what does the future hold?' In considering contrasting data between 2002 and 2009, the report makes a number of positive statements. Such positives include the allocation of more discrete curriculum time for citizenship, increasing evidence of a more strategic approach to integrating citizenship education within and beyond the curriculum, improved links between citizenship and wider school activities and initiatives, and greater levels of, and opportunities for, student participation and pupil voice (Keating *et al.*, 2009: 10, 21, 36, 48). Similarly, the most recent Ofsted (2010: 5) subject report for citizenship education also presents a number of positive developments. Most fundamentally, its first key finding is that '[T]here is evidence that provision and outcomes for students are improving overall. Progress in establishing citizenship securely in the curriculum has been steady. Even in the schools where provision was weak, there was mostly an encouraging direction of travel'. However, evidence also suggests that, aside from an uncertain policy context, serious challenges remain for citizenship education in schools in terms of conceptual definitions, curriculum construction, and pedagogy. Notably, as Keating *et al.* (2009: 10, 21, 36, 48) make clear, where citizenship education is less established such learning is not always explicit for pupils, is characterised by less active forms of learning, may have low status, and has little discrete curriculum time. Moreover, there is consistent evidence that the teaching of citizenship and its place within a school's curriculum, culture and community is likely to be of higher quality where there are specialist teachers and a committed senior management team, and of less quality where these are not in place (cf. Faulks, 2006).

It goes beyond the scope of this chapter to consider more than a few responses to the question 'Where now for citizenship education?' The content here is for this reason selective. The chapter focuses primarily, though not exclusively, on the context of citizenship education in secondary schools in England, and has started by briefly considering the current context of this. It now proceeds to discuss two issues – aims and purpose, and the nature of active citizenship – which are essential foci if citizenship education is to further cement and develop its place in the curriculum of schools.

Citizenship: aims and purpose?

In their report entitled *Towards Consensus?*, Ofsted (2006: i) made clear that, at that time, there was 'not yet a strong consensus about the aims of citizenship education'. It is noteworthy, however, that more recent reports on citizenship education (Keating *et al.*, 2009; Ofsted, 2010) remain largely silent on the aims and purposes of the subject beyond simply the content of the Crick Report and the National Curriculum programmes of study. In doing so, such reports carry the implicit suggestion that the aims and purposes of citizenship education have not changed since 1998 and are agreed (even if they are not shared). This is despite a large amount of academic discourse which either questions the content of the Crick Report (Faulks, 2006; Gillborn, 2006; Osler, 2000; Tooley, 2000) or which recognises that the aims and purposes set out within it are open to interpretation (Arthur, 2000; McLaughlin, 2000; Peterson, 2009). For this reason, there is some justification in approaching such perceptions with a level of scepticism. The intention in this section is to suggest why present presentations of the aims and purpose of citizenship education are problematic and, following this, to offer some tentative suggestions about possible ways forward in this area.

A frequent starting point for considering the aims of citizenship education in English schools is the Crick Report which, in its most famous statement, asserted that:

> We aim at no less than a change in the political culture of this country both nationally and locally: for people to think of themselves as active citizens, willing, able and equipped to have an influence in public life.
>
> (QCA, 1998: 1.5, 7–8)

Whilst spiriting and engaging, this aim is broad in nature. Similarly, the less frequently referenced 'aim and purpose', which the Advisory Group set out in their proposed framework for citizenship education, is open to a number of interpretations:

> The purpose of citizenship education in schools and colleges is to make secure and to increase the knowledge, skills and values relevant to the nature and practices of participative democracy; also to enhance awareness of rights and duties, and the sense of responsibilities needed for the development of pupils into active citizens; and in doing so to establish the value to individuals, schools and society of involvement in the local and wider community.
>
> Democratic institutions, practices and purposes must be understood, both local and national, including the work of parliaments, councils, parties, pressure groups and voluntary bodies; to show how formal political activity relates to civil society in the context of the United Kingdom and Europe, and to cultivate awareness and concerns for world affairs and global issues.

Some understanding of the realities of economic life is needed including how taxation and public expenditure work together.

(QCA, 1998: 6.6, 40)

As McLaughlin (2000: 553) suggests the Crick Report 'did not articulate its conceptions in theoretical terms'. This permitted a number of benefits. Not least, flexibility was provided for schools and teachers in interpreting these in the context of their own communities. Crick (2000: 80) reflected in relation to the Citizenship Order (Education (National Curriculum) (Attainment Target and Programmes of Study in Citizenship) (England) Order 2000), the 'virtue of the Order is that the generality of its prescriptions will leave the school and the teacher with a good deal of freedom and discretion'. The open nature of the aim and purpose of citizenship education also reflected Crick's own belief that 'in a free country ... citizenship education must not be centrally directed in detail, only in broad but clear principles' (2000: 9). The original programmes of study established by the statutory Citizenship Order, as one would perhaps expect with curricular documentation, did not include a justification or conceptual definition of the subject. More recently, the revised National Curriculum for Citizenship (QCDA, 2007: 27) contains an importance statement which sets out the key foundations of the subjects. However, the content of this statement is expressed largely in terms of outcomes. For example, pupils are to 'take an interest in topical and controversial issues', 'engage in discussion and debate', 'learn about their rights, responsibilities, duties and freedoms and about laws, justice and democracy', and are equipped to 'engage critically with and explore diverse ideas, beliefs, cultures and identities and the values we share as citizens in the UK' and to 'evaluate information, make informed judgements and reflect on the consequences of their actions now and in the future'. There is a danger that it is the outcomes which themselves become understood as the aims and purpose of the subject. Whilst the revised National Curriculum programmes of study explain that the importance statement 'reflects the three principles of effective citizenship education set out by the Advisory Group' there is limited prospect that teachers of citizenship beyond those who have followed specialist initial teacher education programmes will read the report in full (cf. Keating et al., 2009: 28). Presenting the aims and purpose of citizenship in such open terms has left the subject without a clear underpinning philosophy. This means that key elements of the subject do not have the conceptual or pedagogical clarity necessary to meaningfully inform the subject's practical application in schools in a coherent way. We should remember that '[W]henever societies seek to educate children for citizenship they always have a particular model or conception of citizenship in mind, implicitly or explicitly' (Kymlicka, 2003: 47). But what conception, or indeed conceptions, of citizenship underpins citizenship education in England?

The most common theoretical position identified as underpinning the nature of citizenship education has been a 'civic republican' model of citizenship (Crick, 2000, 2003; Lockyer, 2003; Annette, 2008; Peterson, 2009). The premise for this has been largely identified in the Advisory Group's extolling of the extent to which education for citizenship could, and should, engender a commitment to the common good within pupils. Central to this was the recognition that citizens possess a civic responsibility to participate within their political communities, and that education for citizenship should prepare pupils for this. To this end, the approach to citizenship established within the Crick Report and the Citizenship Order further included a commitment that pupils should learn certain values, attitudes, and skills necessary for political participation and 'sharing in rule as well as in being ruled' (Lockyer, 2003: 2). The referencing of civic republicanism exemplifies, though, that the theoretical conceptual basis of citizenship education may not be clear or cohesive. As Crick (2003: 21) recognised this 'particular tradition of political thought ... might not have been apparent to the general reader (nor possibly to some members of the Advisory Group itself)', and it was 'not yet current in political and public discourse' (2000: 120). Moreover, in addition to this civic republican focus there was enough in the report for some commentators to identify a liberal element (see for example, Lockyer, 2003: 2) and for others to identify communitarian influences (see for example, Arthur, 2000). One reason for this complexity is the diversity of current theoretical positions in contemporary political thought.

Perhaps even more significantly, what is meant when a broad theoretical position is cited as underpinning curricular aims and purpose is not necessarily immediately clear, and therefore requires some degree of exploration. The 'civic republican conception' of citizenship is open to quite different interpretations (Peterson, 2009). Similarly, the term 'liberal' is used to cover a wide spectrum of positions. Over the last two decades a large corpus of work advanced by liberal scholars has looked to incorporate a concern for active citizenship and what have been termed 'civic virtues'. A central component of this has been the belief that education can play an important formative role in producing an active citizenry. The liberal theorist Will Kymlicka (2003: 57), for example, has suggested that '[C]itizenship education is not just a matter of learning the basic facts about the institutions and procedures of political life; it also involves acquiring a range of dispositions, virtues and loyalties that are intimately bound up with the practice of democratic citizenship'. In a comparable vein, Eamonn Callan (1997: 3) has promoted a 'politics of virtue' aimed at 'creating virtuous citizens'.

A further issue for citizenship education in relation to clarity of aims and purpose lies in the multifarious justifications for the subject. McLaughlin (2000) was right to assert that '[T]he differing reasons invoked for the ... notion of citizenship provide a[n] ... indication of uncertainty and disagreement concerning the concept'; a statement which remains pertinent today. Since the Crick Report, citizenship education has been identified in government and curricular policy as helping to support numerous political, social, economic, and educational concerns. These include (but certainly are not limited to) the following: community cohesion, the promotion of British values, overcoming political apathy in young people, challenging youth and juvenile crime, providing a forum for character education, promoting social and economic inclusion, developing financial capability, engaging young people in community action, supporting the Every Child Matters agenda, supporting democratic structures within schools, peer mediation, school improvement, and improving pupil behaviour and attendance. This reminds us that how citizenship education is conceived, both in terms of its need and its nature, is at least partially dependent on the political and educational concerns of the day. Moreover, a multitude of interests continue to shelter 'under the umbrella' of citizenship education (Frazer, 1999: 99–100). Those interests which can be said to have been identified as (either potentially or actually) shaping approaches to the subject include the following: human rights education, global education, character development, developing an awareness of diversity and equality, education for sustainable development, peace education, the promotion of fair trade and environmental education. Each of these comprises a particular purpose which has the capacity to affect that of citizenship education.

The lack of conceptual clarity and agreement about the aims and purpose of citizenship education raises important practical questions for citizenship teaching. Writing before the introduction of citizenship education, McLaughlin outlined a particular concern about:

> [t]he extent to which a fully articulated conception of an educational pro-
> gramme can be realised in practice, and, in particular about what is required
> if the aims, values and principles of the programme can be grasped, and applied,
> by teachers and educational leaders in a significant and non-platitudinous
> way ... The Crick Report insists that teachers and others be provided with a
> clear conception of citizenship education ... if they are to teach it well and
> not merely follow a prescribed set of procedures. What is involved in this,
> however, may be more difficult to achieve than is generally realised, particu-
> larly given the complexity and controversiality of the notion of citizenship ...
> and the need for complex balancing judgements to be made in relation to it.
> (McLaughlin, 2000: 560)

The resonance of this statement remains. Teachers are largely responsible for the implementation of citizenship education in schools, with the curricular arrangements providing local discretion concerning the detail of curriculum content and approach. Within this environment, it is uncertain whether teachers of citizenship education have engaged, or will have the opportunity to engage, in meaningful reflection concerning the underpinning aims of the Citizenship curriculum, despite this being central to an effective understanding of the subject and the quality of its teaching in schools (cf. Davies et al., 1999).

To arrive at a clear and shared aim and purpose for citizenship education is extremely difficult (some might even argue that it is not possible). There is, however, clear benefit in seeking to provide further conceptual analysis in pursuit of clarity. With this in mind, there are a number of possible ways forward. The first is for schools and teachers to think about the theoretical background which informs the approach to citizenship education within their schools, possibly expressing such thinking in the school citizenship policy. Whilst the content of (and differences between) theoretical conceptions of citizenship within liberal, communitarian, and civic republican political thought are essential to clarifying the nature of citizenship and citizenship education, such theories are dense and complex. As such, they may not be immediately accessible to teachers in schools. However, the type of thinking required can productively start from the premise of certain fundamental and enduring questions concerning the nature of citizenship. These are likely to start with basic questions – how citizenship is defined, what constitutes good citizenship, the nature of the relationships between citizens and their communities – and are likely to progress to associated questions – the relationship between individual rights and the common good, the balance between shared values and plural interests, and the nature and scope of political participation. Without some understanding of these questions and their potential answers, it is difficult to comprehend how schools (whether individually or collectively) can make a concerted and informed effort to produce an active citizenry.

A second way forward is for those engaged in citizenship education to be clearer concerning the pedagogical implications of different aims and purposes. If such differences are not clear, then the whole question will lack relevance to the work of schools and teachers. Pajares' (1992) review of research indicates that teachers' beliefs shape their classroom practices, and there is some evidence to suggest that even when asked teachers 'mostly talk[ed] about concepts related to citizenship in minimalist terms with little attention to more sophisticated and contested understandings' (Evans, 2006: 49). Yet, current research reveals little about citizenship teachers' perceptions of the subject's aims. When teachers make a decision regarding whether to teach human rights as absolute and inalienable or to frame them as dependent on corresponding community responsibilities they do so on the basis (often subconscious or implicit) of theoretical positions. Similarly, particular aims and purpose impact on a teacher's decision to prioritise individual preferences over a responsibility to subjugate these towards the common good. Even a desire for neutrality concerning the inculcation of moral values is dependent on a particular philosophical position. In other words, curriculum models of education for citizenship derive from certain sets of beliefs (Arthur and Davison, 2002: 30; Faulks, 2006; Abowitz and Harnish, 2006). For this reason, those involved in citizenship education can benefit from being clearer as to the aims and purpose (as distinct from the outcomes) of the subject at both a local and national level.

Active citizenship: meaning, scope and practical issues

If there is a common aim and purpose of citizenship education it is that pupils should be, and should become, active within their communities. The pursuit of active citizenship in order to produce active citizens has been much discussed, though not in unified terms. There remains both conceptual contestation and practical problems in ensuring that active citizenship is a meaningful and accessible part of the education for citizenship experienced by young people in England. A thematic study conducted across twenty countries found that '[T]he term "active citizenship" is not yet clearly understood or defined' (Nelson and Kerr, 2006: iv). Whilst this report refers to the lack of shared conceptualisations *across* nations, there is also evidence that, in the context of England, there is a lack of shared understanding of the term *within* a nation (Nelson and Kerr, 2005; Peterson and Knowles, 2009). This section considers active citizenship and suggests that certain definitional and practical problems (not un-connected) must be overcome if citizenship education is to fulfil the expectation of actively engaging pupils in their communities.

The concept of active citizenship has a long historical tradition (Abowitz and Harnish, 2006), characterised by its diffuse usage and articulation. In the UK, the concept re-emerged within the political discourse of the Thatcher and Major Conservative governments in the late 1980s and early 1990s, was adopted by New Labour governments between 1997 and 2010, and has recently featured in the early policy formulations of the newly established Conservative-Liberal Democrat coalition government. However, the concept of active citizenship has not necessarily meant the same thing across these administrations, and as Lawson (2001: 166) reminds us, 'the fact that there does not exist one, universally held, definition of citizenship has meant that beliefs about what active citizenship entails differ greatly'.

Conceptually there remains no singular definition of active citizenship within citizenship education. Part of this complexity owes to the proliferation of terms which have been, and continue to be, used. The Crick Report (QCA, 1998: 12, 2.11), for example, employed the terms 'community involvement and service to the community', whereas Crick (2002) himself subsequently prioritised the term 'active citizenship', by which he meant 'the knowledge, skills and values to be effective in public life'. In making this assertion Crick's intention was to deliberately differentiate active citizenship from volunteering and charitable work without an overtly political aspect. The original programmes of study established in the Citizenship Order (Education (National Curriculum) (Attainment Target and Programmes of Study in Citizenship) (England) Order 2000), referenced 'participation and responsible action', whereas the revised curriculum includes the key processes of 'advocacy and representation' and 'taking informed and responsible action'. Impacting on these definitions has been what constitutes 'active citizenship'. Whilst some commentators and policy documents have sought to distinguish between volunteering and active citizenship (Nelson and Kerr, 2005; DCLG, 2006: 12), others have promoted a wider notion of active citizenship which incorporates altruistic acts such as charitable work and philanthropy (Ellis, 2005; HoC, 2007). In their work, Benton *et al.* (2008: xi) adopt a position which encompasses formal political participation as well as informal civic and civil participation. They define the former as 'narrow participation in civic or state affairs', and the latter as 'broader participation in both civic (state) affairs and community activity'. Included in the latter are 'volunteering, collecting money for a good cause, and taking an interest in local and community issues'.

A further level of complexity owes to a tendency within official reports and policy documents to amalgamate the provision of active citizenship opportunities with the teaching of citizenship using active teaching and learning methods. A result of this practice has been that often, and to quite a large extent, practice in schools which seeks to engage pupils through active teaching and learning methods has been considered as commensurable with the provision of active citizenship activities. Yet, the two elements of citizenship education have important differences. Active citizenship as a learning process can be understood as relating to the idea of *experiential learning*, with students learning through the experience of undertaking active citizenship projects (whether in the school or the wider community). This understanding draws from Kolb's (1998) reflective cycle in which learners start with their own 'concrete experience' and progress through 'reflective observation', 'abstract conceptualisation', and 'active experimentation', before returning to 'concrete experience'. The stages of the cycle involve and support students in drawing out key learning from their activities. This learning includes citizenship knowledge and skills, as well as interpersonal and intrapersonal reflection. The Post-16 Framework (QCA, 2004: 21) for citizenship learning illustrates this approach well, with students asked to 'identify, investigate and think critically about citizenship issues, problems or events of concern to them', to 'decide on and take part in follow-up action, where appropriate', and to 'reflect on, recognise and review their citizenship learning'.

The second understanding of active citizenship – that which presents it in terms of active teaching and learning methods – is different in nature to the first. Here students learn about a citizenship topic or issue through interactive activities, such as discussions, debates, and role-plays. At times within the literature on active citizenship, it is active learning methods, rather than community involvement, which is prioritised. This is illustrated in the 2009 NFER CELS report (Keating *et al.*, 2009) which predominantly conceptualises active citizenship in terms of active teaching methods. This tendency is also evident in Ofsted's response to the difficulties faced by schools in providing pupils with the opportunity to develop skills of 'participation and responsible action'. Recognising that minimal explicit conceptual or methodological guidance had been provided for schools, Ofsted (2004; 2006) established and promoted a range of activities which it suggested were commensurable with the 'responsible action and participation' strand of the original citizenship programmes of study. Significantly, the descriptors proposed by Ofsted relate specifically to classroom and school-based activities within which pupils deploy citizenship knowledge and skills in making responsible suggestions and recommendations through appropriate mechanisms. The descriptors include, for example, 'participation in class debate exercising knowledge and understanding about becoming informed citizens, with pupils making responsible suggestions', 'written and other class and home work arising from work in citizenship taken to sensible conclusions and containing responsible suggestions', and 'drama and other presentations amounting to reflection and conclusions from work undertaken in citizenship'. There are reasons for questioning the application of such descriptors in terms of whether classroom-based teaching and learning activities really meet the original spirit of participation as expressed in the Crick Report, and also in relation to the extent to which practitioners would support them as truly representing active citizenship activities (see Peterson and Knowles, 2009).

A further, more prescient reason for questioning the amalgamation of active citizenship in terms of experiential learning and active teaching and learning methods concerns the legacy of such educational activity. A central feature of the reasoning behind citizenship education has been that enabling pupils to be active citizens whilst at schools will encourage and develop greater levels of participation in future adult life. In other words, participation in civic and civil activity leads to further levels of engagement. The American political and public theorist Benjamin Barber explains that the process involved is one in which '[T]he taste for participation is whetted by participation: democracy breeds democracy' (Barber, 1984: 265), whilst Adrian Oldfield (1990: 155) suggests that the process is not simply 'educative in itself', but that the example set by the initial participators will 'draw ever-widening groups of individuals into the political arena'.

As Wade (2008: 114) points out, there is developing evidence that when pupils engage in service-learning activities which provide opportunities to engage in political activity, positive effects on civic obligation result. We should be careful, therefore, that the educational and societal importance of pupils' experience in active citizenship activities is not reduced by it remaining solely, or even largely, determined in practice by classroom-based active teaching and learning methods. Indeed, case study data from the CELS longitudinal study highlights that the 'link between active citizenship *outside* the classroom and citizenship learning *in* the classroom is not always apparent, to students or staff' (Keating *et al.*, 2009: 57, emphasis in the original). There is clearly further definitional work needed in relation to active citizenship. Most importantly, those engaged in citizenship education (including academics, teachers, schools, and pupils) must seek to understand both the differences between active citizenship and interactive teaching and learning methods, and the relationship between the two.

Perhaps of even more immediate concern for practitioners in school are the practical issues. Such practical issues are numerous. The first is the difficulty of finding curricular time and space for pupils to undertake experiential learning activities. Second, it is a real challenge for many schools to provide experiential learning opportunities for *all* pupils (Keating *et al.*, 2009: 34). Third, assessment of such activities can be problematic (Keating *et al.*, 2009: 30; see also Harrison, this volume) and, perhaps more importantly, can at times detract from pupils' enjoyment of the activity undertaken. Each of these reasons means that active citizenship opportunities are more easily achieved within the context of the school. Whilst this is understandable, it does raise the question of whether the Community Involvement strand of citizenship education prioritised in the Crick Report (QCA, 1998: 12, 2.11) – defined as 'learning about and becoming helpfully involved in the life and concerns of their communities, including learning through community involvement and service to the community' – remains an unfulfilled expectation. What is needed, and is most likely to overcome the challenges identified here, is expertise in providing pupils with a clear methodology for active, meaningful, and enjoyable experiential learning. Often such expertise lies within the third sector, and the models of experiential learning developed and provided by organisations such as Community Service Volunteers, Envision, and Changemakers provide blueprints for effective experiential learning within citizenship education. The key is to ensure that such expertise is drawn into schools to support pupils' involvement within the community in a sustainable way.

Conclusion

These are interesting times for citizenship education. The subject has been a statutory curriculum subject for nearly a decade, and has made some significant progress in many schools. Such positive progress is not, however, universal and it is clear that there are senior leaders and teachers who have not embraced the importance and value of the subject. As it has been argued in this chapter, the progress of citizenship education is not simply affected by matters at the level of educational implementation and policy, but also by the wider political agenda and discourse of the day. This results in a complex context within which the subject's aims are multiple. Despite this, citizenship educators are tasked with being clearer and more explicit concerning the fundamental purpose of their subject and how these relate to wider communities. Of interest to those involved in citizenship education will be how the subject, intimately tied to the New Labour project, will translate into the new Conservative-Liberal Democrat coalition administration. There is a need for those responsible for the teaching of citizenship education to engage in the areas considered within this chapter and, most significantly, for there to be greater clarity concerning how conceptual definitions relate to and impact upon teaching and learning in school. Without such work it is difficult to see how citizenship education will continue its significant recent progress over the forthcoming decade.

Questions for further investigation

1 Consider the aims of citizenship education, as discussed in this chapter in the context of the Crick Report. How does this compare to the conception of citizenship held in your school by teachers, pupils, senior leaders, governors, and parents?
2 Revisit the Crick Report. To what extent are its aims and purpose still relevant for citizenship education today?
3 Selecting an individual scheme or unit of work, consider the extent to which the content promotes particular aims and purposes for citizenship education.

4 How are active citizenship opportunities, of which you are aware, underpinned by a clear methodology, and to what extent are community organisations involved in these?

Suggested further reading

Benton, T. *et al.* (2008) *Young People's Civic Participation In and Beyond School: Attitudes, Intentions and Influences.* London: DCSF. A detailed examination of the National Foundation for Educational Research's Citizenship Education Longitudinal Study. The report draws on a large data set to outline young people's perceptions of civic participation.

McLaughlin, T.H. (2000) 'Citizenship education in England: Crick Report and beyond', *Journal of Philosophy of Education, 34,* 4, pp. 541–70. An accessible and perceptive philosophical exploration of the content of the Crick Report and the citizenship curriculum, which also contains a practical focus. Although written some time ago, the article holds much of interest, particularly in relation to the aims and purpose of citizenship education.

Qualifications and Curriculum Authority (QCA) (1998) *Education for Citizenship and the Teaching of Democracy in Schools: Final Report of the Advisory Group on Citizenship.* London: QCA. The central report which informed the introduction of citizenship education; much of its content and reasoning endures. The report is notable for its breadth and for its definitional illustration of central elements of citizenship education.

References

Abowitz, K.K. and Harnish, J. (2006) 'Contemporary discourses of citizenship', *Review of Educational Research, 76,* 4, pp. 653–90.

Annette, J. (2005) 'Character, civic renewal and service learning for democratic citizenship in higher education', *British Journal of Educational Studies, 53,* 3, pp. 326–40.

——(2008) 'Community involvement, civic engagement and service learning', in Arthur, J., Davies, I. and Hahn, C. (Eds.) *Sage Handbook of Citizenship Education and Democracy.* London: Sage. pp. 388–98.

Arthur, J. (2000) *Schools and Community: The Communitarian Agenda in Education.* London: Falmer Press.

Arthur, J. and Davison, J. (2002) 'Experiential learning, social literacy and the curriculum', in Scott, D. and Lawson, H. (Eds.) *Citizenship Education and the Curriculum* (International Perspectives on Curriculum Series: Vol. 3). Westport, CA: Greenwood Publishing. pp. 27–44.

Barber, B. (1984) *Strong Democracy: Participatory Politics for a New Age.* Berkeley, CA: University of California.

Benton, T., Cleaver, E., Featherstone, G., Kerr, D., Lopes, J. and Whitby, K. (2008) *Young People's Civic Participation In and Beyond School: Attitudes, Intentions and Influences.* London: DCSF.

Callan, E. (1997) *Creating Citizens: Political Education and Liberal Democracy.* Oxford: Clarendon Press.

Crick, B. (2000) *Essays on Citizenship*. London: Continuum.

——(2002) *A Note on What Is and What Is Not Active Citizenship*. London: LSDA.

——(2003) 'The English Citizenship Order 1999: context, context and presuppositions', in Lockyer, A., Crick, B. and Annette, J. (Eds.) *Education for Democratic Citizenship: Issues of Theory and Practice*. Aldershot: Ashgate. pp. 15–29.

Davies, I., Gregory, I. and Riley, S. (1999) *Good Citizenship and Educational Provision*. London: RoutledgeFalmer.

Department for Communities and Local Government (DCLG) (2006) *Take Part: The National Framework for Active Learning for Active Citizenship*. Rotherham: Take Part network.

Education ((National Curriculum) (Attainment Target and Programmes of Study in Citizenship) (England) Order 2000). SI 2000/1603.London: HMSO.

Ellis, A. (2005) *Active Citizens in School: Evaluation of the DfES Pilot Programme*. London: DfES.

Evans, M. (2006) 'Characterizations of citizenship education pedagogy in Canada and England: implications for teacher education', *Citizenship Teaching and Learning*, 2, 1, pp. 40–54.

Faulks, K. (2006) 'Education for citizenship in English secondary schools: a critique of current practice', *Journal of Education Policy*, *21*, 1, pp. 59–74.

Frazer, E. (1999) *The Problems of Communitarian Politics: Unity and Conflict*. Oxford: Oxford University Press.

Gillborn, D. (2006) 'Citizenship education as placebo: "standards", institutional racism and education policy', *Education, Citizenship and Social Justice*, *1*, 1, pp. 83–104.

House of Commons Education and Skills Select Committee (HoC) (2007) *Citizenship Education: Government Response to the Committee's Second Report of Session 2006–2007*. London: The Stationery Office.

Keating, A., Kerr, D., Lopes, J., Featherstone, G. and Benton, T. (2009) *Embedding Citizenship Education in Secondary Schools in England (2002–2008): Citizenship Education Longitudinal Study Seventh Annual Report*. London: NFER.

Kolb, D. (1998) *Experiential Learning*. Eaglewood Cliffs, NJ: Prentice Hall.

Kymlicka, W. (2003) 'Two dilemmas of citizenship education in pluralist societies', in Lockyer, A., Crick, B. and Annette, J. (Eds.) *Education for Democratic Citizenship: Issues of Theory and Practice*. Aldershot: Ashgate. pp. 47–63.

Lawson, H. (2001) 'Active citizenship in schools and the community', *The Curriculum Journal*, 12, 2, pp. 163–78.

Lockyer, A. (2003) 'Introduction and review', in Lockyer, A., Crick, B. and Annette, J. (Eds.) *Education for Democratic Citizenship: Issues of Theory and Practice*. Aldershot: Ashgate. pp. 1–14.

McLaughlin, T.H. (2000) 'Citizenship education in England: Crick Report and beyond', *Journal of Philosophy of Education*, *34*, 4, pp. 541–70.

Nelson, J. and Kerr, D. (2005) *International Review of Curriculum and Assessment Frameworks. Active Citizenship: Definitions, Goals and Practices. Background Paper*. London: QCA.

——(2006) *Active Citizenship in International Review of Curriculum and Assessment Frameworks Countries: Definitions, Policies, Practices and Outcomes. Final Report*. London: QCA.

Ofsted (2004) *Update 43*. London: Ofsted.

——(2006) *Towards Consensus? Citizenship in Secondary Schools,* Her Majesty's Inspectorate Report 2666. London: Ofsted.

——(2010) *Citizenship Established? Citizenship in Schools 2006/09.* London: Ofsted.

Oldfield, A. (1990) *Citizenship and Community, Civil Republicanism and the Modern State.* London: Routledge.

Osler, A. (2000) 'The Crick Report: difference, equality and racial justice', *Curriculum Journal, 11,* 1, pp. 25–37.

Pajares, F. (1992) 'Teachers' beliefs and educational research: cleaning up a messy construct', *Review of Educational Research, 62,* pp. 307–32.

Peterson, A. (2009) 'Civic republicanism and contestatory deliberation: framing pupil discourse in citizenship education', *British Journal of Educational Studies, 57,* 1, pp. 55–69.

Peterson, A. and Knowles, C. (2009) 'Active citizenship: a preliminary study into student teachers' understandings', *Educational Research, 51,* 1, pp. 39–59.

Qualifications and Curriculum Authority (QCA) (1998) *Education for Citizenship and the Teaching of Democracy in Schools: Final Report of the Advisory Group on Citizenship.* London: QCA.

——(2004) *Play Your Part: Post-16 Citizenship.* London: QCA.

Qualifications and Curriculum Development Authority (QCDA) (2007) *The National Curriculum for Citizenship* (Key Stages 3 and 4) [online]. Available at: http://curriculum.qca.org.uk/key-stages-3-and-4/subjects/key-stage-3/citizenship/index.aspx (accessed 14th September 2010).

Tooley, J. (2000) *Reclaiming Education.* London: Cassell.

Wade, R.C. (2008) 'Service-learning', in Levstik, L. and Tyson, C. (Eds.) *Handbook of Research in Social Studies Education.* New York, NY: Routledge. pp. 109–23.

Chapter 17

Conclusion

Hilary Cremin

UNIVERSITY OF CAMBRIDGE

Introduction

This book has provided much food for thought and reflection. Fundamentally, there is much debate about what it means to be a citizen, and therefore what constitutes citizenship, with each contributor making their own case in light of their understandings and research. As Don Rowe points out, if the purpose of schooling and the ways in which education should be organised are contested, it is not surprising that there are different ideas about the nature and processes of citizenship education (CE). In addition, some of the complexity in the field is due to the growth in international and comparative perspectives on CE that David Kerr highlights. This has made the field more interesting and diverse, but also more complex and harder to pin down. Whilst Andrew Peterson is optimistic that in the UK there is evidence that CE provision and outcomes for students are improving overall, he nevertheless acknowledges that the lack of conceptual clarity and agreement about its aims and purpose raise important practical questions for citizenship teaching. Reassuringly, Ian Davies reminds us that it would be neither realistic nor desirable to expect a simple resolution to the debates that have been highlighted in this book.

This concluding chapter provides an overview of some of the themes that have emerged here. These are grouped as: wider political issues; issues to do with time and place; issues of social justice and participation; and professional and pedagogical issues. The chapter will conclude with some final thoughts about two possible stances that CE teachers might take towards these debates.

Wider political issues

Part of the controversy over CE derives from the fact that citizenship values and ideologies are contested. Ian Davies identifies two competing perspectives that focus on rights and duties in private and public contexts in different ways. These are liberal perspectives, which foreground the rights a private citizen has with minimal intervention from the state, and the civic republican perspective, which emphasises the duties or responsibilities of citizens towards others, with a greater role for the state in maintaining social order and equity. Both John Beck and Mark Pike talk about a tension between cultural and religious traditions on the one hand (for example tightening of blasphemy laws) and universal notions of rights (for example free speech) on the other. These tensions have been seen as related to a public/private divide in citizenship. Ian Davies asks: What is the interface between citizenship and concepts of character, morality and religion, and should the latter be taken into account in thinking about what it is to be a good citizen? Hilary Cremin argues that we can no longer universalise the ideal citizen as white, middle-class, heterosexual and male. To continue to be useful, the concept of citizenship needs to take account of more feminised perspectives which make the interaction between public and private aspects of life more dynamic. This would involve, for example, consideration of domestic violence and on-going inequalities in divisions of labour in the home. In a similar vein, Max Biddulph argues that lesbian, gay, bisexual and transgender perspectives should inform ideas around what it means to be a citizen, and that young people have an entitlement to knowledge and understanding about the plurality of sexuality, and the political implications of this.

These are difficult issues. As Don Rowe points out, the service model of citizenship (community volunteering for example) has a long tradition in the UK. This is associated with religion and the Church, and many teachers find it easier to engage with this than with the teaching of political literacy, identity politics and the practices of democratic participation.

Mark Pike challenges us to reveal the Judaeo-Christian source of many British values, and to acknowledge and respect them as shared values in a liberal demo-cratic society without seeking to impose Christianity on students or eschewing their religious sources. Many teachers who have reservations about promoting character education, religious teachings, patriotism and personal virtue, he argues, have no qualms about inculcating democratic values. Alveena Malik sug-gests that white people should consider white identity, and 'who we think we are' in order to engage in more meaningful dialogue about community cohesion with people from British Minority Ethnic communities. Integration between people of different ethnicities is limited, she suggests, with dangers of 'sleepwalking our way to segregation'. Schools deal with issues of rapid population churn, segre-gated communities, extremism and manifestations of identity crises, including the rise of gang culture, on a daily basis. Their role is important in educating the future workforce to respond positively to diversity and difference.

Issues to do with time

Another set of issues is to do with time. These concern both the past and the future. As John Beck points out, CE is not part of British tradition. British people have traditionally been framed as subjects not citizens, and there has been no government control over the Citizenship curriculum until recently. Civic life in the UK has been strong substantively and procedurally, however, with practices of colonialism and institutions like the National Health Service forming British identity over many years in ways that continue to have influence. Challenges for the future concern the ways in which young people now express their civic identities through patterns of consumerism, identity politics, single-issue politics and the internet. Paul Warwick questions whether notions of national citizenship or even anthropocentric notions of global citizenship are adequate conceptual models for the challenges of life in the 21st century. He points to 'mega-problems', or macro-problems that cross international boundaries and time, and that are becoming ever more pressing.

Issues to do with place

International and comparative perspectives on citizenship and CE also provoke debate. Alveena Malik raises issues to do with changes in the notion of 'community'. Communities are now perceived as being more diverse, and are not bound by physical or geographical restrictions. Most people are subject to diasporic influences and identify with multiple communities. The word 'community' used in educational contexts ranges from meaning the community of the school, to the community in which the school is embedded, to the community of Britain, to the global community. Different people will feel attachment to community at these levels to different degrees and in different ways. David Kerr identifies the need to respond to global issues such as terrorism, climate change, migration and the growth of fledgling democracies. He cautions against western bias in the collection and interpretation of comparative and international perspectives on citizenship education. When western civic republican and liberal traditions of citizenship interact with eastern Confucian-based traditions of duty and reciprocity, notions of citizenship expand and become problematical, or can result in 'educational borrowing' from western countries, in ways that are unhelpful and restrictive to eastern countries.

Related to this are ideas around the role of a nation state, and the extent to which it should continue to dominate what it means to be a citizen. Moira Faul and Hilary Cremin suggest that critical and mindful application of concepts of govern*ance* and govern*ing* can support practitioners and young people in recognising and engaging in new public spaces for democratic engagement beyond national govern*ment*, including in their own classrooms.

Others argue that the messy interaction between activity within individual schools and the macro-environment within which they operate has largely negative effects. Moira and Rob Hulme point out that despite various policy initiatives to 'personalise' education, and to act on student voice and consultation, schools remain fundamentally undemocratic, indeed authoritarian places, and that many teachers and pupils feel that they have very little real say in the running of the school. Successive policy interventions emanating from government have influenced school cultures to the extent that they are characterised by performance and compliance, which creates a negative or inhibiting climate for student voice/s. The case study given by Hilary Cremin and Moira Faul of a school council on school governance is evidence of this phenomenon. Don Rowe argues that, ideally, citizenship schools should ensure consistency of message between the citizenship curriculum and the life of the school in respect of the key citizenship concepts which include rights, responsibilities, justice, democracy, power, equality, diversity and rules/laws. There are, however, those who regard these aims as subsidiary to, or even a distraction from, the school's core business of promoting academic excellence in a social and political climate which appears not to value such wider ambitions. Putting democracy into practice within hierarchical institutions like schools is therefore problematic and controversial. Thus, schools differ in their ability to provide opportunities to participate in the civic life of their communities, and in their understanding of the role of learning through community involvement.

Terry Haydn adds in his chapter that there is a significant (digital) divide which challenges citizenship education and citizenship educators, between citizens who are able to use Information Technology effectively in order to engage with others in an attempt to become more effective citizens, and those who are unable or unwilling to do so. As Haydn concludes, given the vast potential of ICT, there is a debate to be had on the relationship between the opportunities and the risks to young people.

Issues of social justice and participation

Carolynne Mason shows that socio-economic status is more important than other factors in predicting the types of activities, such as voluntary and charity work, that young people are engaged in. Young people from socio-economically deprived communities face challenges to their civic engagement, including a lack of money for travel and fees, lack of time because of need to earn money or look after family members, lack of access to the internet and, perhaps most importantly, a lack of the kinds of social and cultural capital that are needed to value and access these opportunities. They are, however, more active than many media commentators suggest. Issues of epistemology and measurement are significant in explaining the diversity of views about whether or not young people are civically engaged. There is a need to value, support and recognise some of the more informal and private activities that these young people are engaging in, if they are not to lose out to their more privileged peers.

John Beck points to tensions between localism (and nostalgic references to the past) and the dominance of trans-national corporations and an environmentally reckless consumer culture. Rob and Moira Hulme suggest that ideas of localism, 'responsibilisation' and 'Big Society' are part of a unifying neoliberal agenda in which citizens manage their own risks and have a duty to avoid sickness or unemployment. Failed citizens are now those who fail to manage their own care. Despite apparent increases in new localism and opportunities for self-government and democracy, they suggest, opportunities for 'deliberative democracy', in which citizens learn, on their own terms, to be active in their own communities, workplaces and social movements as well as the wider body politic, have, in effect, been closed down.

Professional and pedagogical issues

There are also debates that centre on the professional identities of citizenship teachers, and how citizenship is taught and assessed in schools. Tom Harrison addresses the thorny issue of assessment and calls for greater clarity about what elements of citizenship education are of value before any attempt can be made to draw up coherent assessment models. Beck points out that CE was slow to take off due to subject rivalries within the subject associations in the humanities and social sciences, and due to feelings that the school curriculum was being politicised, which continue to have influence. There is on-going evidence that provision, whilst improving, remains uneven, and continuing debate about what is taught and how, and the extent to which it should be formally recognised and mandated. As Ian Davies suggests, how citizenship is taught may be as important, if not more important, as what is taught. Active citizenship education, which many citizenship educators favour, emphasises learning by doing, encourages discussion, debate and critical thinking and employs collaborative learning. It focuses on issues that are relevant to young people's lives, and provides opportunities for them to participate in civic life. This is hard to achieve in practice, but, arguably, should continue to be the goal of citizenship teachers.

Kathy Bickmore provides one model of active citizenship teaching based on a recognition of different kinds of conflict talk, including debate, constructive controversy, issues discussion, conflict resolution and deliberation. There are, she suggests, different ways of supporting young people to develop conflict resolution skills, including initiatives such as peer mediation which focus on actual disputes between young people, and curricular initiatives, which introduce conflictual perspectives into subjects like Science and English. Young people are only likely to develop nonviolent democratic engagement skills and inclinations when they have regular opportunities to practise voicing and discussing contentious questions, and yet learning activities that risk provoking strong emotions are often avoided or prematurely curtailed in schools. She calls for research to provide a well-grounded theoretical framework for understanding why these pedagogies are so rare, especially in under-resourced public schools serving diverse populations, and what can be done about it.

Conclusion

In true CE style, this chapter will end by presenting two stances that teachers might take as citizenship educators. The first is suggested by Mark Pike. His stance is not values-neutral – indeed the opposite – and he argues that such a stance is an impossible one to adopt. No tool is neutral once it is in human hands, he argues, and no curriculum is neutral in the hands of government or teachers. In light of this:

> I suggest that if citizenship is to be taught in school, teachers must be open with students about the beliefs and values upon which their citizenship education is based. Arguably, to seek to influence a child or young person's beliefs and values through a particular curriculum without sufficient transparency about the values underpinning that curriculum is to treat such a learner more like a 'subject' than a 'citizen'.
>
> (Pike, this volume: 181)

Drawing from *On Liberty*, by John Stuart Mill, he points out that anyone who does something because it is the custom makes no choice. Certain interpretations of democratic values have become so 'customary' in our society that they are rarely 'chosen'.

The other stance is taken by John Beck, who argues that it is not in the values or content of CE that agreement will be found, but in the processes:

> Indeed, it has often been argued that citizenship, at least in the modern world, is an *essentially contested concept* (Gallie, 1955) – i.e. one about which there will always be disagreement between equally well-informed and equally serious people. An important implication of this may be that it is difficult in modern pluralistic societies to justify educating *for* a specific 'thick' form of citizenship, and that efforts might better be focused on equipping pupils to understand what political questions are, and why they are often contested, and to prepare them to become, as far as possible, active participants in such debates – at every level from school and local community to the national and even the global.
>
> (Beck, this volume: 13)

These two stances lie at the heart of CE debates. Perhaps they are antithetical; perhaps they can be united in some way. The challenge ahead lies with the next generation of citizenship educators.

Index